TRISH BURR is a self-taught and renowned embroiderer. Through research and practice she has developed this individual technique of surface embroidery. She is the author of several highly successful books including *The Kew Book of Embroidered Flowers* and *Trish Burr's Embroidery Transfers*. Trish lives and works in Cape Town, South Africa. For more information on Trish and her work visit www.trishbembroidery.com

Also by Trish:

 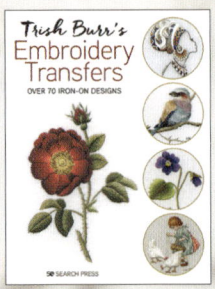

978-1-78221-906-4   978-1-78221-903-3

THE KEW BOOK of NATURE SAMPLERS

TRISH BURR

DEDICATION

For all lovers of nature.
'Let the field be joyful, and all that is in it. Then all the trees of the woods will rejoice.'
Psalm 96:12

ACKNOWLEDGEMENTS

'Appreciation is a wonderful thing. It makes what is excellent in others belong to us as well.' – Voltaire

I would like to thank all those involved in the creation of this book, in particular Katie French and Becky Robbins from Search Press and Gina Fullerlove from the Royal Botanic Gardens, Kew, who initiated and helped to bring this book to fruition.

To Betsy Hosegood who proofread all the projects in this book: thank you for your expertise. What would I do without you?

To my daughter Stacey, who once again agreed to shoot all the photos for this book. Thank you for capturing my embroidery so beautifully. I love that we are able to share this process!

On a more personal note: to my husband Simon, my girls Stace, Tess, Katie, and Mum – I know I keep saying this will be the last one but here I am again! You are my nearest and dearest and I love you all. Katie, I love that we had this year to spend quality time together during the Covid-19 lockdown. Thank you for introducing me to the world of Korean dramas and for keeping me company while I stitched.

This book is also dedicated to the memory of my Dad, who passed on in 2020. You are missed, but will always live on in our hearts.

Last but not least, to my customers, students and readers who are always supportive and encouraging of my work. These pages are, as always, for you.

THE KEW BOOK of NATURE SAMPLERS

TRISH BURR

SEARCH PRESS

First published in 2023

Search Press Limited
Wellwood, North Farm Road,
Tunbridge Wells, Kent TN2 3DR

Text and illustrations © Trish Burr 2023
Photographs by Stacey Burr
Photographs and design ©
Search Press Ltd. 2023

With special thanks to Rachel Pedder-Smith, Carolyn Jenkins, Wendy Hollender, Amy Rose Geden and Jane Carkill for permission to reproduce their paintings in stitch, as detailed within each project.

All rights reserved. No part of this book, text, photographs or illustrations may be reproduced or transmitted in any form or by any means by print, photoprint, microfilm, microfiche, photocopier, video, internet or in any way known or as yet unknown, or stored in a retrieval system, without written permission obtained beforehand from Search Press. Printed in China.

Folder with transfers edition ISBN:
978-1-78221-949-1
Hardback edition ISBN: 978-1-80092-030-9
ebook ISBN: 978-1-78126-946-6

Please note, iron-on transfers are only available with the folder edition of this title.

The Publishers and author can accept no responsibility for any consequences arising from the information, advice or instructions given in this publication.

Readers are permitted to reproduce any of the work in this book for their personal use, or for the purpose of selling for charity, free of charge and without the prior permission of the Publishers. Any use of the work for commercial purposes is not permitted without the prior permission of the Publishers.

Suppliers
Visit Trish's website:
www.trishbembroidery.com

Alternatively, visit the Search Press website:
www.searchpress.com

Extra copies of the templates are available to download free from the Bookmarked Hub: www.bookmarkedhub.com

ABOUT THE ARTISTS

I would like to give a special mention to the artists who so kindly allowed me to re-create aspects of their beautiful paintings in embroidery: Rachel Pedder-Smith, Carolyn Jenkins, Wendy Hollender, Amy Rose Geden and Jane Carkill. Without your beautiful artwork and the inspiration it provided, none of these embroidery samplers would have been possible. Here is some information on each of these talented artists:

Rachel Pedder-Smith
www.rachelpeddersmith.com
Rachel is a botanical artist who received a PhD at the Royal College of Art, London. Rachel's work is in the collections of the Royal Botanic Gardens, Kew, Shirley Sherwood and many other private collections worldwide. She has won four RHS gold medals for her botanical paintings and is best known for her ground-breaking and exquisite 18-foot Herbarium Specimen Painting, displayed at Kew.

Carolyn Jenkins
www.carolynjenkins.co.uk
Carolyn studied Art and Graphic Design at St Martin's School of Art in London and Bath Academy of Art. She is also a professional gardener and studied for a diploma in Botanical Painting at the English Gardening School, for which she was awarded 'Distinction' and 'Best Student'. She has won two RHS medals for her botanical paintings and was commissioned to illustrate the book *Highgrove, A Garden Celebrated* by H.R.H. King Charles III and Bunny Guinness. Carolyn is an artist who is highly regarded for her botanical watercolour paintings, which often include mind-boggling detail.

Wendy Hollender
www.wendyhollender.com
Wendy is a botanical artist, illustrator, author and instructor. She is known for her finely detailed botanical drawings seamlessly blended with coloured pencil and watercolour, but somehow managing to achieve a manner similar to oil painting. Her illustrations have been widely published and her work has been included in the 13th International Exhibition at Hunt Institute for Botanical Documentation, Royal Botanical Gardens, Kew, and the Smithsonian National Museum for Natural History. She is the author of several books, including *The Joy of Botanical Drawing*, *Botanical Drawing in Color* and *Botanical Drawing, A Beginner's Guide*. She is an instructor of Botanical Art and Illustration at the New York Botanical Garden and leads workshops at her farm in Accord, NY, as well as in locations such as Greece, Spain, Hawaii and many nature preserves, botanical gardens, arts centres and colleges around the world.

Amy Rose Geden
www.etsy.com/shop/Amyrosegeden
Amy Rose is best known for her stunning botanical prints, which attract thousands of followers on Pinterest, Etsy and Instagram. Amy Rose is an artist, illustrator and printmaker living and working in the Cotswolds, UK. Her work is inspired by botany, nature and changing seasons and has a Victorian, antique feel. She tries to capture the textures and colours of the plants and objects she paints, and collects lots of vintage natural-history books for inspiration. She lives in a beautiful village surrounded by fields and countryside, which inspires her work.

Jane Carkill
www.etsy.com/ie/shop/LambLittleShop
Jane is an illustrator from Kilfenora, Ireland, and the unique terrain of her homeland is her first memory of belonging in the natural world. She is an artist and printmaker who attracts thousands of followers on Instagram and sells her work through her Etsy shop. Flora and fauna have always been the ultimate inspiration for Jane's work. A graduate of Textile Art, Critical Theory and Professional Arts Practice, Jane has a preference for natural ephemeral beauty and intricate details, and is inspired by illustrations of the 1800s, folklore, ancient myths, stories from Irish history and personal memories.

'If you truly love nature, you will find beauty everywhere'.
– Laura Ingalls Wilder

CONTENTS

Foreword	6	Simple projects	42
Introduction	8	Starter stitch sampler	44
What is needle painting?	10	Poppy sampler	54
Tools and materials	10	Wildflower sampler	60
Preparation	16	Sacred lotus flower sampler	68
Stitch instructions	22	Breadseed poppy sampler	76
Outlines	32	Intermediate projects	88
Raised embroidery	34	Barn owl sampler	90
Natural dyeing	36	Bunny sampler	104
Stitching the projects	40	Butterfly sampler	118
Useful advice before you start	40	Advanced projects	134
		Pelargonium sampler	136
		Dragonfly sampler	152
		The templates	168
		Using iron-on transfers	176

FOREWORD

The Royal Botanic Gardens, Kew is world-renowned in the study of plants and fungi. Kew and Wakehurst, its wild botanic garden in Sussex, attract over 2.5 million visitors annually to spectacular gardens and living plant collections. Through our collections we support the study of biodiversity, conservation and sustainable development, seeking nature-based solutions to the challenges presented by climate change. Kew undertakes scientific research to protect plants across the globe and preserve species through initiatives such as the Millennium Seed Bank project. The gardens serve as spaces for the dissemination of plant knowledge and encourage visitors to connect and marvel at nature.

Kew's Library and Archives is one of the foremost botanical research resources in the world, holding references for the taxonomy and systematics of wild plants from all parts of the globe. It represents seminal botanical literature from throughout the ages, including illustrated works such as *Curtis's Botanical Magazine*, first published in 1787, which holds the accolade of the longest running illustrated botanical periodical. The collection spans centuries, continents, and languages, and includes 185,000 monographs and rare books, 200,000 botanical illustrations and an incredible seven million pages of archive material. This rich resource attracts researchers from a diverse range of disciplines including plant scientists, horticulturalists, historians, authors and artists.

In her second embroidery book with Kew, Trish Burr examines the relationships of plants, animals and fungi found within the Gardens while continuing to build upon the visual language practised by artists associated with Kew and the field of botany. The discipline of scientific botanical illustration demands strict levels of attention to detail and accuracy, and Trish's embroidered designs faithfully recreate the illustrations from which they draw influence while providing a further dimension in celebration of the plant form. Trish takes inspiration from the work of botanical illustrators such as Rachel Pedder-Smith, who uses dried plant specimens to inform her work, reinvigorating the pressed plant through her meticulous studies of colour and structure.

We are delighted that Trish has taken inspiration from the gardens and collections at Kew. Her exquisite and detailed embroideries showcase the infinite range of colour and detail found within the kingdoms of plants and fungi and reflect a deep-seated admiration for their subject. Her descriptions of plant dyes serve as just one example of the myriad of ways in which we are indebted to plants for their properties. Her embroidered samplers remind us of the interdependency of flora and fauna and our own place within the natural world.

Julia Buckley
Library and Archives
Royal Botanic Gardens, Kew

INTRODUCTION

As I sit down to write this introduction, I pause for a moment and think back on the impact that the Covid-19 pandemic has had on our lives. For many, it has been a time of uncertainty, loss and separation from loved ones. But the lockdown period also brought with it some surprisingly positive side effects. Here in South Africa, we had extended periods of isolation, and this quiet time enabled me to slow down, appreciate nature more, spend quality time on my embroidery, and to share my work with the world in the form of an online stitching journal. As a result of this journal, a whole new community took up needle and thread and discovered the joys of embroidery!

Embroidery is a wonderful form of relaxation that takes you to a happy place where you can set aside the cares of the world for a while. Can we ever have too many embroidery projects, too much inspiration, too much happiness? I know I can't! One of the ways I can continue to provide this inspiration is through my books. This is the second embroidery book that I have created in collaboration with the Royal Botanic Gardens, Kew. The first book, *The Kew Book of Embroidered Flowers*, featured botanical paintings. This title comprises nature-inspired embroidery samplers that depict the diversity of plants, fungi, insects and birds that can be found in the natural area and woodlands of the Royal Botanic Gardens, Kew, in London.

It has been a joy to design and stitch these embroideries, although I must confess that some features did present a bit of a challenge: how to stitch the hedgehog's spiky quills or how to achieve those twisty 'roots' on a pod, for example, but it was fun coming up with solutions!

These projects cater for all levels of expertise from beginner to advanced. If you are new to embroidery you could begin with the starter stitch sampler on page 44, which will enable you to familiarize yourself with all the stitches before moving on to the main projects. More experienced stitchers may relish the opportunity to jump straight into the more complex samplers. Either way, I hope you will enjoy the diverse embroidery projects from our natural world. The samplers can be stitched as a whole, or you may like to choose elements from each sampler and create your own piece of embroidery.

If you find that the information in this book differs slightly from any of my previous books, this is because I am always learning new and improved ways of doing things, or better materials to work with. Happy stitching!

WHAT IS NEEDLE PAINTING?

Needle painting is a surface embroidery technique – it is like painting a picture on fabric with a needle and thread. An outline of the image is first traced and transferred onto the fabric, then filled with embroidery using the original image as a reference. Needle painting is also referred to as silk shading, long-and-short shading or thread painting – these are just different names for the same technique. The main stitch used for needle painting is long-and-short stitch, which is normally worked in one strand of cotton or silk thread. Long-and-short stitch allows you to fill an area with subtle blends of colour, which results in the realistic 'painted' finish and the beautiful shading for which it is renowned.

Of course, a few other stitches are used to best mimic the object to be stitched and create a realistic, lifelike effect. You can find more information on the stitches used in the section on stitch instructions (see pages 22–35).

TOOLS AND MATERIALS

FABRICS

Pure natural fibres, such as 100 per cent linen, cotton or silk, are ideal for needle painting embroidery. Generally, the fabric you use should be very closely woven to allow for the precise placement of each stitch and have very little stretch in it to prevent distortion when mounted into the hoop. Although I prefer to use quite specific fabrics for needle painting, there are many other fabrics that could be used, and I don't want to limit you. You may find fabric sources in unlikely places. For example, you might find an old sheet or pillowcase that is perfect, or you may be lucky enough to have an old linen tablecloth that is made from beautiful antique linen. I recently purchased some antique, monogrammed linen from France, which I was able to cut up and use for embroidery projects – the quality was superb and certainly not something that is still available today. Here are some features to look for when purchasing your own fabric:

- **Good quality:** always use the best-quality fabric you can afford. Beware of cheap imitations as they may look fine, but once the embroidery is complete they may cause puckering or distortion and cause all sorts of problems.

- **Pure fibres:** where possible, use pure natural fibres such as cotton, linen and silk; avoid synthetic fibres.

- **Close weave:** make sure the fabric has a very tight, close weave; generally, if it is a heavy fabric, it will have a looser weave. Avoid gauzy, translucent, flimsy, soft or floppy fabrics – you want fabric with a bit of body so it will support the embroidery. If in doubt, look in the quilting section for good-quality cottons.

- **The stretch test:** make sure the fabric has little or no stretch in it – if the fabric is stretchy, it will distort in the hoop and cause major puckering. Do the 'stretch test': pull and stretch the fabric along both sides along the grain – if it stretches a lot, it is not suitable. You want the fabric to be quite crisp. If in doubt, purchase several samples and try them out at home before using.

- **Not suitable:** evenweave linens for counted thread embroidery or cross stitch are not suitable. The weave will be too loose, and you will not have enough placement for your needle.

LINEN

Linen is my fabric of choice. The linen you use for needle painting should have a very high thread count, be of medium weight to support the stitching and have a very tight, smooth weave. Linens with a loose weave, textured linens or linens for dressmaking are not suitable.

PROS: linen is very resilient and a joy to work on as the fibres will spring back into shape when washed or ironed. It is a strong, robust fabric that does not mark easily and, for some reason, iron-on transfers seem to work better on linen than cotton, giving a clear and strong print.

CONS: fine-quality linen that was produced in the past for use in bedsheets and tablecloths – the type of linen used by our grandmothers for embroidery – is no longer produced due to a lack of demand in the commercial world. It is only available from specialist outlets, and is therefore expensive and can be difficult to obtain.

NB: at the time of going to press I have a premium, Belgian linen fabric available for sale in my online store. The closest alternative (but not as fine) is an Irish linen or church linen, which can be ordered from online church suppliers.

COTTON

A good-quality cotton muslin (also known as calico), such as that used for heirloom embroidery and quilting, can be successfully used for needle painting. It should be at least 200 count and evenly woven across the weft and warp to prevent distortion in the hoop. Cotton satin also works well, as, despite its name, it is a pure cotton fabric – the term 'satin' describes the weave. Other cotton fabrics such as denim or poplin that are mediumweight and have a very close, smooth weave could also be used – make sure they are pure cotton, not mixed, and have no stretch in them.

PROS: cotton muslin is easy to source, less expensive than linen and provides a nice smooth, tight weave for needle painting. It is a good fabric to start with for beginners in embroidery.

CONS: cotton is not as strong and durable as linen and may distort and mark more easily. Iron-on transfers will work well on cotton but the print will not be as defined as it is on linen.

SILK AND SATIN

A good-quality natural silk dupion can also be used for needle painting. The silk should preferably be the powerwoven kind (not handwoven) so that it has fewer slubs and a nice smooth finish. It should be of a medium weight and 100 per cent pure silk, not mixed or synthetic. Other silk and satin fabrics such as good-quality silk tafetta or pure silk duchesse satin can also be used successfully.

PROS: silk is divine to stitch on as the needle glides through the fibres with no resistance. It comes in a large selection of colours and has good body with a very tight weave, which provides a supportive ground fabric for needle painting.

CONS: silk marks easily, as I have found out! You need to be mindful of stains while stitching as it is difficult to remove the marks and great care needs to be taken when washing silk fabric. Good-quality, pure silk fabrics are expensive, and will need to be purchased from a specialist shop or outlet, preferably one that supplies wedding fabrics.

NB: you cannot use iron-on transfers on silk – you will have to transfer design outlines by hand.

BACKING FABRIC

If you are using a medium-weight, close-weave fabric that is sturdy enough to support the stitching, it is not necessary to use a backing fabric. I prefer not to use one but the choice is yours. If you do decide to use a backing fabric, choose a fine cotton muslin or similar.

PROS: backing fabric can provide extra support if your ground fabric is too thin or flimsy. If your ground fabric has a loose or rough weave, a backing fabric can create a smoother consistency to stitch on.

CONS: it is difficult to line up the main and backing fabrics correctly, which can result in puckering when removed from the frame or hoop. When mounting your embroidery, you will need to stretch and mount both the backing and ground fabrics separately to achieve a good result.

THREADS

DMC and Anchor stranded cottons are used for the projects in this book. Stranded cotton is readily available from online needlework stores or your local highstreet store in most countries.

DMC STRANDED COTTON (OR FLOSS)

DMC stranded cotton is the most commonly used brand of stranded cotton. It offers a huge variety of colours and lends itself perfectly to needle painting. Cotton thread is easy to use, durable, colourfast, washable and can resist exposure to light. DMC threads are made from the best long-staple cotton in the world and mercerized twice to give an exceptional sheen. The thread is comprised of six easily separated strands, and you will normally use one strand in your embroidery, unless otherwise directed. Anchor is another brand of good-quality stranded cotton that can be used instead of, or combined with, DMC. If you choose to use any other brand, be sure that it is colourfast and good-quality.

THREAD NAP

All thread has a nap, which is the direction in which the fibres lie. It helps to achieve smoother stitching if you thread the yarn in the same direction each time, as this allows the nap to remain in the same direction while stitching. The photograph opposite shows how to do this.

SUBSTITUTING THREADS

If you are unable to find Anchor threads you can use the conversion chart provided on my website (www.trishbembroidery.com), which will give you the closest match to DMC stranded cotton. Please be aware that it is not possible to provide exact colour matches, so if you choose to use substitutes your embroidery will invariably look different to mine.

A rainbow of DMC stranded cotton threads and sewing threads, which I use for fine details.

HOW TO USE COTTON THREAD

Pull out a length of thread from the skein – about 50–60cm (20–24in) is good. Separate one strand from the six. Cut this off and thread into the needle. Use one strand of thread throughout unless otherwise instructed in the pattern.

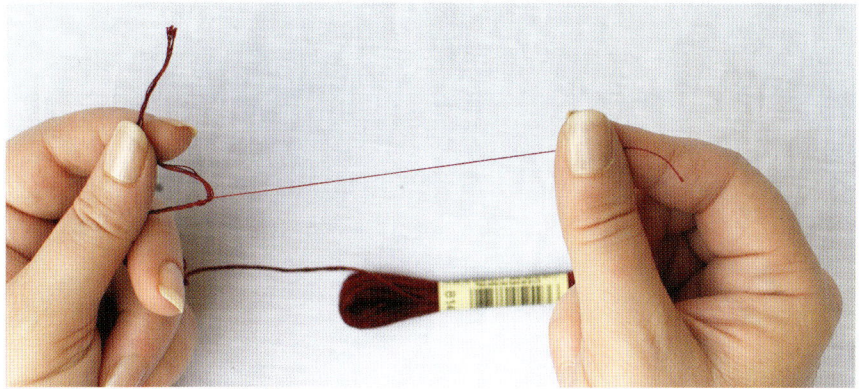

POLYESTER SEWING THREAD FOR OUTLINES

One strand of stranded cotton can normally be used for outlining, but sometimes even this is too thick and you may need a more delicate outline for specific areas. When required, you can split one strand of polyester sewing cotton into two and use one of these very fine threads for outlining. To split a polyester thread, follow the instructions given below. Any good-quality sewing thread such as Gütermann, Mettler, DMC or Coats can be used.

HOW TO SPLIT POLYESTER SEWING THREAD

- Cut a length of sewing thread.
- Tease open the ends with the blunt end of a needle – you will see that it can easily be separated into two.
- Pull the strands apart, separate one, and thread it into the needle.

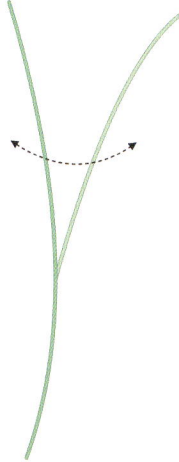

A selection of polyester machine threads, which are sometimes needed for outlining.

HOOPS AND FRAMES

SUPER GRIP HOOP (1)
The best type of hoop to use for surface embroidery is a super grip hoop such as Susan Bates Hoop-La™ or similar. This hoop will grip your fabric and keep it absolutely drum-tight, which is necessary to prevent puckering of your embroidery. These hoops can be purchased online or from any good needlework store.

PROS: quick and simple to use, these keep your fabric drum-tight. You can easy adjust your tension while stitching.

CONS: they can leave a hoop mark that is difficult to remove. To prevent this you will need to bind the hoop and make a hoop cover (see page 16).

WOODEN HOOP (NOT SHOWN)
Wooden hoops are available in different sizes and are perfect for framing your completed embroidery (see page 20). These hoops can be purchased online or in any good needlework store; I would recommend brands such as Elbesee or Nurge.

PROS: they are good for framing your completed embroidery.

CONS: if you are using them for embroidery, they don't keep fabric as drum-tight as a super grip hoop and will need regular adjusting.

STRETCHER FRAME (2)
Stretcher bars come in pairs of different lengths so you can connect them together to make the size you want. They should be very light and as thin as possible, so that they are easy to hold in the hand. Brands such as Siesta Frames in the UK and Edmunds in the US are ideal because they are very lightweight, but any similar stretcher bars will do. If you can't find these, you can buy a lightweight artists' canvas frame from an art shop and remove the canvas.

PROS: do not leave a hoop mark. Can be assembled to fit the size of the embroidery and keep embroidery fabric aligned with the grain of the fabric. Do not require a hoop cover or binding on the frame.

CONS: a little extra preparation is required to stretch and insert thumb tacks. Thumb tacks need to be removed to adjust the tension.

THUMB TACKS (NOT SHOWN)
You will need thumb tacks to secure the fabric to the stretcher frame. The steel ones with a flat top are ideal, but you can also buy a thumb-tack kit, which includes a magnetic tool to push the tacks in and a tack extractor – these save a lot of wear and tear on your fingers!

NEEDLES (3)
You will need a sharps needle (also known as a general sewing needle) for needle painting. It has a round eye and short shaft, which allows for the stabbing motion you use in needle painting and is easier to control when creating smaller stitches. Sizes range from 2–12: the larger the number, the smaller the needle. You should use sharps numbers 10–11 for one strand of thread, and sharps numbers 9–10 for two strands of thread.

If you find it difficult to see the eye of the needle you could also use a crewel embroidery needle with a longer eye in sizes 9–11. Crewel embroidery needles can be useful if using more than one strand of thread in specific circumstances.

I like Bohin needles because they go through the fabric like a hot knife through butter and do not tarnish or bend, but any good brand of needle such as John James, Richard Hemming or Clover can be used. It is recommended that you dispose of your needle when it starts to tarnish and use a new needle for each project so that it does not damage your thread or fabric.

SCISSORS (4)
You will need a small sharp pair of embroidery scissors. I like the Kai curved scissors, as they cut cleanly and sharply and are good for unpicking too, but any good-quality embroidery scissors will do.

MAGNIFYING LIGHT (NOT SHOWN)
This is one of the most important tools for this style of embroidery and will be the best investment you ever make! It is virtually impossible for you to see the fine stitches in your needle painting without one. The belief that simply magnifying your work makes it easier to see is not true – sitting in a badly lit area and trying to magnify a dark image will not help. What makes your work easier to see is light – the combination of bright light and magnification is ideal and will reduce eye strain while stitching. You need a magnifying light that has daylight or white light equivalent so that it does not distort the colours you are working with.

WHICH MAGNIFYING LIGHT?
I often get asked this question as there are many magnifying lights on the market to choose from. I would recommend that you get the best you can afford. I have tried many lights, some more expensive than others, but I now use the Daylight Slimline LED Magnifying Lamp with a 13cm (5in) glass and 21 LEDS. The new LED lights are great – they provide a bright, white light so there are no shadows on your work and the bulbs do not need replacing. I like to sit comfortably in my armchair while stitching, so I have a light on a floor stand that I can adjust to my needs, but you could use either a table clamp, desktop or floor stand, whatever you feel most comfortable with. Any good online craft/needlework store is a good place to find a variety of magnifying lamps to suit your pocket and preference.

If for any reason you are unable to use a magnifying light, ensure that you work under a bright light and consider using reading spectacles for magnifying your work. These come in different magnifications, so find the ones that suit you. If you already use spectacles, the reader spectacles can be placed on top of your regular spectacles to magnify the viewing area.

PREPARATION

PREPARING YOUR FABRIC

- Wash and iron your fabric to remove creases and pre-shrink it. It is not advisable to wash silk or satin, but both can be pressed lightly with an iron (not a steam iron).
- Line up the grain – to do this, pull a thread on two sides at right angles to ensure that it is on the straight grain before mounting in the hoop. This is an essential step, as if you mount your fabric across the grain, it will cause puckering in your embroidery piece.
- Overcast the edges of the fabric with a sewing machine, or use masking tape, a glue stick or fray-stop to prevent fraying.

TRANSFERRING THE OUTLINE BY HAND

To transfer a design outline using the templates on pages 168–175, here is a simple method:

- Trace the outline onto a piece of tracing paper or have it photocopied.
- Place the outline onto a lightbox or on a window and secure with masking tape.
- Place your fabric centrally on top of this and again tape in place.
- With the light showing through you will easily be able to see the lines – trace over these lines with an HB pencil or a fine micron pen size 005.

For advice on using iron-on transfers, see page 176.

PREPARING A HOOP

BIND THE HOOP

To prevent damage to your fabric, bind the inner hoop with strips of white or off-white fabric. You can use fabric glue to secure the end and prevent unravelling.

HOOP COVER

To prevent hoop marks on your fabric while stitching, make a hoop cover:

- Cut a piece of scrap fabric the same size as your embroidery fabric: it is best to use white or off-white.
- Cut a small hole in the centre of the fabric.
- Place your embroidery fabric over the inner hoop and the scrap fabric on top of this.
- Centre the design in the hoop.
- Cut away the excess fabric to reveal your design, as shown.

PREPARING YOUR FABRIC IN A HOOP

- Both pieces of fabric – main and cover – need to be mounted into the hoop together, so place both fabrics over the inner hoop, lip facing up.
- Place the outer hoop over this.
- Push it down and you will feel the outer hoop slip under the lip of the inner hoop (if you are using a super grip hoop).
- Tighten the screw and stretch the fabric, then repeat this until the fabric is drum-tight. The fabric needs to be very taut to provide a good tension.
- Stretch the fabric on the straight grain, across and down as shown. Do not stretch on the bias, as the fabric will overstretch and result in distortion when removed.

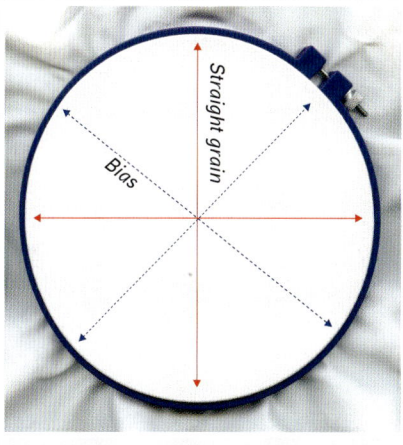

Here, the straight grain is shown with red arrows; the bias is shown with blue arrows.

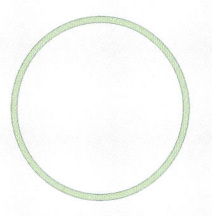  

PREPARING YOUR FABRIC IN A FRAME

- Place the fabric face down on a table (the embroidery outline will be facing down).
- Place the frame on top of this (on the back of the fabric). Ensure that the outline is centred within the frame.
- Pull the fabric on each side over the bars and secure with tacks, easing the fabric into place so that it is very taut.
- Adjust the fabric as necessary until it is tightly stretched across the frame.

The back of the embroidery, mounted in a frame.

WASHING YOUR EMBROIDERY

- Soak your embroidery in warm water using a mild soap (I use an organic castile soap).
- Rinse thoroughly in cold water.
- Wrap in a fluffy towel to remove excess moisture.
- Place face down on a towel and either block (see below) or leave to dry.

Please note that if you have used silk thread, it is not advisable to wash your embroidery as the colours tend to run – you will have to dry clean it or steam as outlined for blocking, below.

BLOCKING YOUR EMBROIDERY

There may be times when your completed stitching is badly puckered or distorted, or there is a stubborn hoop mark that is hard to remove. Blocking your embroidery is an easy way to freshen and restore it to its original shape. If DMC stranded cotton has been used for the embroidery, it can be washed and then blocked, but if silk threads have been used, it is not advisable to wash it, but it can be blocked using the method below. All you need is a cork or polystyrene board and some map pins.

COTTON THREAD METHOD

- Wash your embroidery as outlined above.
- Place the damp fabric on a surface such as cork or foam – make sure it has a straight edge.
- Line up your embroidery on the straight edge on one side and place pins at each corner, then pin all along the first edge.
- Do the same on the other three sides – stretch the fabric as you go and move your corner pins if you need to. Ensure that the fabric is stretched tight with no creases.
- Leave until completely dry or use a hairdryer if you are in a hurry.
- Remove the pins and, if necessary, press lightly with a hot iron on the wrong side.

Here, the embroidery has been blocked and mounted, giving it a beautifully taut finish.

MOUNTING YOUR EMBROIDERY ON ACID-FREE BOARD

This is a simple but effective way to mount your completed embroidery ready for framing or storing.

MATERIALS REQUIRED
- Acid-free board or foam core
- Felt or thin quilt wadding/batting
- Glue
- Stitchers' tape or acid-free double-sided tape
- Map pins or thumb tacks
- Artists' tape or masking tape

METHOD
- Cut a piece of board to the required size. Cut a piece of felt or wadding/batting the same size. Glue the felt to the top of the board.
- Place your embroidery centrally over the board.
- Insert a few pins along one side to keep it in place.
- Turn over and apply double-sided tape on either side. Pull the fabric up over the tape and secure it in place.
- Repeat on the opposite side – stretch the fabric, pressing and smoothing it down as you go. Repeat this on the other two sides. Make sure the fabric is taut on the board and there are no creases. Adjust the fabric if necessary.
- Add some artists' or masking tape along the edges of the fabric to neaten on the back. Your embroidery is now mounted and ready to frame.

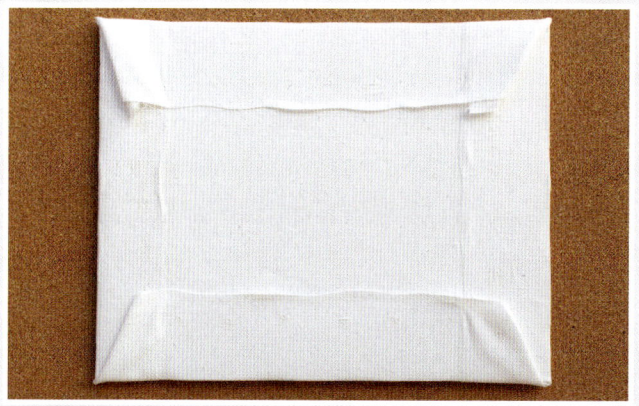

MOUNTING YOUR EMBROIDERY IN A WOODEN HOOP

These hoops can be purchased online or in any good needlework shop, and are available in different sizes. This is the mounting method I prefer as the embroidery can be removed for laundering in the future if it gets dusty.

INSTRUCTIONS

1. Cut a piece of cotton fabric in a colour that matches the fabric used for your embroidery – here I have used white. This will be used as a backing for the completed embroidery. Line up the two pieces of fabric and trim to ensure they are about the same size. Mount both pieces of fabric into the hoop, using the cotton fabric as a backing, ensuring it is drum-tight. Tighten the screw as tight as you can get it, using a screwdriver. Trim around the excess fabric leaving approx 4cm (1½in) of fabric.

2. Thread a needle with two strands of cotton – make sure there is enough cotton to go all the way around the hoop. Secure the thread and sew tacking/basting stitches (running stitches) around the edge. They should be about 1cm (½in) away from the cut edge. When you reach the starting point, pull the thread tight to gather the fabric evenly, and secure with a few running stitches.

3. This last step is optional but does provide a nice neat finish for the back. Cut a circle of felt fabric that will fit just inside the back of the hoop. You can embroider your initials or the date on the back if you like, or leave it as is. Attach this circle to the back of the gathered fabric with slip stitches all around the edge.

4. Your mounted embroidery is now complete. To remove for laundering, unpick all the stitches, wash your embroidery and, once dry, repeat steps 1–3 to mount it again.

STAINING THE HOOP

You may want to leave your hoop in its natural state or you may prefer to stain it a different colour. Here is my method for staining, which must be done before you mount your work:

MATERIALS REQUIRED
- Wood stain in your choice of colour
- Small regular paintbrush
- Disposable gloves
- Paper towel for cleaning

METHOD
- Either hold the metal piece at the top or attach the hoop to a clothesline or similar with a peg while you paint it.
- Apply a nice even layer of stain around the outer hoop only (you do not need to stain the inner hoop). Paint the outside and then the inside of the hoop.
- Leave the stain for about 15 minutes to absorb into the wood and, if required, add a second coat.
- Finish it off with a varnish/sealer or leave as is. Allow to dry for at least 12 hours before use.

STITCH INSTRUCTIONS

These are the five stitches that I use most frequently when needle painting: long-and-short stitch, split stitch, French knots, satin stitch and bullion stitch.

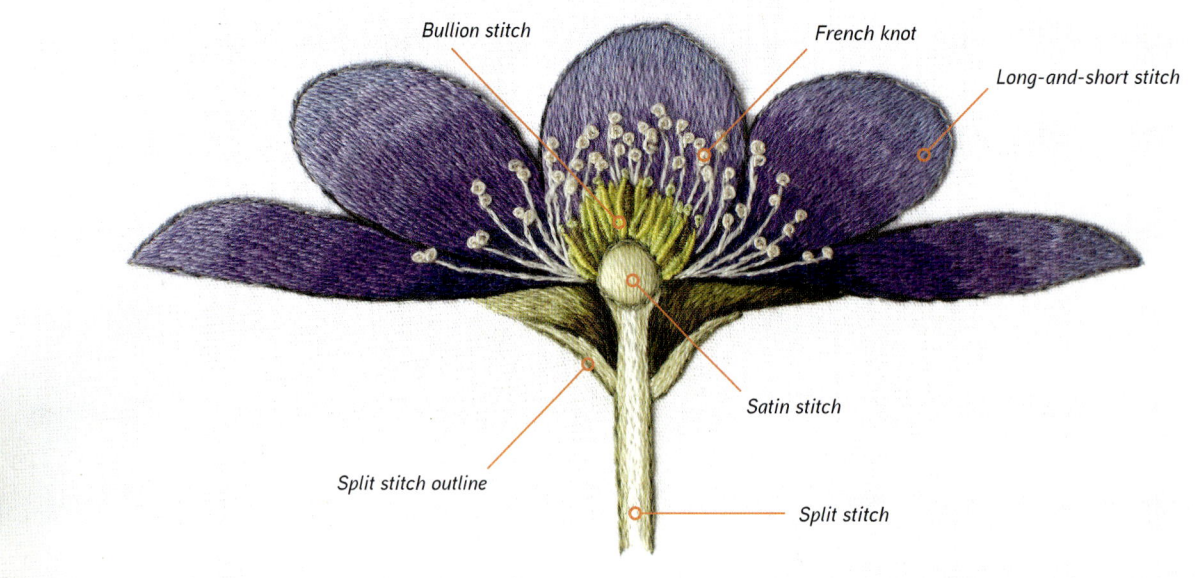

SECURING YOUR THREAD

This method of securing your thread does not leave any lumps or bumps – do not use a knot.

METHOD
- Make a tiny stitch close to the edge of the shape – up at A and down at B. This stitch must be in an area that will be covered by embroidery. Leave a small tail at the back.
- Make a second stitch close to this – up at C and down at D, into the centre of the first stitch.
- Give the thread a tug: it should be secure. Cut off the tail at the back.
- To finish and start a new colour, run your needle and thread under a few stitches at the back of the work to secure.

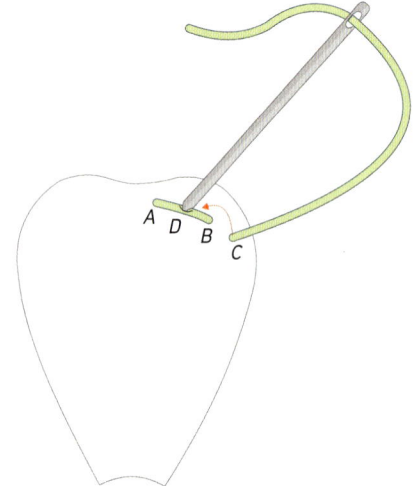

LONG-AND-SHORT STITCH

Long-and-short stitch shading is worked in rows of stitches that softly blend into each other. The colours gradually change through the rows to produce a smooth transition of colour. This colour gradient results in the beautiful shading that long-and-short stitch is so well known for. It can be adapted to fill different shapes and to achieve different effects within individual elements of a design – these are discussed in more depth on the pages that follow.

BASIC LONG-AND-SHORT STITCH: FILLING A SIMPLE PETAL

The term 'long-and-short' is confusing, as it is more like staggered satin stitches – so let go of the idea that you need to stitch one long stitch then one short stitch across the row. The stitches in each new row cover the base of the stitches in the previous row.

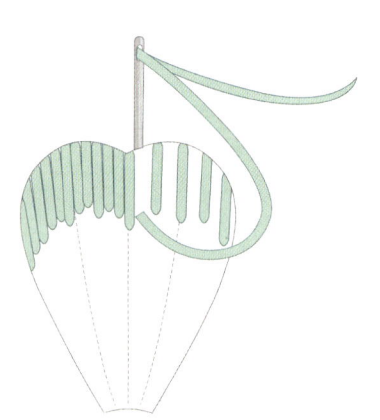

METHOD

Row one: start in the centre of the shape on one edge and work out towards each side. Using the lightest shade of colour, add random stitches across the shape to establish the direction of your stitching. Each stitch should be approximately 1cm (½in) in length, up at A and down at B. Continue filling in the gaps with long-and-short stitches across the shape until the row is complete. The stitches in the first row should be very close together to establish a firm foundation for the next rows.

Row two: turn your work around so you are working away from you and looking out onto your stitching. Thread the second shade of colour and, again, add random stitches across the row as before. Bring the needle up through the previous stitching at A and down into the fabric at B. It works best if you come *up* into the previous stitching and not down. Going down into stitches causes little holes like small pepper marks, which make your stitching look rough and uneven.

Continue filling in the gaps with long-and-short stitch across the shape until the row is complete. Keep your stitches in line with the guidelines, adjusting as necessary to fit the shape. Work every other row as for row two, changing to the next shade of colour each time.

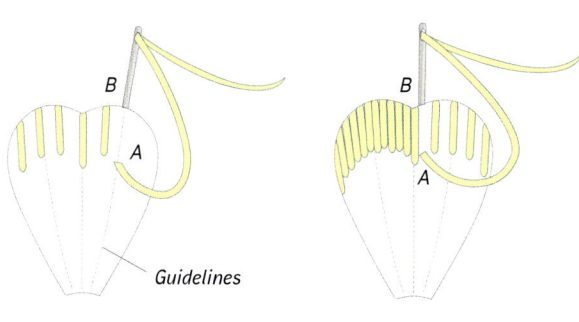
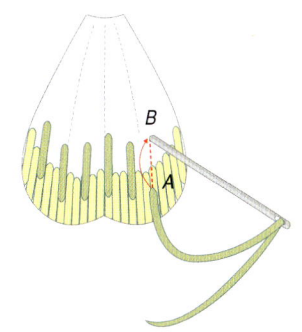
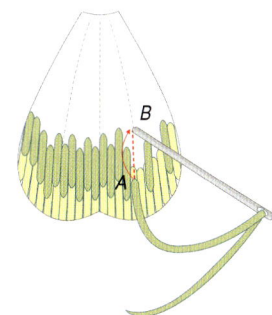

GUIDELINES FOR LONG-AND-SHORT STITCH

Long-and-short stitch shading does not always follow straight lines – sometimes we need to adjust the stitches to follow the direction of a shape and achieve a more natural look. If you look at a petal, for example, you will see that it most often tapers towards the centre. It helps to draw in guidelines to direct your stitches. These can be drawn in with an HB pencil, as shown in the example.

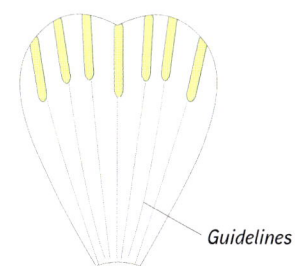

TIPS FOR LONG-AND-SHORT STITCH

Wherever possible, stitch from the wider area to the narrow area of a shape. It is much easier to reduce stitches than it is to increase them. There may be instances where you have no choice due to the nature of the shape, but generally it is easier to stitch from a wide to a narrow area.

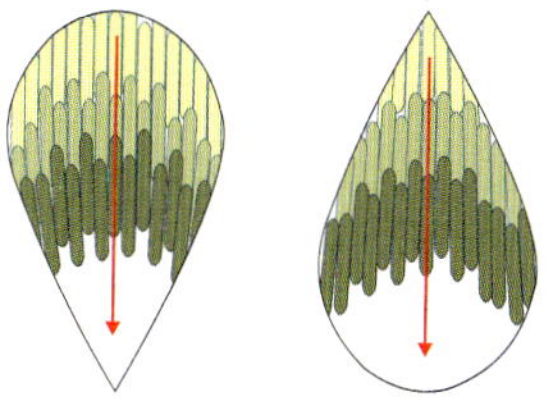

Always stagger the stitches in each row to create a soft blending of shades. Avoid rigid bands of stitching. If your rows look straight, go back and add the odd staggered stitch to break up the line.

Always fill each row (particularly the first row) adequately. Avoid leaving gaps in between the stitches, otherwise when you stitch the next row there won't be any thread to go into, just a space. If you see a gap, go back and add in a stitch to fill it.

The stitches in each row should lie parallel to each other. Sometimes you need to gradually change the slant of the stitches to fit a shape but, wherever possible, avoid abrupt changes of angle as this will cause your stitching to look messy.

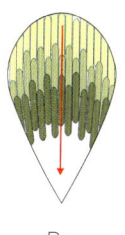
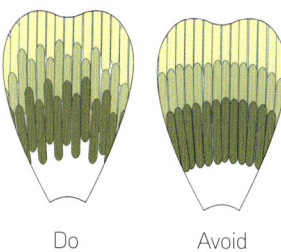
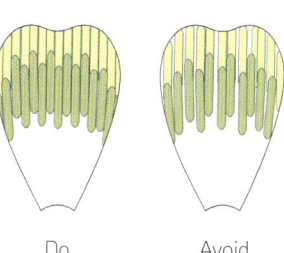
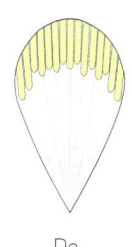
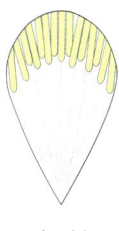

Do   Avoid   Do   Avoid   Do   Avoid   Do   Avoid

PRACTISE YOUR LONG-AND-SHORT STITCH

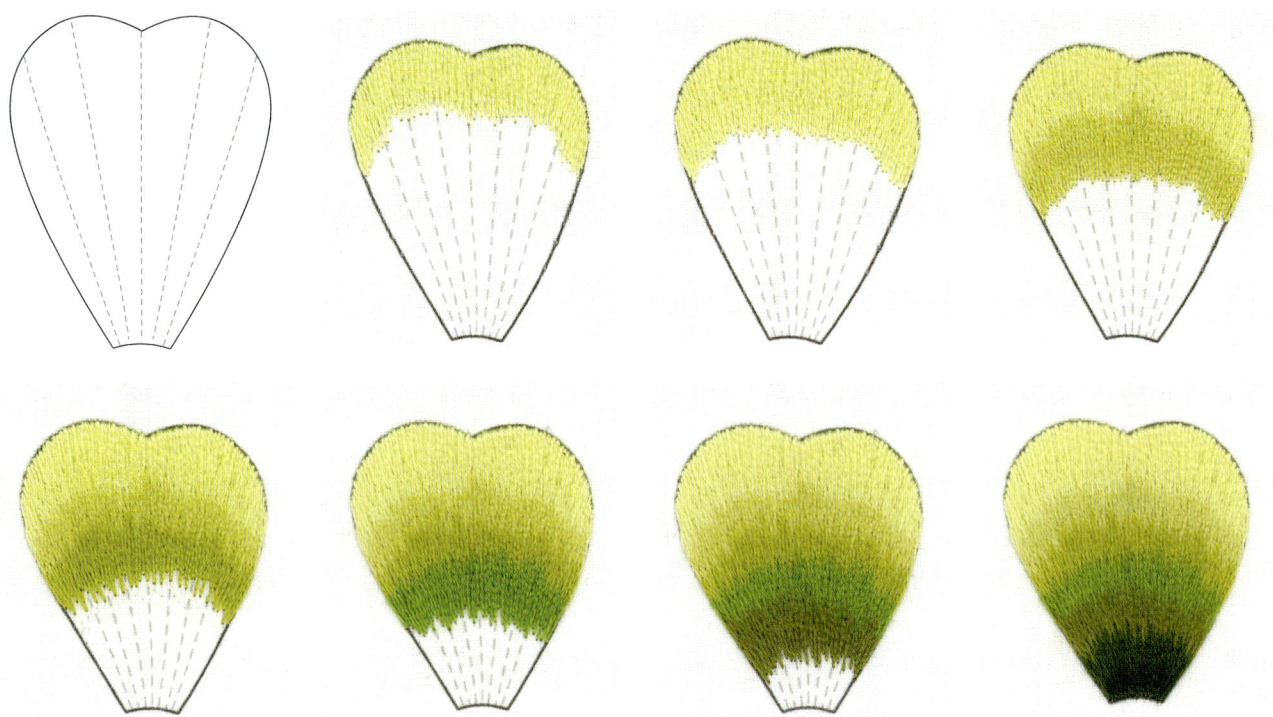

If you are new to embroidery, you may like to familiarize yourself with the basics of long-and-short stitch. Transfer this petal outline with an HB pencil to a scrap of fabric, draw in some guidelines and practise filling it with long-and-short stitch using five shades from light to dark of any colour. Use the step-by-step photographs above as a guide. Don't worry if it does not look right the first time – it will come with a bit of practice!

LONG-AND-SHORT STITCH FOR FLOWERS

Start with the petals that are at the back or bottom and work up to the petals in the front. You can also add a split stitch outline to define each petal (see page 29). Stitch from the outside edge of the petal in towards the centre, as shown in the diagrams.

LONG-AND-SHORT STITCH ON A BUTTERFLY

Here is an example of the stages of working long-and-short stitch on a butterfly.

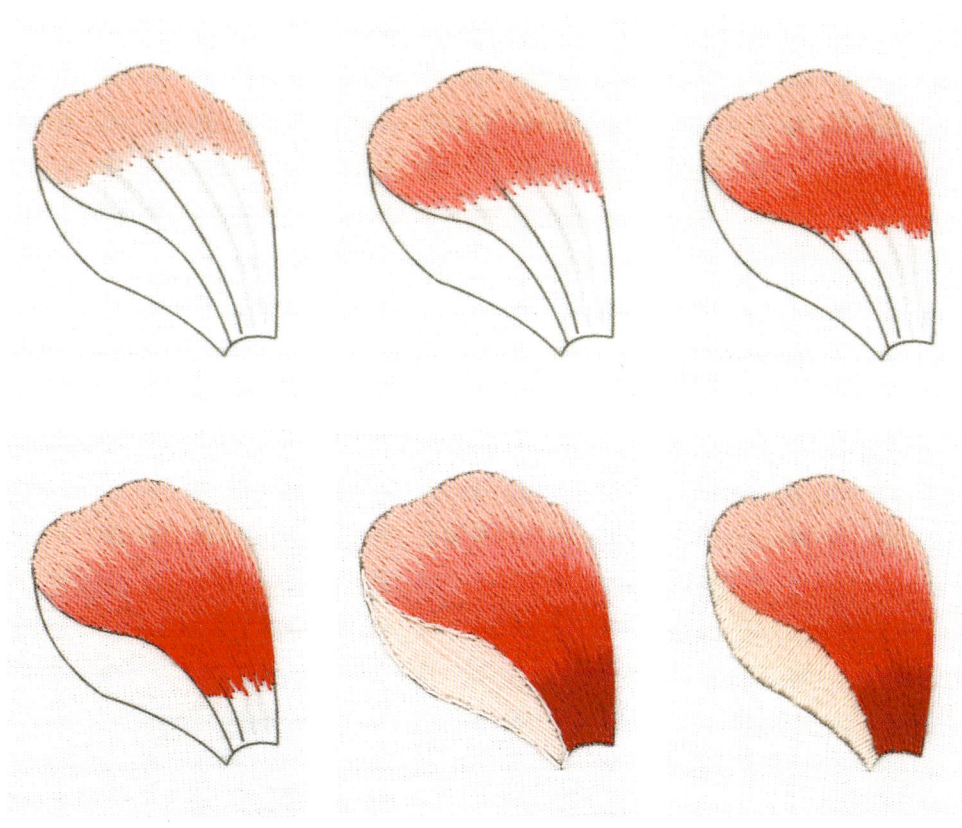

LONG-AND-SHORT STITCH FOR PETALS WITH A TURNOVER

Stitch the petal first and then the turnover.

- Fill the petal with long-and-short stitch, following the steps on pages 22–23 and opposite.
- Outline the turnover with split stitch. Pad the turnover with long straight stitches to raise it slightly above the petal (see also pages 34–35).
- On top of this and over the split stitch outline, add long-and-short stitches or satin stitches if space does not allow.

LONG-AND-SHORT STITCH FOR LEAVES

Fill both sides of the leaf, on either side of the centre vein, with long-and-short stitch. Start from the outside edge and work in towards the centre vein. When one side is complete, go back and stitch the other side. The centre vein is stitched with split stitch.

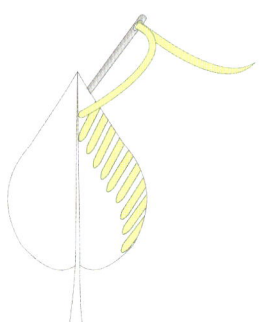 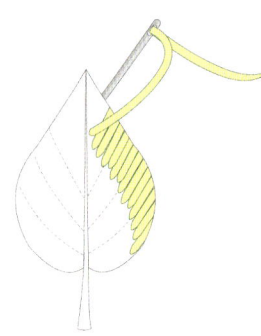 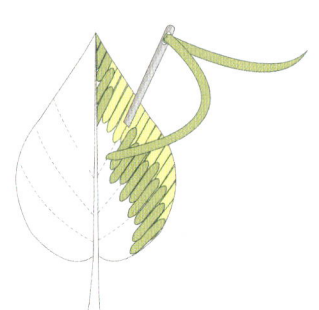 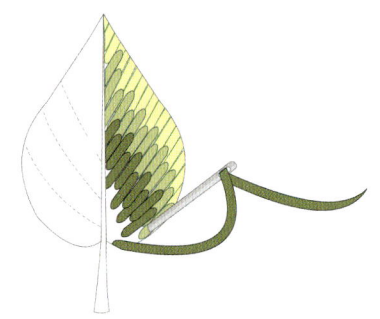

LONG-AND-SHORT STITCH FOR SIMPLE LEAF SHAPES

Draw in guidelines to direct your stitching. Fill each side of the leaf with long-and-short stitch from the outside edge in towards the centre vein, using your guidelines to direct your stitches. Stitch the centre vein with split stitch.

 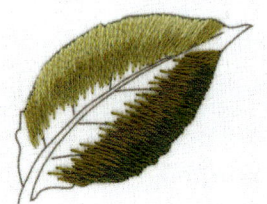  

LONG-AND-SHORT STITCH FOR IRREGULAR LEAF SHAPES

To stitch a leaf that has an irregular shape, it is easier to divide each section and stitch individually. You can draw in pencil lines to separate each section, as shown in red in the diagram. Again, start from the outside edge and work in towards the centre vein. Once all the stitching is complete, stitch the centre vein and outlines with split stitch.

LONG-AND-SHORT STITCH FOR SMALL SHAPES

To fill a small shape such as a bud or sepal with more than one shade of colour, do not shorten your stitches to try to fit all the shades into the space. Rather, fill the shape with the two lightest colours, then add a few straight stitches at the base on top of this in the darker shade(s), as shown in the example, right.

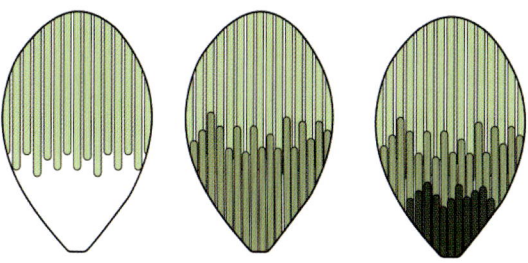

LONG-AND-SHORT STITCH FOR CURVED SHAPES

To fill a curved shape such as a petal, you will need to shorten the stitches and stitch more than one row of each shade. Shortening the stitches helps them to hug the shape of the curve.

- Stitch a row of short stitches (A).
- Stitch another row of short stitches in the same colour (B).
- Stitch a row of short stitches in the next colour (C).
- Stitch another row of short stitches in the same colour (D).

Continue like this until the shape is complete.

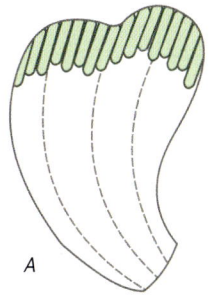
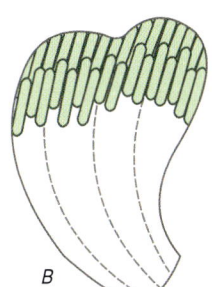
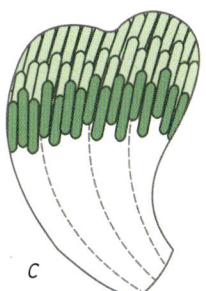
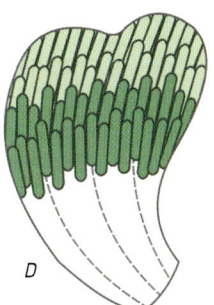

A B C D

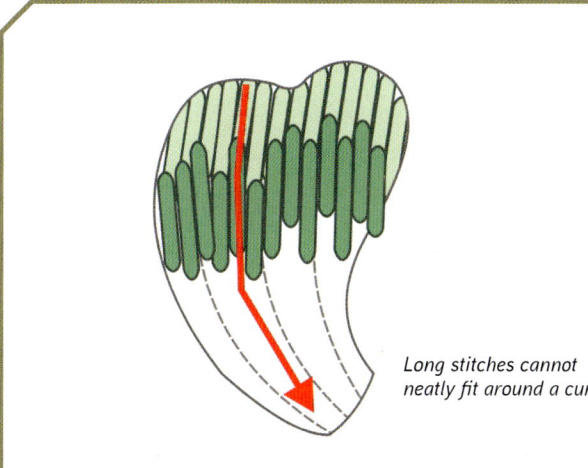

Long stitches cannot neatly fit around a curve.

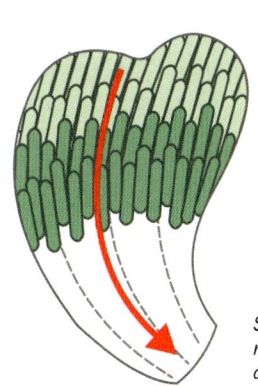

Shorter stitches can more easily follow a curve.

COLOUR AND SHADING FOR LONG-AND-SHORT STITCH

LIGHT AND SHADOW

Light shines on everything, providing highlights in some areas and shadows in others; without light and shadow everything would appear flat and dull. To achieve a realistic three-dimensional appearance in our embroidery we need to include both light and shadow. The example on the right shows where both the light and shadow would fall when the light source is to the left-hand side.

COLOUR

Contrary to popular belief, long-and-short shading itself is not smooth; as each row encroaches into the previous one it will be slightly raised. It is the smooth transition of colour that makes your shading *appear* smooth. If the shades are correctly blended, they will appear to melt into each other and glow. These are the most important factors:

1. RIGHT BLEND OF SHADES

When shading from light to dark, the values should be of similar tones so that they blend easily. You can change contrast, for example from pale pink into medium/dark pink and it will look fine, but if you change tones abruptly it will look wrong. On the right are examples of a successful blend of fuchsia shades, and an unsuccessful blend of fuchsia shades. In the first petal you will see that similar tones in the fuchsia pink family create a nice transition of colour, but in the second petal there is a jump from fuchsia pink into coral/garnet tones which breaks the continuity of shading. One of the reasons this can happen is if you substitute one brand of thread for another, as the colours in each brand use different dye lots and rarely match.

Right blend   *Wrong blend*

2. GOOD BALANCE OF SHADES

Achieving the right balance in your shading can contribute enormously to the visual smoothness of the stitching. A simple guide that will help to achieve a good balance is: wherever possible, fill the shape with two-thirds light or medium shades and one-third dark shades, as shown in the example right.

3. MIXING CLEAN AND DUSTY SHADES

Using a mix of clean and dusty shades can often create a more realistic effect. As shown in the example below right, the lighter shades of pink are clean, but the darker shades are 'dusty'. The dusty shades give the impression of a shadow, which is the way it would be seen in nature. Mixing clean and dusty shades of colour can also create a vintage look, whereas using all clean colours tends to look more modern.

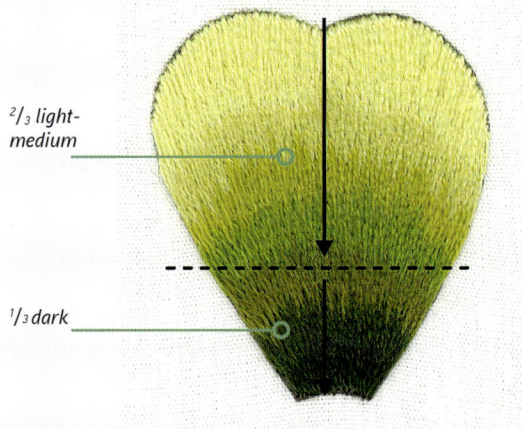

Good balance of shades

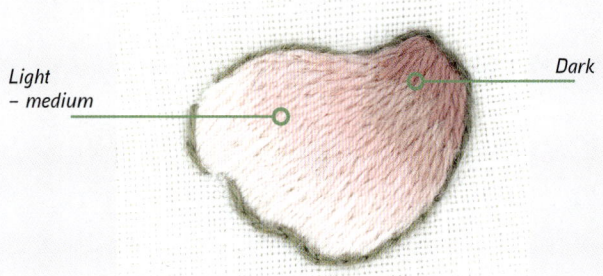

Mixing clean and dusty shades

SPLIT STITCH

Split stitch is a very useful stitch as it can be used both for outlines and to fill a shape. When adjacent lines of split stitch are worked in a shape it resembles fine, long-and-short stitch so it is good for filling stems or areas where a lot of shading is required in a small space. There are different versions of split stitch; I use the split backstitch variation as it allows me to control the stiches from the top. Split stitch is like backstitch, except instead of coming back at the end of the previous stitch you come back *into* the previous stitch (about two-thirds back).

METHOD
Bring the thread up at A and down back into the previous stitch at B. Bring the thread up at C ready to make the next stitch. Repeat for all stitches.

SPLIT STITCH OUTLINES
Sometimes you might want to use a split stitch outline under your long-and-short stitch to define the edge of a shape. This can be particularly useful when you are stitching a flower with petals that lie one on top of the other. The edge of each petal needs to be raised slightly to define it, otherwise they will look like they all merge into each other.

METHOD
Outline the shape with split stitch, as indicated in yellow in the diagram, right. You can use one strand of thread for this but, if the shape is quite large, you can use two strands to make a very raised edge. The long-and-short stitches, indicated in green, will go over the split stitch outline to cover it.

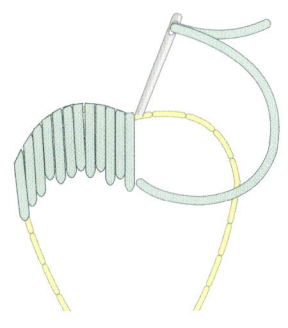

You can also add a split stitch outline around the completed stitching to define the edges, as shown in this example, right.

SPLIT STITCH FILLING
This can be used to fill shapes such as a stem, or when an area is too small for long-and-short stitch.

METHOD
Stitch a line of split stitch. Next to this add another line of split stitch – continue adding adjacent lines of split stitch one next to the other to fill the shape. Please note, you can change the shades of colour (light to dark) either horizontally or vertically in the split stitch lines to create a shaded effect, as shown in the examples.

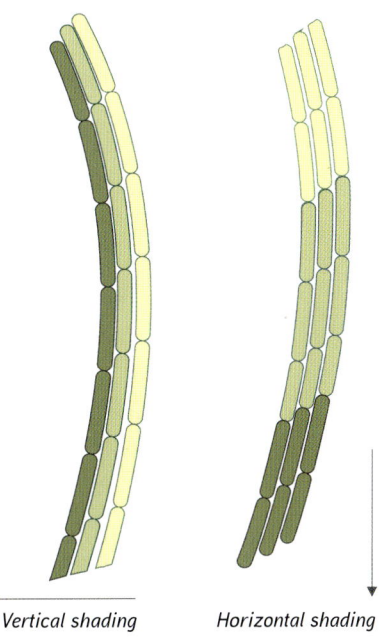

Vertical shading   *Horizontal shading*

Split stitch filling on a stem

SATIN STITCH

Satin stitch is used to fill shapes with straight parallel stitches. It can be useful if the shape is too small for long-and-short stitch or if the shape to be filled needs a smooth filling.

METHOD

Start slightly away from the end to establish the direction of your satin stitches; you can go back and fill in the first few stitches afterwards. Come up at A and down at B, as shown in the diagram. Continue to work parallel stitches across the shape.

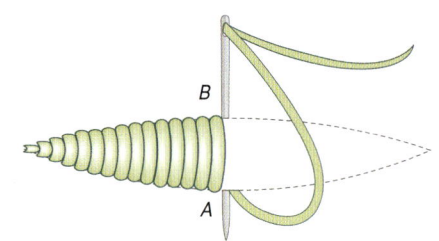

FRENCH KNOTS

French knots are used to add texture to an area. They are useful for imitating areas like flower centres, pollen or seeds. French knots can be stitched in different shades of colour to produce a shaded or graduated effect.

METHOD

- Use one strand of thread and two twists. Bring your needle up at A and then wrap the thread around your needle twice.
- Insert your needle tip into the fabric very close to the original hole, at B.
- Pull your thread quite firmly to form a knot against the fabric, then pull the needle through to the back of your fabric to complete the knot.

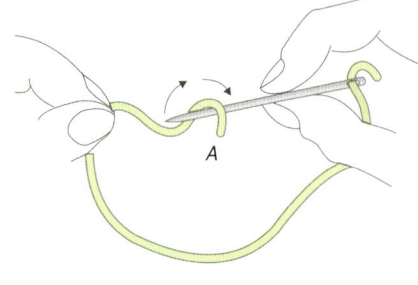
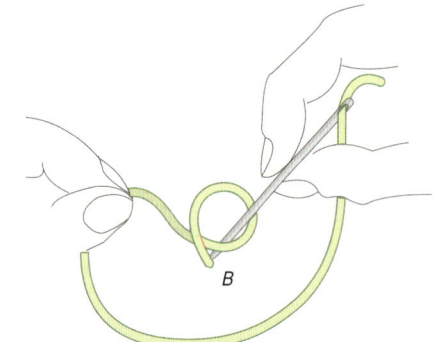
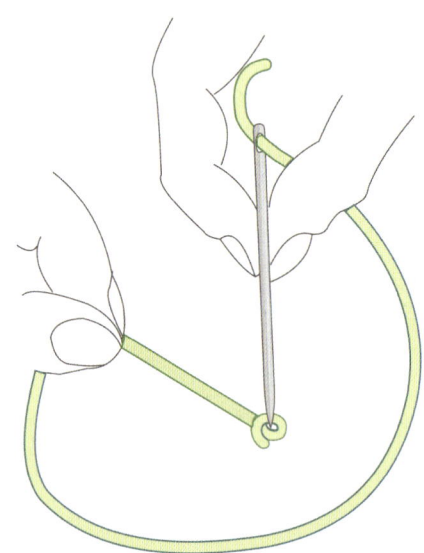

BULLION STITCH

Bullion stitches are used to create coil-like shapes, which can be useful for imitating areas of a flower such as an anther. Note that you will need to slacken the fabric in the hoop or frame to stitch bullions; I often leave them until last so I can do this.

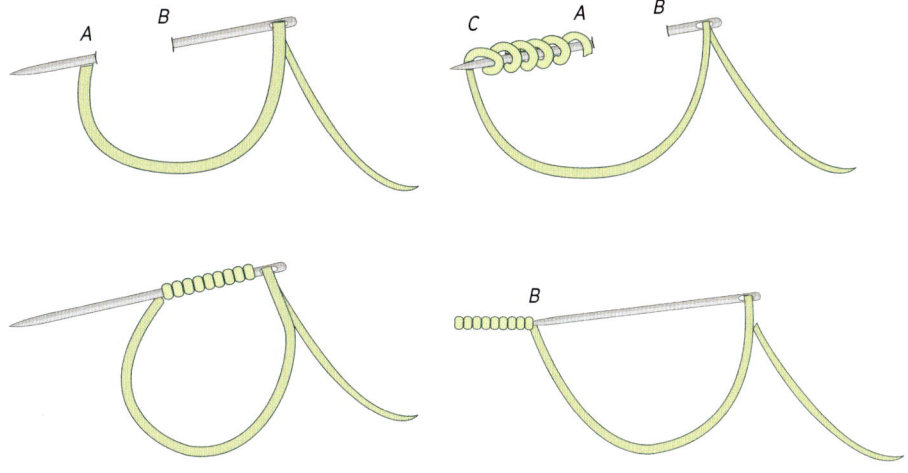

METHOD

- Bring your needle up at A, go down at B and partway up at A – this will be the length of your bullion. Only push your needle three-quarters of the way through, leaving a long loop.
- Wind your thread around the needle in an anti-clockwise direction (C). The number of loops will depend on the length of the bullion knot.
- Pull your needle gently through the coil of loops and adjust your thread at the same time.
- Pull your needle completely through. Push the top of the coil down while pulling your thread through to even out the coil. Re-insert your needle into the fabric to complete.

PRACTISE THE STITCHES

If you are new to embroidery you may like to familiarize yourself with split stitch, satin stitch, French knots and bullions. Transfer these outlines to a piece of scrap fabric and stitch them using one strand of thread or two if you find it easier to start with. Don't worry if they don't look perfect first time – it will come with a bit of practice. Use the stitch sampler on page 44 as a guide.

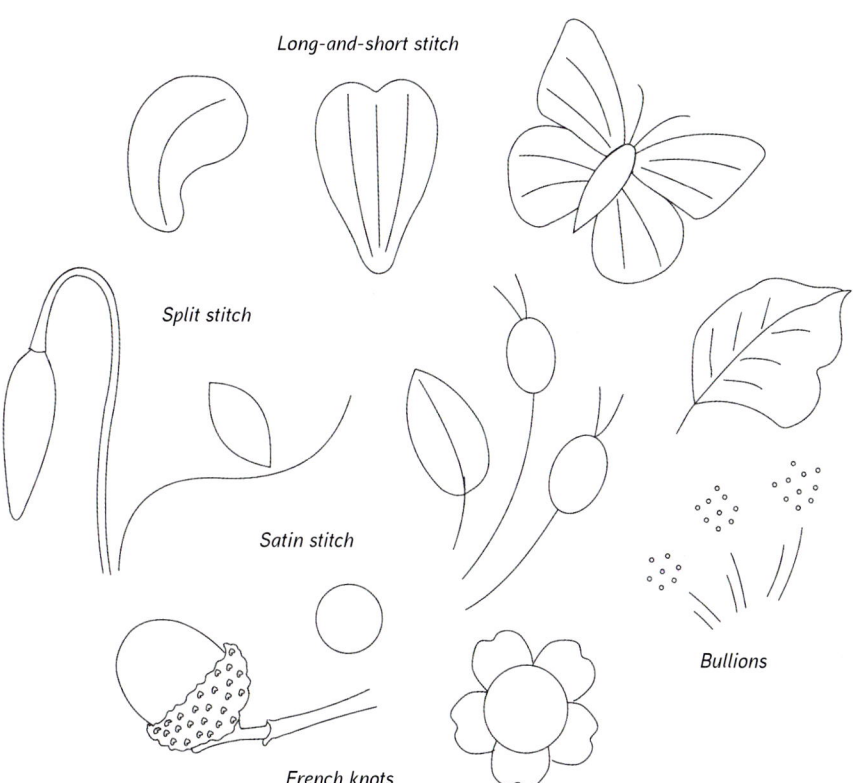

Long-and-short stitch

Split stitch

Satin stitch

French knots

Bullions

OUTLINES

Outlines are an effective way of adding details, defining a shape or distinguishing individual aspects of your embroidery. The outlines are added using split stitch or, if the area is very small, a straight stitch. Outlines can make your embroidery pop and add interest to a picture, by making it look more realistic. You can see this in these before-and-after examples.

Before and after adding outlines.

ADDING DETAILS WITH OUTLINES

Here, I have added outlines and other details to give shape and form to an area of the design. I have embroidered the dragonfly wings and then added fine veins on top of these using a split sewing thread. In the second example, I have added fine hairs to the stem and bud, again using a split sewing thread.

METHOD

The outlines should not dominate your embroidery; they should always be fine and subtle. To achieve this, use one strand of thread, or if a very delicate outline is called for you can split a strand of polyester sewing thread (see page 13). Rather than stitching a solid line, break up the line occasionally to create a more natural look, as seen in this example, right.

32

RAISED EMBROIDERY

To create a three-dimensional effect in your embroidery, padding can be added under long-and-short stitch or satin stitch to make shapes look as though they are raised above the fabric. The raised shape creates its own little shadows, which makes it look more lifelike. This is especially effective when used for shapes such as flower buds, sepals, seeds and petal turnovers.

PADDED LONG-AND-SHORT STITCH

Shapes can first be padded with long, straight stitches and then long-and-short stitch worked on top of the padding. It is not recommended that you add more than one or two layers of padding for long-and-short stitch as, if it is too thick, it will be very difficult to get the needle through.

METHOD
- Outline your shape with split stitch so that it will hug the padding and define the edge.
- Fill your shape with straight stitches across the shape – this is the padding, which is always worked at right angles to the long-and-short stitches – as shown in the diagram.
- Stitch long-and-short stitch on top of this and over the split stitch outline.

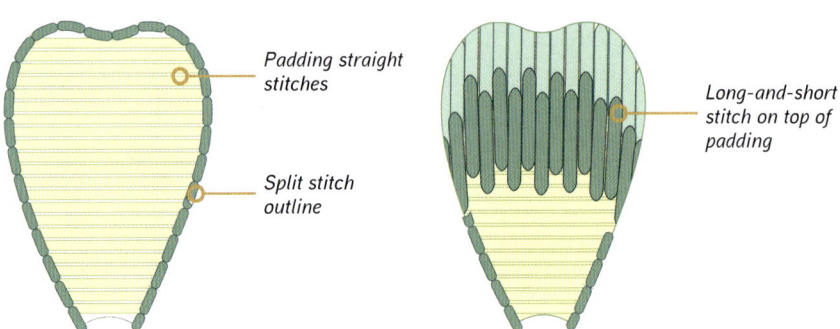

Here are two examples of padded long-and-short stitch on a bud and a beetle.

34

PADDED LONG-AND-SHORT STITCH VARIATIONS

Here are two alternative methods for padding underneath long-and-short stitch.

METHOD ONE
In this example, I have created two layers of straight stitches at right angles to each other using two strands of thread. This raises the petals slightly. Add straight stitches along the length of the shape (A). Add straight stitches across the width of the shape on top of the previous stitches (B).

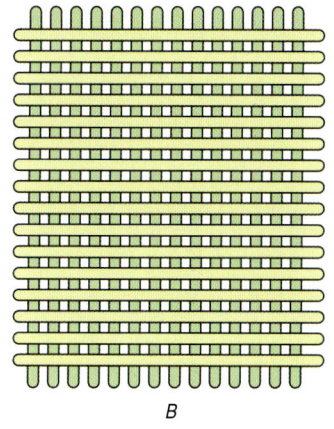

A *B*

METHOD TWO
In the second example, shown right, I have used a piece of felt to create a dome-like effect for a mushroom or toadstool cap. Cut out a piece of felt that is slightly smaller than the cap shape and secure the felt by hand using slip stitches around the edge.

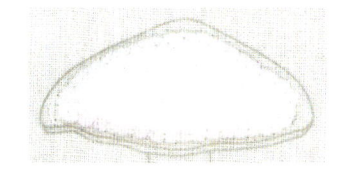

PADDED SATIN STITCH

METHOD
- Outline the shape with split stitch or double running stitch, so that it will hug the padding and define the edge.
- Fill the shape with straight stitches across the shape – this padding should always be worked at right angles to the satin stitch. You can add one, two or three layers of padding for satin stitch.
- Stitch the satin stitch on top of this and over the outline.

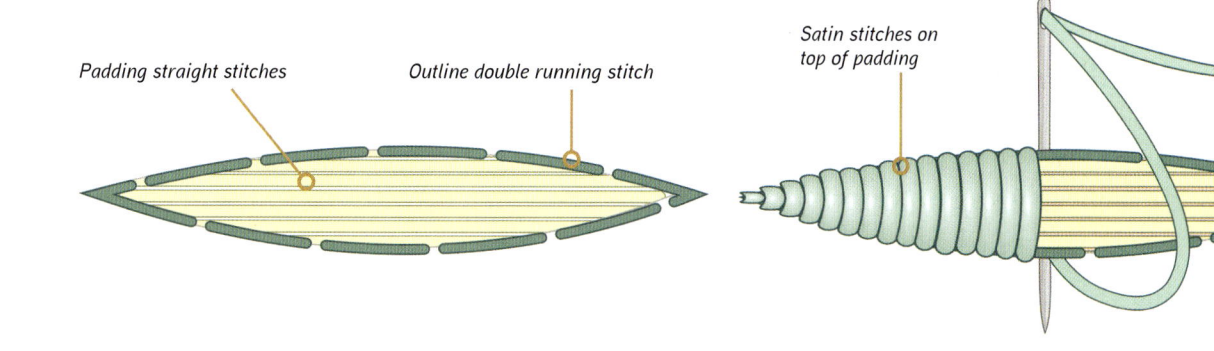

Padding straight stitches   *Outline double running stitch*

Satin stitches on top of padding

NATURAL DYEING

I mainly use white or ecru fabrics as backgrounds for my embroideries, as I believe these show them off to their best advantage. However, there are times when using different coloured backgrounds can create interesting visual results. If you want to explore this, here are some instructions for dyeing your fabric with natural dyes.

I have done extensive research into using natural dyes, and although there are numerous methods, I have found the following to be the simplest and most effective. I have tried many different plant materials, but some of them were not terribly successful, or faded over time, so here I will detail only the dyeing materials that turned out well, and which provide a nice selection of background colours for embroidery.

Most of these materials can be found in your kitchen or are easy to obtain: blackberries, turmeric powder, tea bags and coffee. If you want to experiment with other plant materials, you will find lots of information online.

SAFETY FIRST
Keep a separate set of equipment for dyeing - don't use the pots, pans and spoons that you use to prepare food.

FIRSTLY, A LITTLE DISCLAIMER

Natural dyes are quite unpredictable and inconsistent. Their success depends on many factors including the pH of your water, how you prepare your fabric and which dye materials you use. Natural dyes do fade over time and will naturally become lighter with washing and exposure to light. I have used tea and coffee often in the past and it has remained stable over the years, but I cannot, of course, guarantee that this will be the case for every dye in every situation. I dye white premium linen from my online store – if you choose to use other linen or cotton, the results may differ.

YOU WILL NEED

- Linen or cotton fabric for dyeing
- A medium/large saucepan
- A bucket
- Large glass/porcelain bowls
- Rubber gloves and an apron
- Mordant: alum powder (aluminium acetate)
- Optional: bicarbonate of soda (baking soda) or vinegar if dyeing with turmeric
- Natural dye materials: for example, blackberries, turmeric powder, tea bags, pure instant coffee (not chicory)

PREPARATION

Before you can dye your fabric you will need to wash it to remove any chemical sizing. You will also need to pre-soak the fabric in a mordant (here I have used alum powder), which will help to fix the dye colour and prevent it from fading.

1. Wash the fabric in a washing machine or by hand using hot water.

2. Fill the saucepan with hot water (enough to cover your fabric) and bring to the boil. Add three teaspoons (12g/½oz) of alum powder. Mix thoroughly until it is completely dissolved. This is enough for about 500g (17½oz) of fabric: the ratio is roughly 1 tsp (5g/0.14oz) of alum to 100g (3½oz) fabric.

3. Wet your fabric – make sure it is completely soaked before adding to the pan.

4. Place the fabric in the pan and soak for about 1–2 hours.

5. Move the fabric around every now and then to ensure the mordant is evenly distributed – this will help to evenly distribute the colour as well.

6. Allow to cool and remove. Rinse thoroughly in cold water. Place the fabric in a bucket of cold water, ready for dyeing.

DYEING

BLACKBERRIES

Blackberries provide shades of pink and purple; you can get very similar results with red cabbage.

1. Rinse the blackberries in cold water then liquidize or mash them. I use this mixture as it is, but you could strain it if you prefer.

2. Place in the dye pot (saucepan) with about 2–3 cups (475–700ml) of water.

3. Bring the mixture to the boil.

4. Add the pre-treated fabric to the dye solution and soak for about an hour.

5. Remove the fabric and allow to cool.

6. Rinse the fabric in cool water until the water runs clear.

7. Wash the fabric with a mild laundry soap, and again rinse until clear.

8. Hang the fabric out of direct sunlight to dry.

9. Iron on a hot setting to set the colour.

TURMERIC

Turmeric provides shades of yellow and orange.

1. Boil water in a kettle.
2. Add a ratio of two tablespoons of turmeric to two cups (475ml) of boiling water – you will need enough water to cover your fabric. Stir well to ensure it is completely dissolved.
3. Add the fabric to the dye solution. For an orange shade: add one tablespoon of bicarbonate of soda to the prepared dye – this changes the pH of the dye and turns it orange. If you add a tablespoon of vinegar it will change it to a very fluorescent yellow. Allow to soak for 30 minutes.

4. Remove the fabric and allow it to cool.

5. Rinse the fabric in cool water until the water runs clear.

6. Wash the fabric with a mild laundry soap, and again rinse until clear.

7. Hang the fabric out of direct sunlight to dry.

8. Iron on a hot setting to set the colour.

TEA BAGS

Tea bags provide a range of shades, from cream and tan to off-white. Experiment with different types of tea; opposite you can see the results of using several different types of tea bag, all dyed following the method below.

1. Boil water in a kettle.

2. Add a ratio of one tea bag to one cup (230ml) of boiling water – you will need enough water to cover your fabric.

3. Steep the tea bags until the water colour is quite strong. Remove the bags and stir until completely dissolved.

4. Add the fabric to the dye solution and soak for 15–45 minutes. The longer you soak, the stronger the colour will be: if you want a light, creamy shade, only soak for 15 minutes.

5. Remove the fabric and allow to cool.

6. Rinse the fabric in cool water until the water runs clear.

7. Wash the fabric with a mild laundry soap, and again rinse until clear.

8. Hang the fabric out of direct sunlight to dry.

9. Iron on a hot setting to set the colour.

COFFEE

Coffee provides various shades of cream and pale tan.

1. Boil water in a kettle.

2. Add a ratio of two teaspoons of coffee to two cups (475ml) of boiling water – you will need enough water to cover your fabric.

3. Stir until the coffee is completely dissolved.

4. Add the fabric to the dye solution and soak for 15–45 minutes. The longer you soak, the stronger the colour will be: if you want a light, creamy shade, only soak for 15 minutes.

5. Remove the fabric and allow to cool.

6. Rinse the fabric in cool water until the water runs clear.

7. Wash the fabric with a mild laundry soap, and again rinse until clear.

8. Hang the fabric out of direct sunlight to dry.

9. Iron on a hot setting to set the colour.

DYED FABRIC RESULTS

Here are the results of my natural dyes, from top to bottom:
Blackberries, after 1 hour
Five Roses Tea, after 15 minutes
Coffee, after 15 minutes
Rooibos tea, after 30 minutes
Turmeric, after 30 minutes
Turmeric and bicarbonate of soda, after 30 minutes
Coffee, after 30 minutes
Five Roses Tea, after 45 minutes
Black Tea, after 15 minutes.

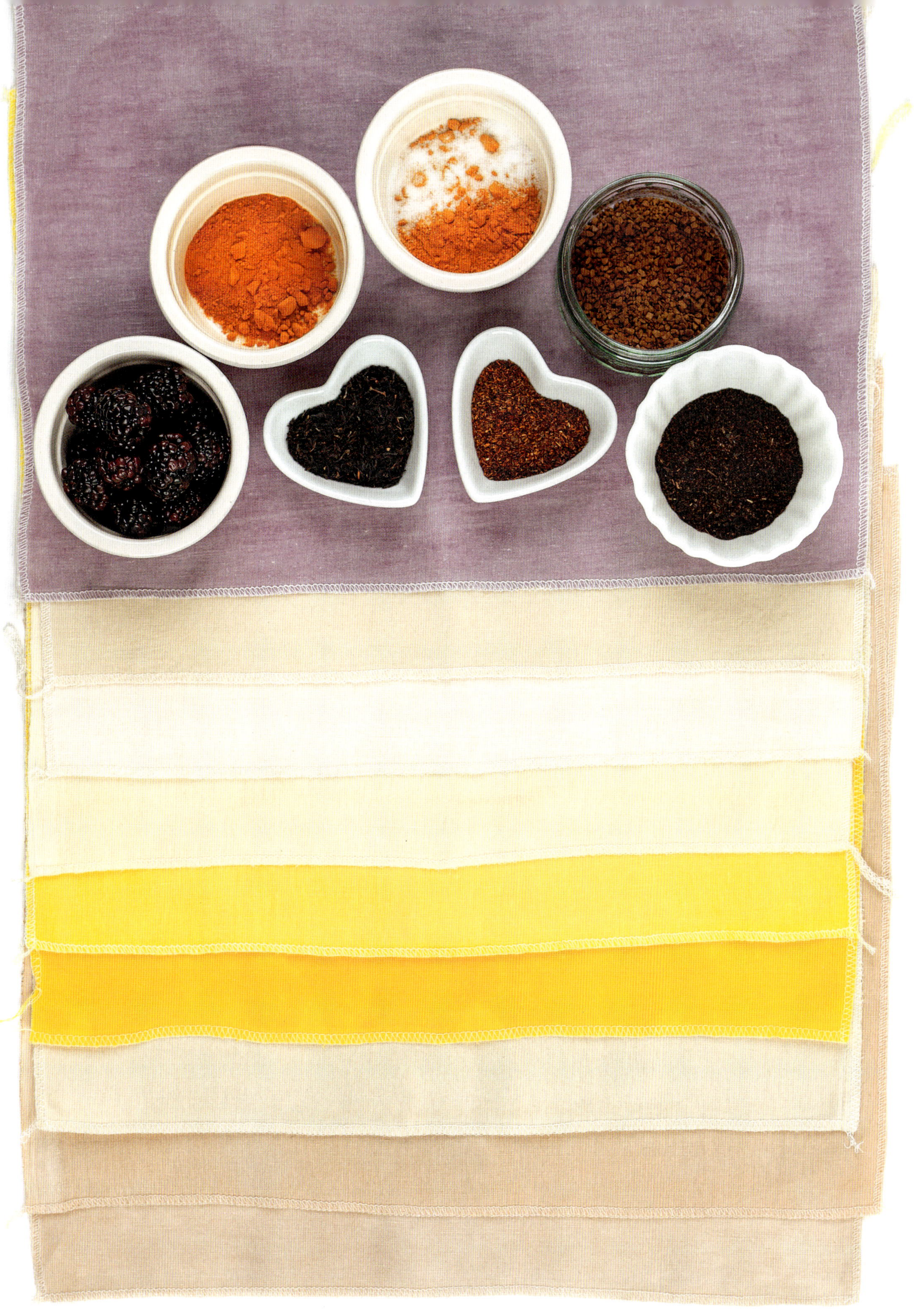

STITCHING THE PROJECTS

- Transfer the outline to your fabric (see pages 16 and 176).
- Mount your fabric in a hoop or frame (see pages 16–17).
- If desired, add directional lines with a sharp pencil (see page 23).
- Refer to the order of work and follow the step-by-step directions given for each project.

USEFUL ADVICE BEFORE YOU START

- Keep your hands clean.
- Keep your embroidery clean: store in a white cotton bag or pillowcase.
- Always keep your fabric taut in the hoop/frame.
- Ensure that you are sitting comfortably and take regular breaks. To prevent neck and shoulder tension, try placing a small cushion under your armpit (the side that holds the hoop). This encourages your arm and shoulder into a more relaxed position.
- Stop stitching occasionally and hold your work away from you so you can view it from afar – this gives a truer impression of what it looks like, rather than close up under the magnifying glass.
- If your embroidery doesn't look right, take a photograph of it with your smartphone; if something is wrong, you will immediately see it in the photograph and can then correct it. The wonderful thing about needle painting is that you can often add stitches on top of the previous embroidery or make corrections without unpicking… I really hate unpicking!
- Put on some good music, a podcast, audio book or movie, and enjoy your stitching time.

TBURR21

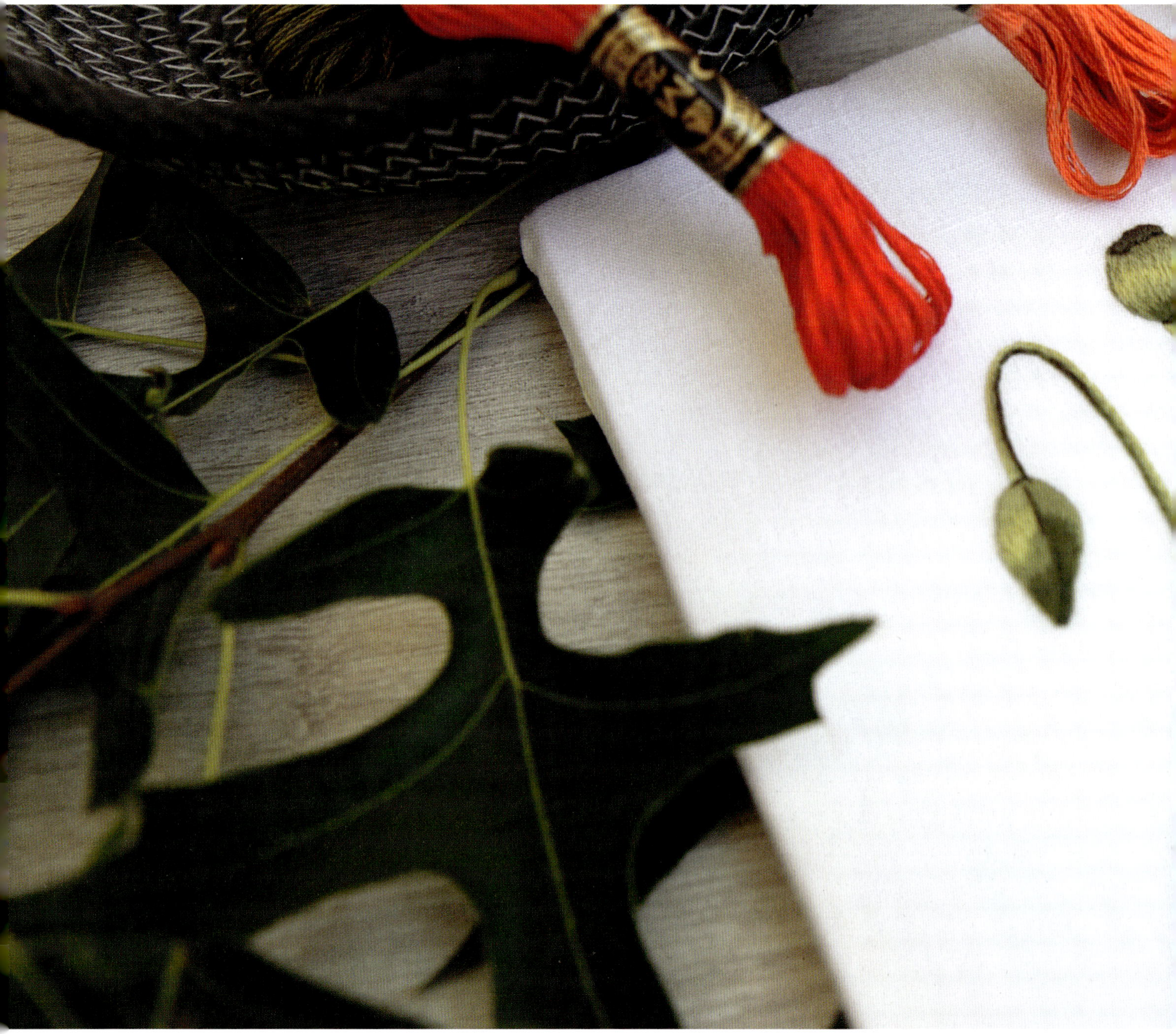

SIMPLE PROJECTS

STARTER STITCH SAMPLER

Use this sampler to practise all the stitches. It could also be used as a reference for future projects.

PROJECT SIZE

15 x 15cm (6 x 6in)

YOU WILL NEED

- Piece of fabric, 30 x 30cm (12 x 12in)
- Threads as per list
- A super grip hoop, size 18 or 20cm (7 or 8in)
- Template, see page 168

PREPARATION

- Transfer the outline to the fabric (see pages 16 and 176).
- Add directional lines in pencil, as required (see page 23).
- Mount your fabric in the hoop or frame (see pages 16–17).
- Follow the step-by-step instructions on pages 46–52.
- Use one strand of thread throughout unless otherwise specified.

ORDER OF WORK

Actual size.

1
SPLIT-STITCH BUD AND STEM

THREAD LIST

DMC
- 22
- 351
- 469
- 470
- 844
- 922
- 935
- 936
- 3825

Step 01c
3825, 922, 351, 22;
outline 844

Step 01b
470, 469, 936, 935

Step 01a
936, 935

Step 01d
3825, 922, 351, 22;
outline 844

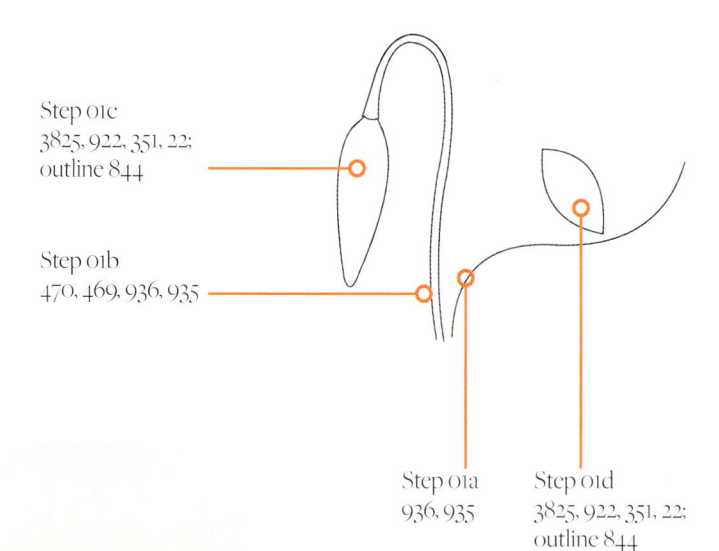

STEP 01: SPLIT-STITCH BUD AND STEM
1a. Fill the right-hand stem with adjacent lines of split stitch.
1b. Fill the left-hand stem with adjacent lines of split stitch.
1c. Fill the bud with lines of split stitch. Start at the outside and work into the centre – use the photographs below to guide you; outline with split stitch.
1d. Fill the leaf with adjacent lines of split stitch; outline with split stitch.

HINT
Shorten the stitches when stitching around a curve; lengthen them when on a straight path.

46

2. LONG-AND-SHORT STITCH PETAL

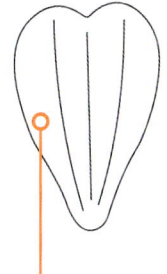

Step 02
472, 471, 470, 469, 936;
outline 844

THREAD LIST

DMC
- 469
- 470
- 471
- 472
- 844
- 936

STEP 02: LONG-AND-SHORT STITCH PETAL

Use the photographs, left, as a guide to colour placement. Fill the shape with rows of long-and-short stitch; outline with split stitch.

3. CURVED LONG-AND-SHORT STITCH PETAL

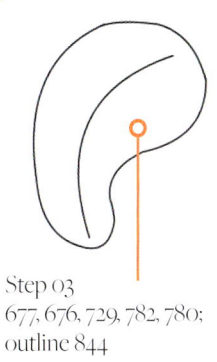

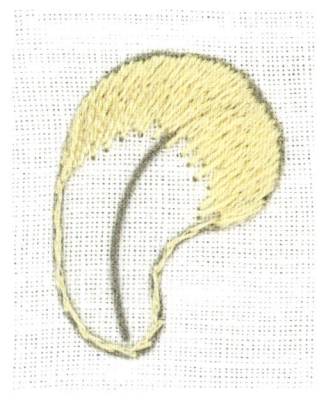

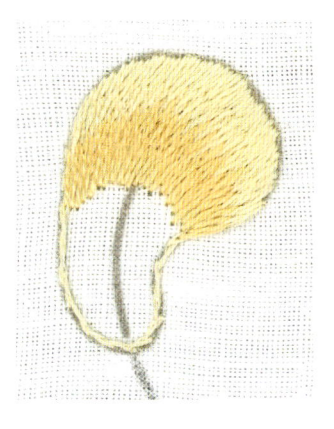

Step 03
677, 676, 729, 782, 780;
outline 844

THREAD LIST

DMC
- 676
- 677
- 729
- 780
- 782
- 844

STEP 03: CURVED LONG-AND-SHORT STITCH PETAL

Fill the shape with rows of long-and-short stitch. To get around the curve you need to shorten the stitches in each row – stitch at least two rows of each shade as shown in the photographs, left. Outline the shape with split stitch.

4 LONG-AND-SHORT STITCH BUTTERFLY

THREAD LIST

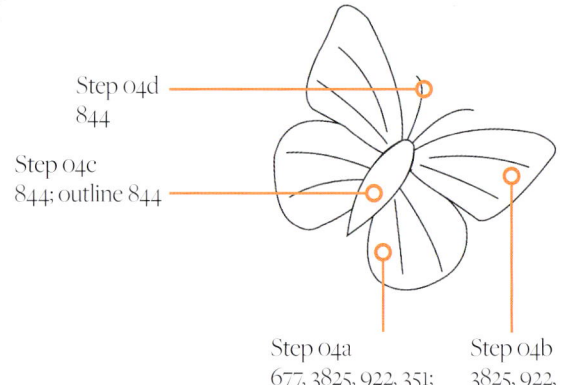

DMC
- 22
- 351
- 677
- 844
- 922
- 3825

Step 04d
844

Step 04c
844; outline 844

Step 04a
677, 3825, 922, 351;
outline 844

Step 04b
3825, 922,
351, 22

STEP 04: LONG-AND-SHORT STITCH BUTTERFLY

4a. Fill the bottom wing portions with long-and-short stitch; outline with split stitch.
4b. Fill the top wing portions with long-and-short stitch. Do not outline this wing, as we want it to appear lighter.
4c. Fill the body with padded satin stitch, then outline with split stitch.
4d. Work the antennae with split stitch.

5 LONG-AND-SHORT STITCH LEAF

Step 05b
524, 3053;
outline 844

Step 05a
471, 470, 469,
936; outline 844

Step 05c
935

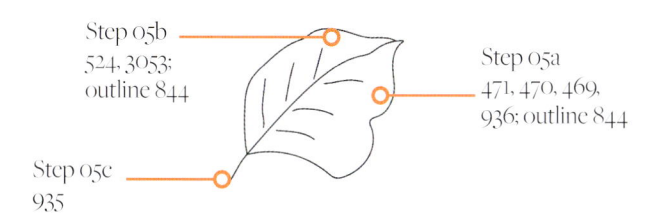

THREAD LIST

DMC
- 469
- 470
- 471
- 524
- 844
- 935
- 936
- 3053

STEP 05: LONG-AND-SHORT STITCH LEAF

5a. Fill the right-hand side of the leaf in long-and-short stitch; outline in split stitch.

5b. Fill the left-hand side of the leaf in long-and-short stitch; outline in split stitch.

5c. Fill the stem and centre vein with split stitch.

49

6 SATIN-STITCH PODS

THREAD LIST

DMC - 844
- 524   - 936
- 676   - 3052
- 729   - 3825

Step 06c
3052; outline 844

Step 06b
524; outline 844

Step 06f
3825, 844

Step 06e
676; outline 844

Step 06d
729; outline 844

Step 06a
936, 844

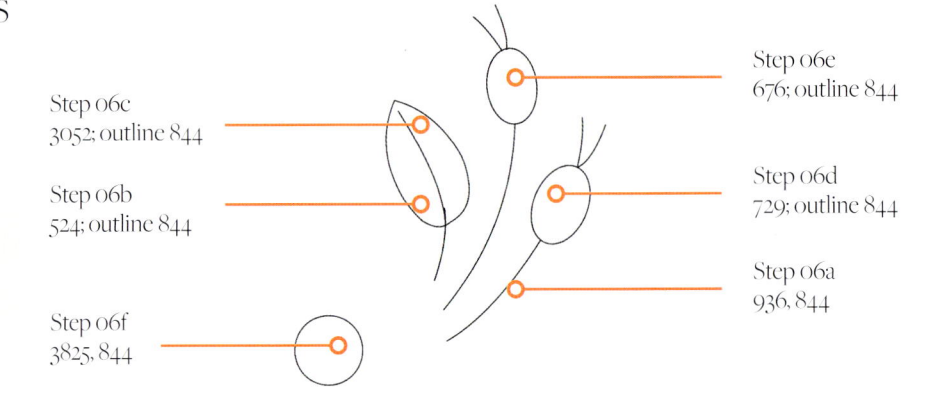

STEP 06: SATIN-STITCH PODS

6a. Create the stems with one or two rows of split stitch.
6b. and **6c.** Fill each side of the leaf with padded satin stitch; outline with split stitch.
6d. Fill the bud with padded satin stitch; outline with split stitch.
6e. Repeat as for step 6d.
6f. Fill the dot with padded satin stitch. First, outline the dot with split stitch. Make a star shape in the centre as shown in the photograph, right. On top of this add straight satin stitches. On top of this add another layer of straight satin stitches at right angles to the previous one – these stitches must go over the outline; outline with split stitch.

50

7. FRENCH-KNOT FLOWER

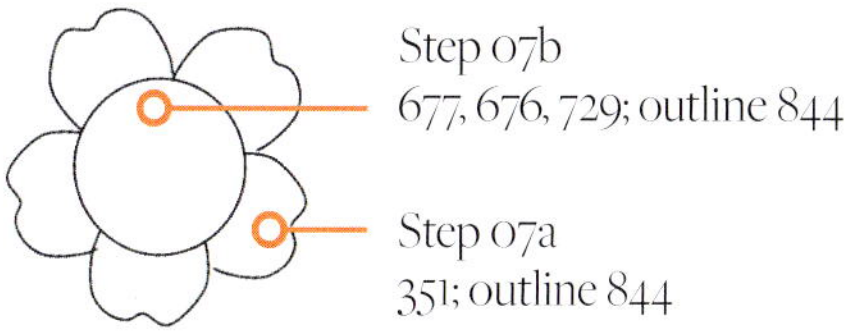

Step 07b
677, 676, 729; outline 844

Step 07a
351; outline 844

THREAD LIST

DMC
- 351
- 676
- 677
- 729
- 844

STEP 07: FRENCH-KNOT FLOWER

7a. Fill each petal with padded satin stitch; outline with split stitch.
7b. Fill the centre with French knots. Use two strands and two twists.

8. BULLION FLOWERS

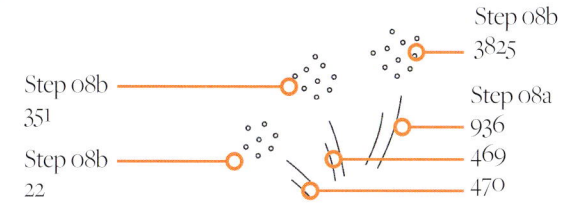

Step 08b
3825

Step 08b
351

Step 08a
936
469
470

Step 08b
22

THREAD LIST

DMC
- 22
- 351
- 469
- 470
- 936
- 3825

STEP 08: BULLION FLOWERS

8a. Loosen your fabric in the hoop to create the bullions. Add two bullions next to each other for each flower.
8b. Fill the flowers with French knots; use two strands and two twists for each.

9 FRENCH-KNOT ACORN

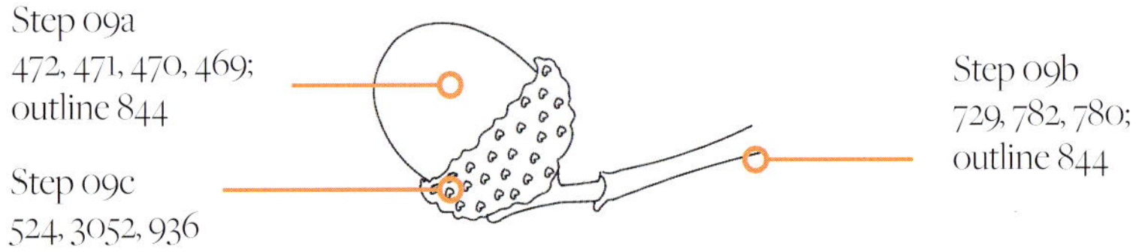

Step 09a
472, 471, 470, 469;
outline 844

Step 09c
524, 3052, 936

Step 09b
729, 782, 780;
outline 844

THREAD LIST

DMC
- 469
- 470
- 471
- 472
- 524
- 729
- 780
- 782
- 844
- 936
- 3052

STEP 09: FRENCH-KNOT ACORN

9a. Fill the nut with long-and-short stitch; outline with split stitch.
9b. Fill the branch with adjacent lines of split stitch.
9c. Fill the acorn cup with French knots. Use two strands and two twists for each.

52

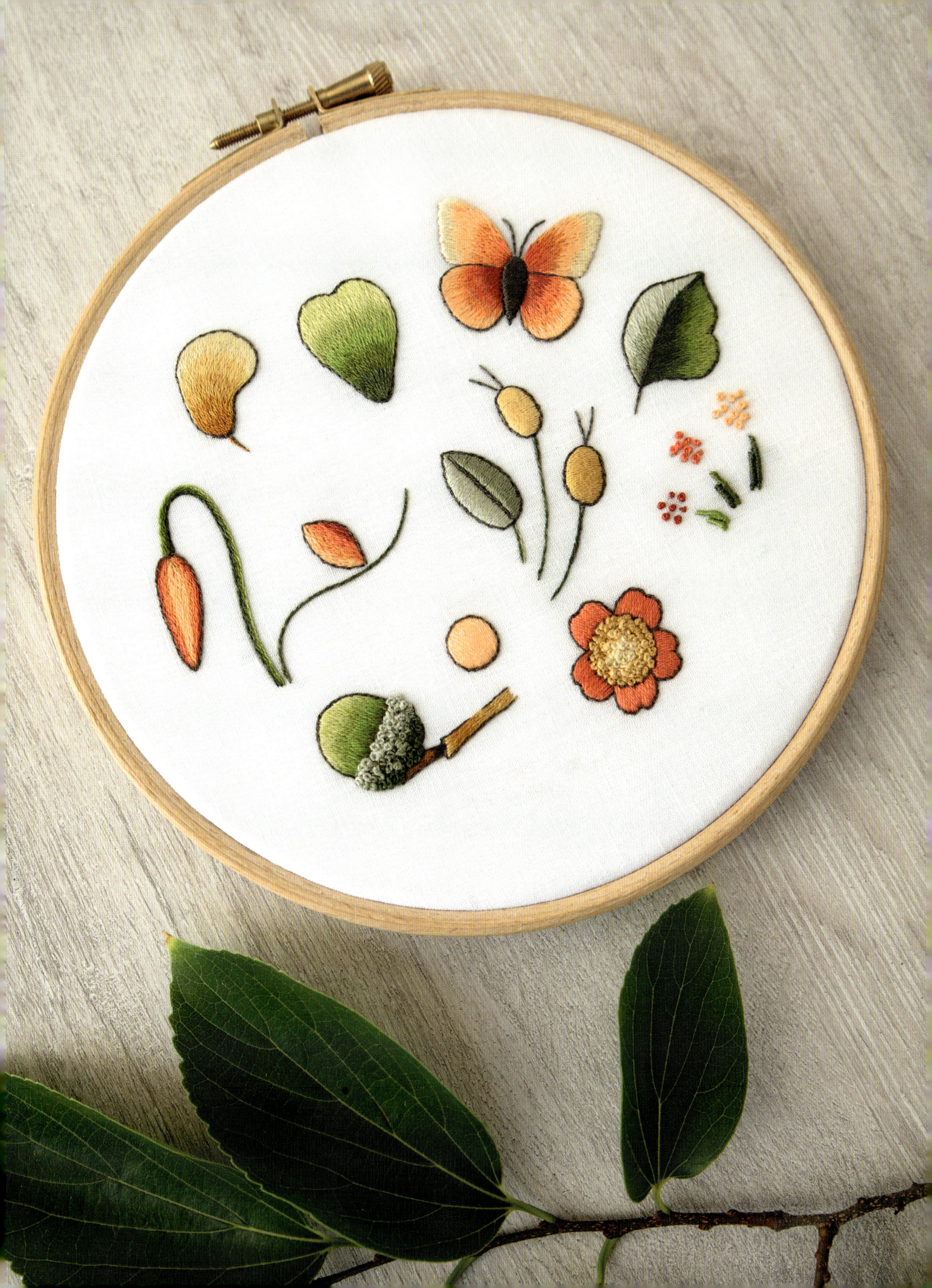

POPPY SAMPLER
PAPAVER SOMNIFERUM

Artwork by Rachel Pedder-Smith.

PREPARATION

- Transfer the outline to the fabric (see pages 16 and 176).
- Add directional lines in pencil, as required (see page 23).
- Mount your fabric in the hoop or frame (see pages 16–17).
- Follow the step-by-step instructions on pages 56–58.
- Use one strand of thread throughout unless otherwise specified.

PROJECT SIZE

11 x 10cm (4¼ x 4in)

YOU WILL NEED

- Piece of fabric, 28 x 30cm (11 x 12in)
- Threads as per list
- A super grip hoop, size 20cm (8in), or stretcher frame
- Template, see page 169

THREAD LIST

DMC	
- 349	- 3051
- 351	- 3052
- 352	- 3053
- 817	- 3348
- 935	- 3777
- 3021	- 3787
	- 3865

ORDER OF WORK

Actual size

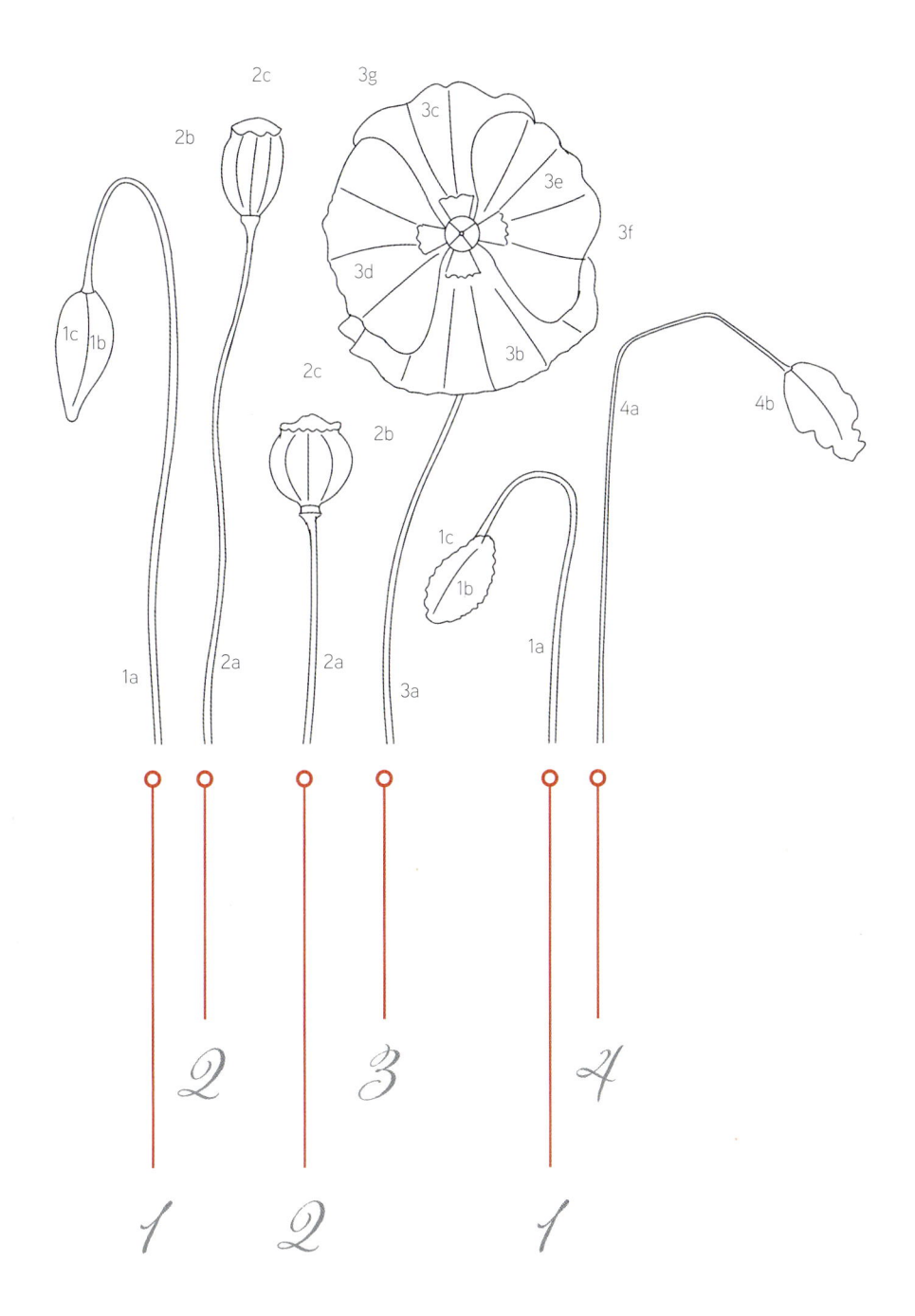

1

Step 01c
3052, 3053, 3348, 3052, 3051;
lines 3021

Step 01b
3052, 3051, 935; lines 3021

Step 01a
3348, 3052, 3051

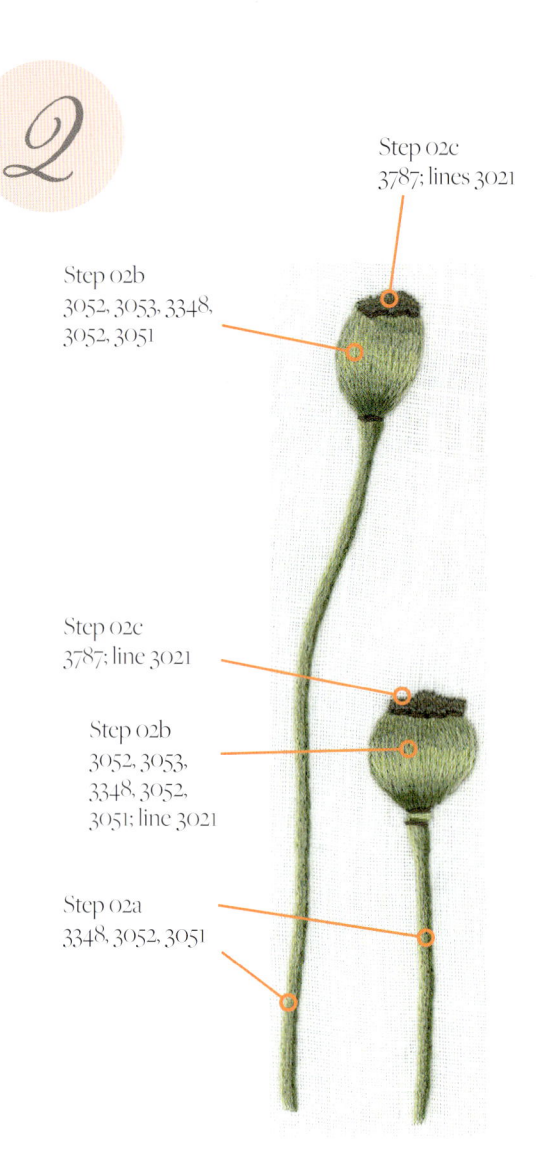

2

Step 02c
3787; lines 3021

Step 02b
3052, 3053, 3348,
3052, 3051

Step 02c
3787; line 3021

Step 02b
3052, 3053,
3348, 3052,
3051; line 3021

Step 02a
3348, 3052, 3051

STEP 01: STEMS AND BUDS
See above and opposite.
1a. Fill the stem with adjacent lines of split stitch.
1b. Fill the right-hand side with long-and-short stitch; add a line of split stitch in 3021.
1c. Fill the left-hand side with long-and-short stitch.

STEP 02: SEEDHEADS
2a. Fill the stem with adjacent lines of split stitch.
2b. Fill the bottom of the seedheads with long-and-short stitch; add a line of split stitch in 3021.
2c. Fill the top of the seedheads with satin stitch. Add outline in split stitch.

3

Step 03e
352, 351, 349, 817, 3777;
outline 3021

Step 03c
352, 351, 349, 817, 3777;
outline 3021

Step 03f
3021, 3865

Step 03g
3348

Step 03d
352, 351, 349, 817, 3777;
outline 3021

Step 03b
352, 351, 349, 817,
3777; outline 3021

Step 03a
3348, 3052, 3051

Step 01c
3052, 3053, 3348,
3052, 3051; lines 3021

Step 01b
3052, 3051, 935

Step 01a
3348, 3052, 3051

STEP 03: POPPY

3a. Fill the stem with adjacent lines of split stitch.
3b. Fill the bottom petal with long-and-short stitch. Add outlines in split stitch.
3c. Fill the top petal with long-and-short stitch. Add outlines in split stitch.
3d. Fill the left-hand petal with long-and-short stitch. Add outlines in split stitch.
3e. Fill the right-hand petal with long-and-short stitch. Add outlines in split stitch.
3f. Fill with straight stitches.
3g. Fill with straight stitches around the centre. Add a small French knot in the centre. Use one strand and two twists.

4

Step 04b
352, 351, 349, 817

Step 04a
3348, 3052, 3051

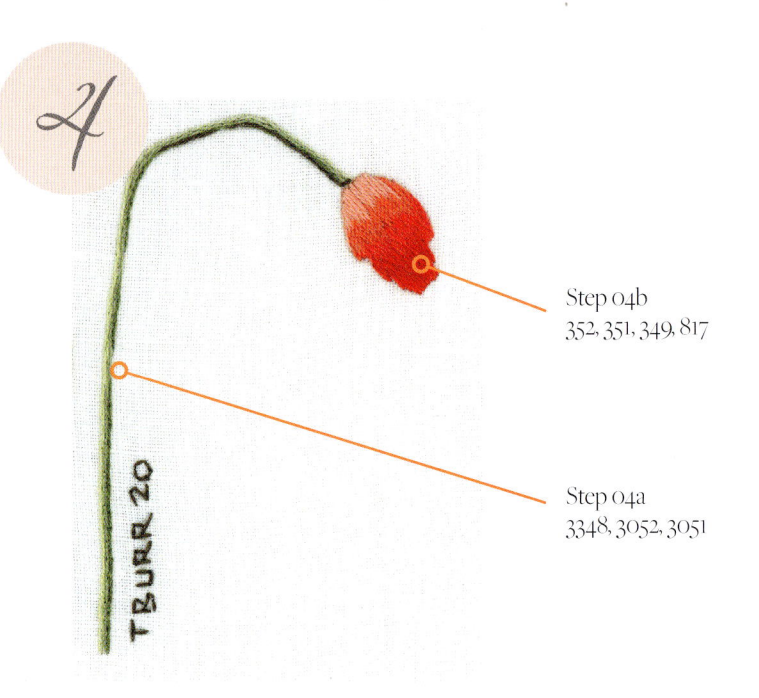

STEP 04: FLOWERING BUD
4a. Fill the stem with adjacent lines of split stitch.
4b. Fill the bud with long-and-short stitch.

58

37

WILDFLOWER SAMPLER

Artwork by Jane Carkill.

PROJECT SIZE
11 x 10cm (4¼ x 4in)

YOU WILL NEED
- Piece of fabric, 30 x 30cm (12 x 12in)
- Threads as per list
- A super grip hoop, size 20cm (8in), or stretcher frame
- Template, see page 169

THREAD LIST

DMC
- 26
- 27
- 29
- 30
- 32
- 341
- 355
- 642
- 919
- 920
- 921
- 922
- 934
- 977
- 3021
- 3032
- 3033
- 3041
- 3042
- 3045
- 3046
- 3371
- 3740
- 3743
- 3747
- 3776
- 3782
- 3787
- 3790
- 3825
- 3827
- 3865

Anchor
- A842
- A843
- A845

PREPARATION

- Transfer the outline to the fabric (see pages 16 and 176).
- Add directional lines in pencil, as required (see page 23).
- Mount your fabric in the hoop or frame (see pages 16–17).
- Follow the step-by-step instructions on pages 62–65.
- Use one strand of thread throughout unless otherwise specified
- Anchor threads are prefaced with an A before each number.

ORDER OF WORK

Actual size

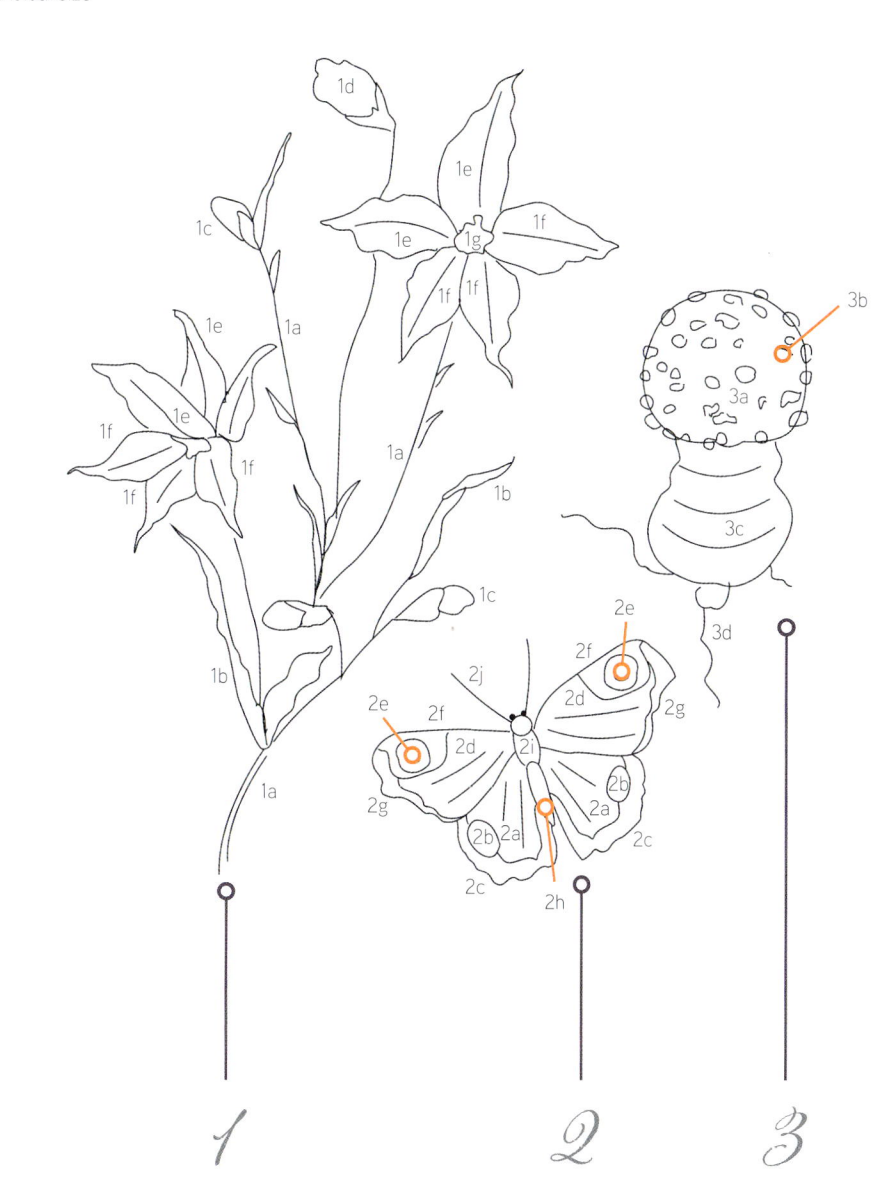

1 *2* *3*

1

Step 01d
3747, 3042, 3041;
outline 29

Step 01c
3747, 3042;
outline 29

Step 01e
29, 32, 30, 26,
3747; outline 29

Step 01f
27, 3743, 3042,
3041, 3740;
outline 29

Step 01b
A842, A843, A845;
outlines 934

Step 01a
A843, A845, 934

Step 01e
29, 32, 30, 26,
3747; outline 29

Step 01g
3046, 3045

Step 01f
27, 3743, 3042,
3041, 3740;
outline 29

Step 01b
3740

STEP 01: FLOWER

1a. Fill the stems with lines of split stitch; outline in split stitch.
1b. Fill the leaves with lines of split stitch; the tip of the right-hand leaf has a purple touch of 3740. Outline in split stitch.
1c. Fill the buds with long-and-short stitch (fill with satin stitch in first shade – add second shade on top of this); outline with split stitch.
1d. Fill the larger bud with long-and-short stitch; outline in split stitch.
1e. Outline the petals in split stitch using one strand. Fill the petals with long-and-short stitch, starting with the petals that are furthest back and working forwards to the petals in the front; outline with split stitch.
1f. Repeat as for step 1e.
1g. Fill the flower centres with French knots, using one strand and two twists.

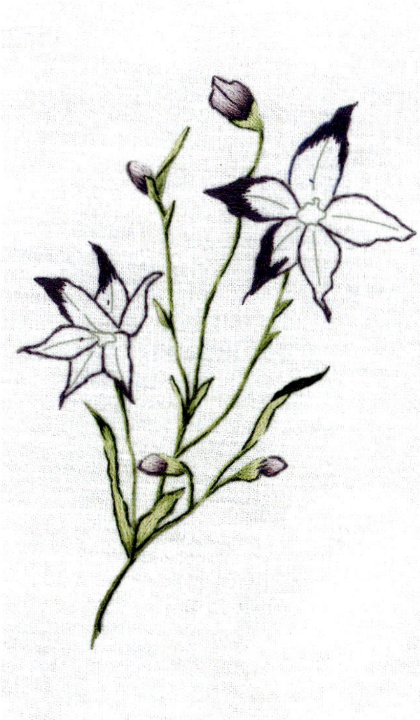
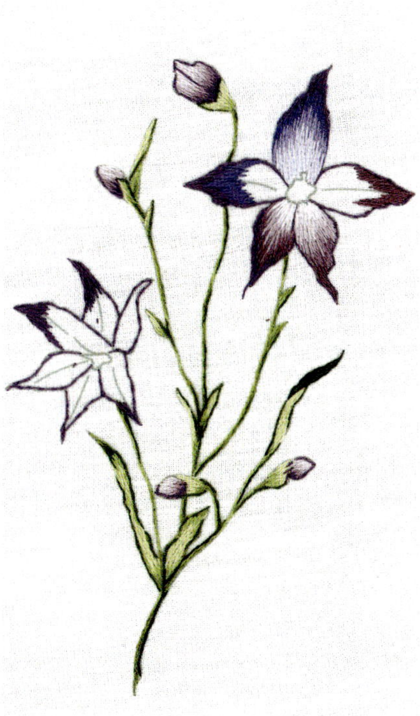
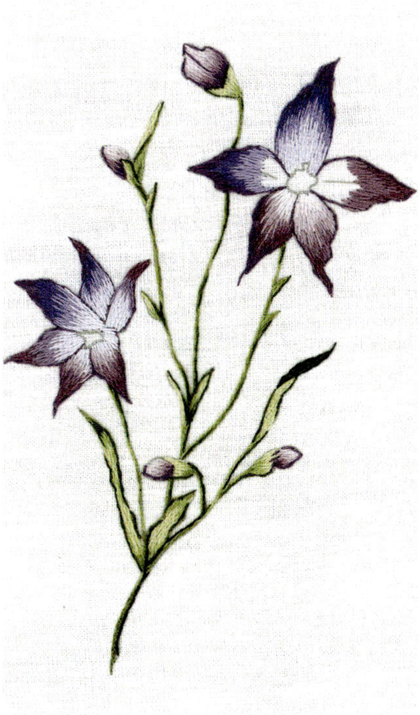
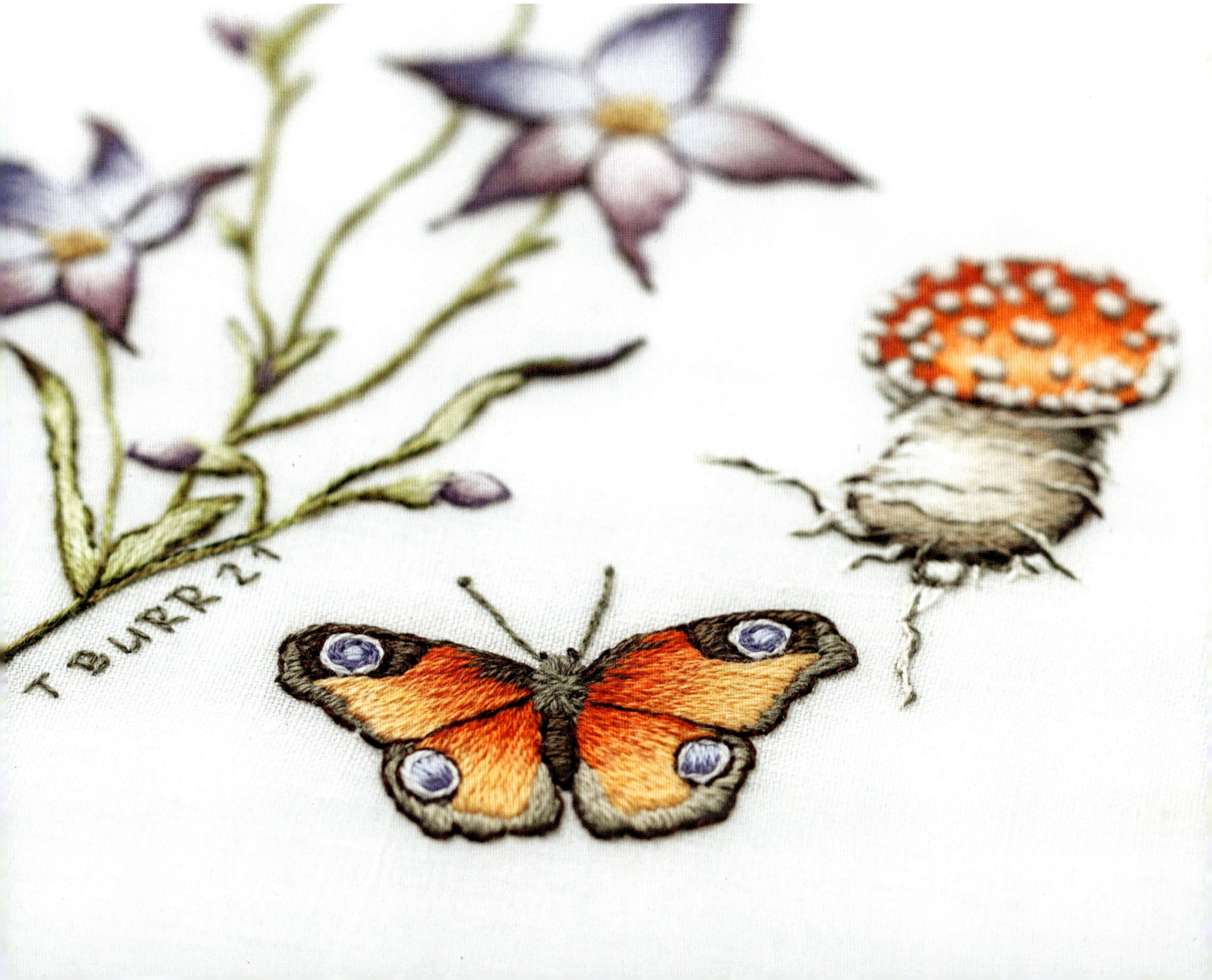
T BURR 21

STEP 02: BUTTERFLY

2a. Fill with long-and-short stitch, from the outside in towards the centre.
2b. Completely fill the area with satin stitch, then add some stitches on top of this in second shade. Add outlines of 3865 in split stitch.
2c. Fill the band with long-and-short stitch, or satin stitch where space does not allow.
2d. Fill with long-and-short stitch, from the outside in towards the centre.
2e. Fill with satin stitch. Add outlines with split stitch. Finally add a line of split stitch around the edge.
2f. Fill with long-and-short stitch or satin stitch where space does not allow. Add outlines in split stitch.
2g. Fill with satin stitch. Use this colour to add broken outlines to the wings in split stitch.
2h. Fill with satin stitch, outline in split stitch.
2i. Fill with straight stitches – these should be angled slightly to create a fluffy effect.
2j. Fill with split stitch. Add the clubs at the tips with two small French knots, using one strand and one twist each.

Step 02g
3787

Step 02j
3787, 3021

Step 02i
3787

Step 02f
3787, 3021; outline 3371

Step 02e
341; outline 32, 3865, 3021

Step 02d
3827, 977, 3776, 921, 919, 3021

Step 02b
341, 32; outline 3865, 3021

Step 02a
3827, 977, 3776, 921, 919

Step 02c
642, 3787

Step 02h
3021; outline 3371

STEP 03: TOADSTOOL

3a. Fill the cap with long-and-short stitch. Outline with split stitch.
3b. Add spots with French knots, using two strands and two twists. Add tiny outlines around these spots in straight stitches.
3c. Fill the stalk with long-and-short stitch. Add lines and outlines with split stitch or straight stitches where required.
3d. Fill the 'roots' with lines of split stitch.

Step 03b
3865; outline 3787

Step 03a
355, 920, 921, 922, 3825; outline 3021, 3371

Step 03c
3865, 3033, 3782, 3032, 3790, 3787; outlines 3021, 3371

Step 03d
3787, 3033, 3865

65

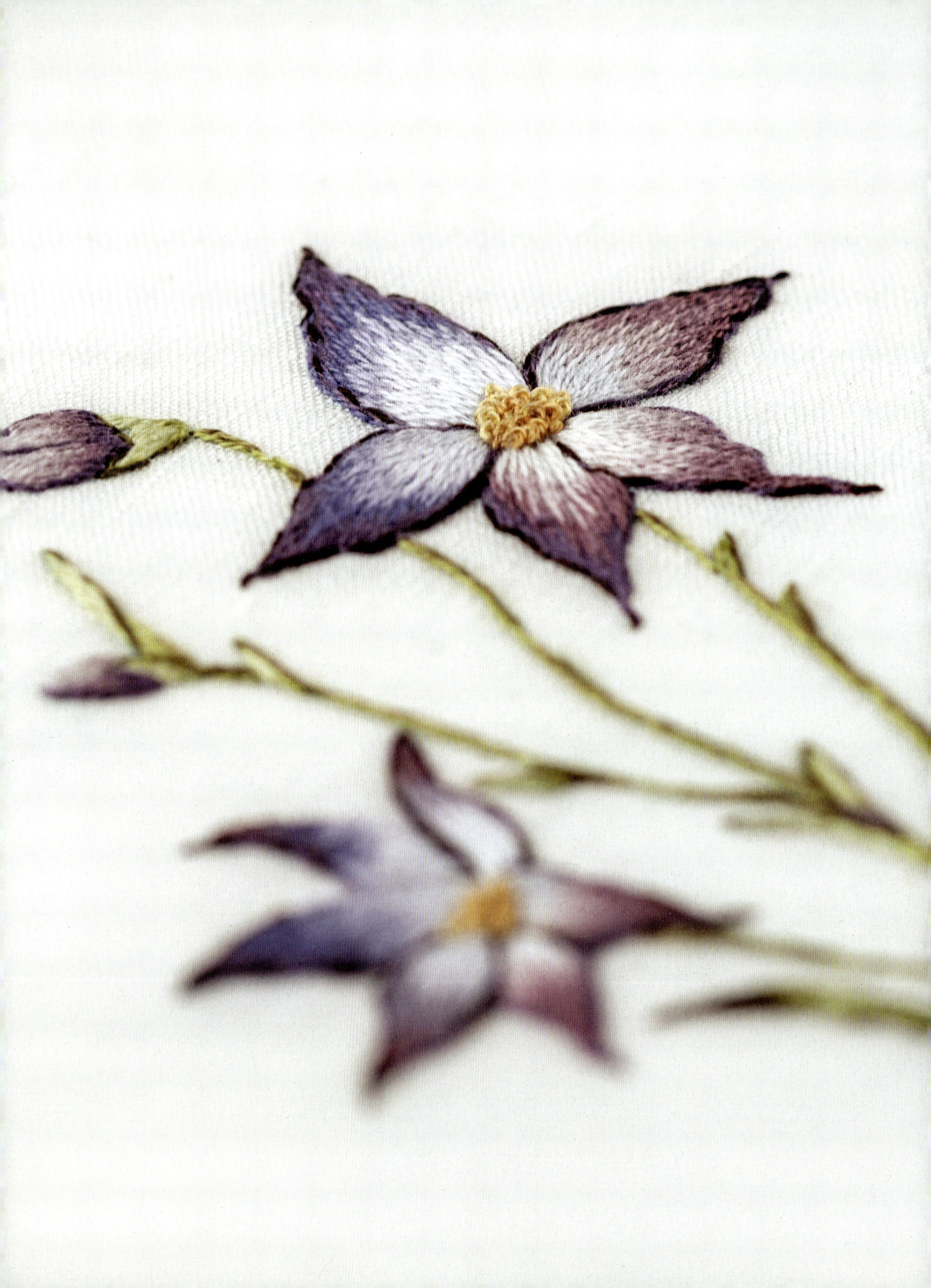

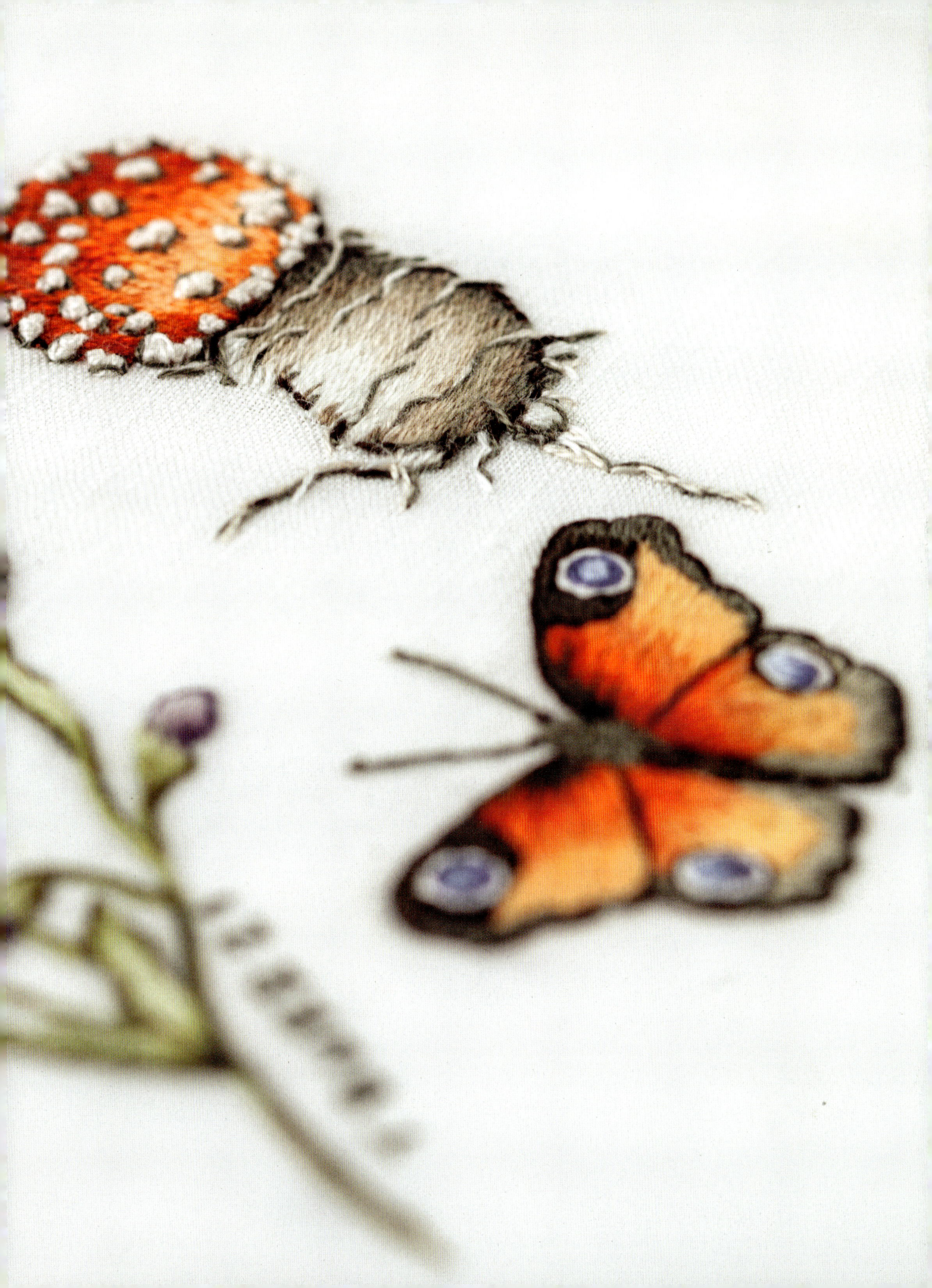

SACRED LOTUS FLOWER SAMPLER

NELUMBO NUCIFERA

Artwork by Wendy Hollender.

PROJECT SIZE
11 x 9.5cm (4¼ x 3¾in)

YOU WILL NEED
- Piece of fabric, 30 x 32cm (12 x 12½in)
- Threads as per list
- A super grip hoop, size 20cm (8in), or stretcher frame
- Template, see page 170

THREAD LIST

DMC
- 10
- 15
- 165
- 315
- 433
- 436
- 471
- 580
- 581
- 600
- 604
- 611
- 640
- 642
- 644
- 746
- 777
- 935
- 936
- 3021
- 3046
- 3047
- 3051
- 3347
- 3348
- 3689
- 3787
- 3805
- 3806
- 3819
- 3865

PREPARATION

- Transfer the outline to the fabric (see pages 16 and 176).
- Add directional lines in pencil, as required (see page 23).
- Mount your fabric in the hoop or frame (see pages 16–17).
- Follow the step-by-step instructions on pages 70–73.
- Use one strand of thread throughout unless otherwise specified.

ORDER OF WORK

Actual size

1

STEP 01: SEEDHEAD 1

1a. Fill the stem sections with long-and-short stitch; outline with split stitch.
1b. Fill the background with long-and-short stitch; outline with split stitch.
1c. Fill each spot with satin stitches; outline with split stitch.
1d. Fill with long-and-short stitch; outline with split stitch.

Step 01a
644, 642, 3787; outline 3021

Step 01a
433, 436, 3787

Step 01d
644, 642, 640, 3787; outline 3021

Step 01b
644, 642, 640; outline 3021

Step 01c
436, 433; outline 3021

Step 01a
644, 642, 3787

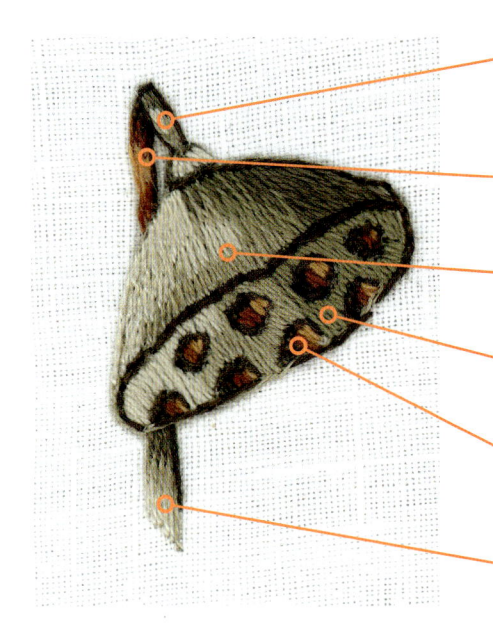

2

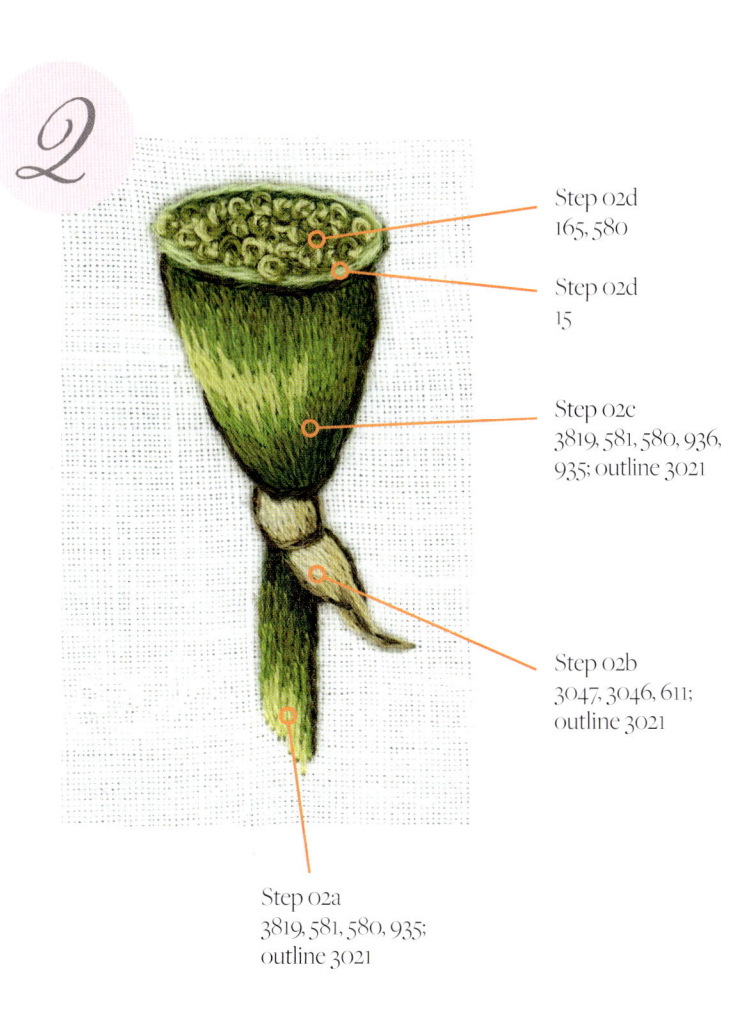

Step 02d
165, 580

Step 02d
15

STEP 02: SEEDHEAD 2
2a. Fill the stem with long-and-short stitch; add a line in split stitch.
2b. Fill with long-and-short stitch; outline in split stitch.
2c. Fill with long-and-short stitch; outline in split stitch.
2d. Fill with French knots – use two strands and two twists. Add band in split stitch.

Step 02c
3819, 581, 580, 936, 935; outline 3021

Step 02b
3047, 3046, 611; outline 3021

Step 02a
3819, 581, 580, 935; outline 3021

3

STEP 03: BUD
3a. Fill the stem with long-and-short stitch; add a line in split stitch.
3b. Fill with satin stitch; outline in split stitch.
3c. Fill with long-and-short stitch; outline in split stitch.
3d. Fill with long-and-short stitch; outline in split stitch.
3e. Fill with long-and-short stitch; outline in split stitch.
3f. Fill with long-and-short stitch; outline in split stitch.
3g. Fill with long-and-short stitch; outline in split stitch.
3h. Fill with long-and-short stitch; outline in split stitch.
3i. Fill with long-and-short stitch; outline in split stitch.

Step 03e
3805, 3806, 604, 3689, 3348, 471, 3347; outline 315, 777

Step 03d
600, 3805

Step 03c
600, 3805

Step 03f
3348, 471, 3347; outline 315, 777, 3347

Step 03i
3348, 471, 3347; tip 604, 3689; outline 315, 777, 3347

Step 03h
3348, 471, 3347; tip 604, 3689; outline 315, 777

Step 03b
3347

Step 03a
3051, 580, 471, 165; line 3021

Step 03g
3348, 471, 3347; tip 604, 3689; outline 315, 777, 3347

71

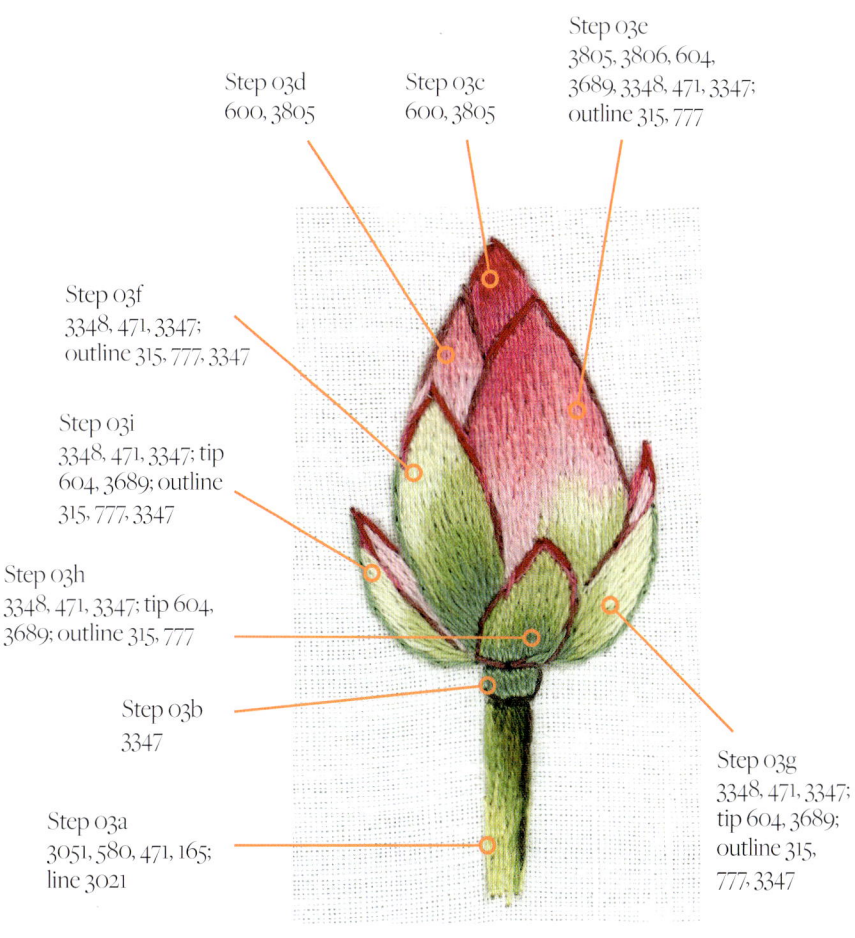

4

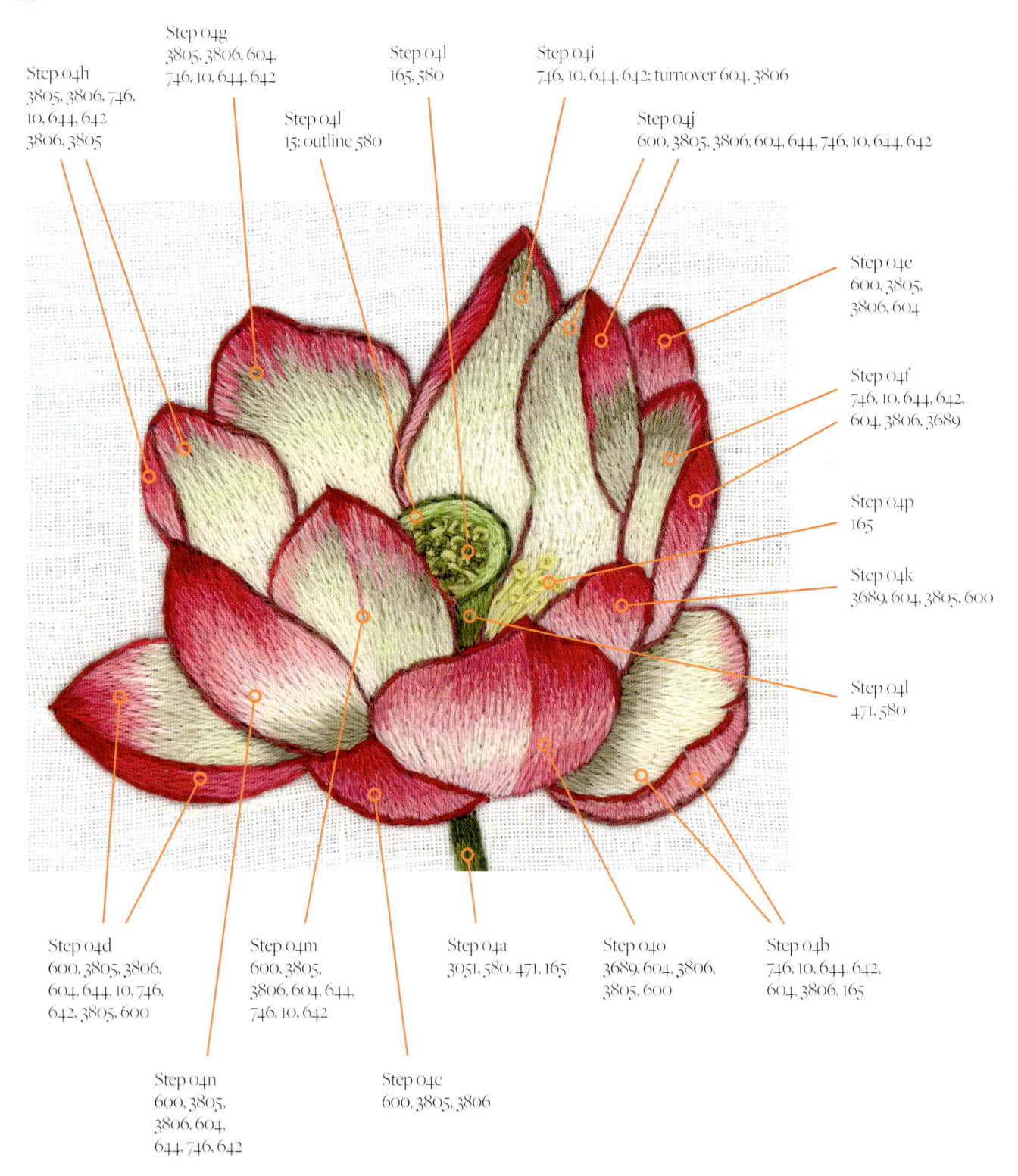

Step 04h
3805, 3806, 746, 10, 644, 642 3806, 3805

Step 04g
3805, 3806, 604, 746, 10, 644, 642

Step 04l
15; outline 580

Step 04l
165, 580

Step 04i
746, 10, 644, 642; turnover 604, 3806

Step 04j
600, 3805, 3806, 604, 644, 746, 10, 644, 642

Step 04e
600, 3805, 3806, 604

Step 04f
746, 10, 644, 642, 604, 3806, 3689

Step 04p
165

Step 04k
3689, 604, 3805, 600

Step 04l
471, 580

Step 04d
600, 3805, 3806, 604, 644, 10, 746, 642, 3805, 600

Step 04m
600, 3805, 3806, 604, 644, 746, 10, 642

Step 04a
3051, 580, 471, 165

Step 04o
3689, 604, 3806, 3805, 600

Step 04b
746, 10, 644, 642, 604, 3806, 165

Step 04n
600, 3805, 3806, 604, 644, 746, 642

Step 04c
600, 3805, 3806

72

STEP 04: FLOWER

4a. Fill the stem with adjacent rows of split stitch.
4b. Fill the petal with long-and-short stitch and turnover in satin stitch. Outline in split stitch (see below, as this is done at the end in step 4o).
4c. Fill the petal with long-and-short stitch; outline in split stitch.
4d. Fill the petal and turnover with long-and-short stitch. Outline in split stitch.
4e. Fill the petal with long-and-short stitch; outline with split stitch.
4f. Fill the petal and turnover with long-and-short stitch. Outline in split stitch.
4g. Fill the petal with long-and-short stitch; outline with split stitch.
4h. Fill the petal and turnover with long-and-short stitch. Outline in split stitch.
4i. Fill the petal with long-and-short stitch and turnover with satin stitch. Outline in split stitch.
4j. Fill the petal and turnover with long-and-short stitch. Outline in split stitch.
4k. Fill the petal with long-and-short stitch; outline with split stitch.
4l. Fill the base with long-and-short stitch. Fill the centre with French knots using two strands and two twists. Fill the rim with lines of split stitch. Outline in split stitch.
4m. Fill the petal with long-and-short stitch; outline in split stitch.
4n. Fill the petal with long-and-short stitch; outline in split stitch.
4o. Fill the petal with long-and-short stitch; outline in split stitch. Add all outlines around petals in split stitch in 315 and 777.
4p. Add in the final stamens with French knots and straight stitches in 165.

STEP 05: BUTTERFLY

5a. Fill the hindwings with long-and-short stitch.
5b. Fill the forewings with long-and-short stitch. Add dark wing tips in satin stitches; outline in split stitch.
5c. Fill the body with satin stitch.
5d. Stitch the antennae with split stitch.

Step 05b
3787, 3021

Step 05d
3787

Step 05b
3865, 746, 644, 642

Step 05c
3021

Step 05a
3865, 746, 644

TBURR 21

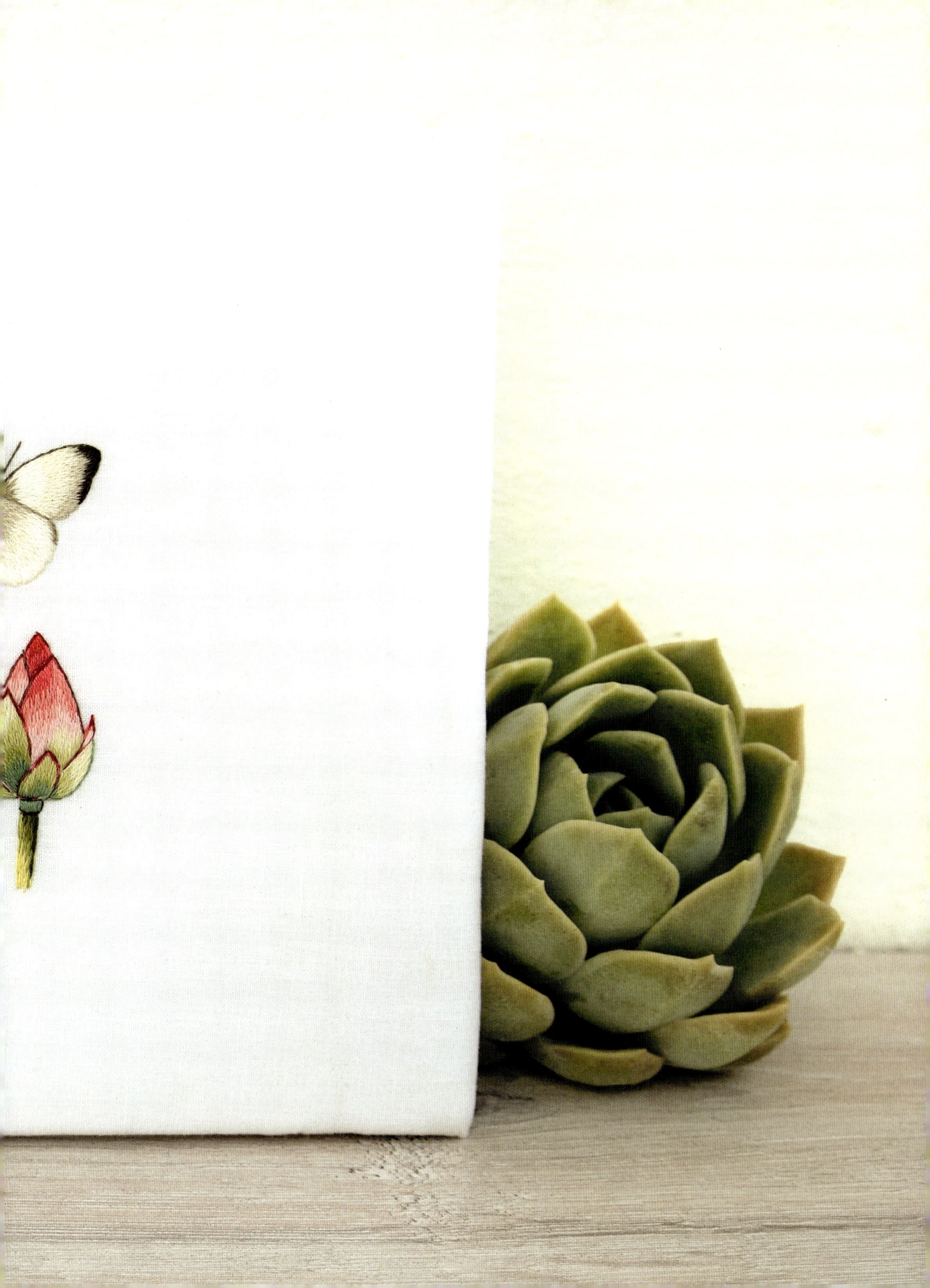

BREADSEED POPPY SAMPLER

PAPAVER SOMNIFERUM

Artwork by Wendy Hollender.

PROJECT SIZE

14 x 9.5cm (5½ x 3¾in)

YOU WILL NEED

- Piece of fabric, 30 x 32cm (12 x 12½in)
- Threads as per list
- A super grip hoop, size 20cm (8in), or stretcher frame
- Template, page 170

THREAD LIST

DMC
- 01
- 03
- 10
- 14
- 15
- 23
- 33
- 164
- 469
- 471
- 522
- 524
- 535
- 640
- 642
- 644
- 772
- 822
- 935
- 936
- 987
- 988
- 989
- 3021
- 3348
- 3363
- 3609
- 3689
- 3787
- 3803
- 3834
- 3863
- 3865

Anchor
- A86
- A87

PREPARATION

- Transfer the outline to the fabric (see pages 16 and 176).
- Add directional lines in pencil, as required (see page 23).
- Mount your fabric in the hoop or frame (see pages 16–17).
- Follow the step-by-step instructions on pages 79–85.
- Use one strand of thread throughout unless otherwise specified.
- Anchor threads are prefaced with an A before each number.

ORDER OF WORK

Actual size

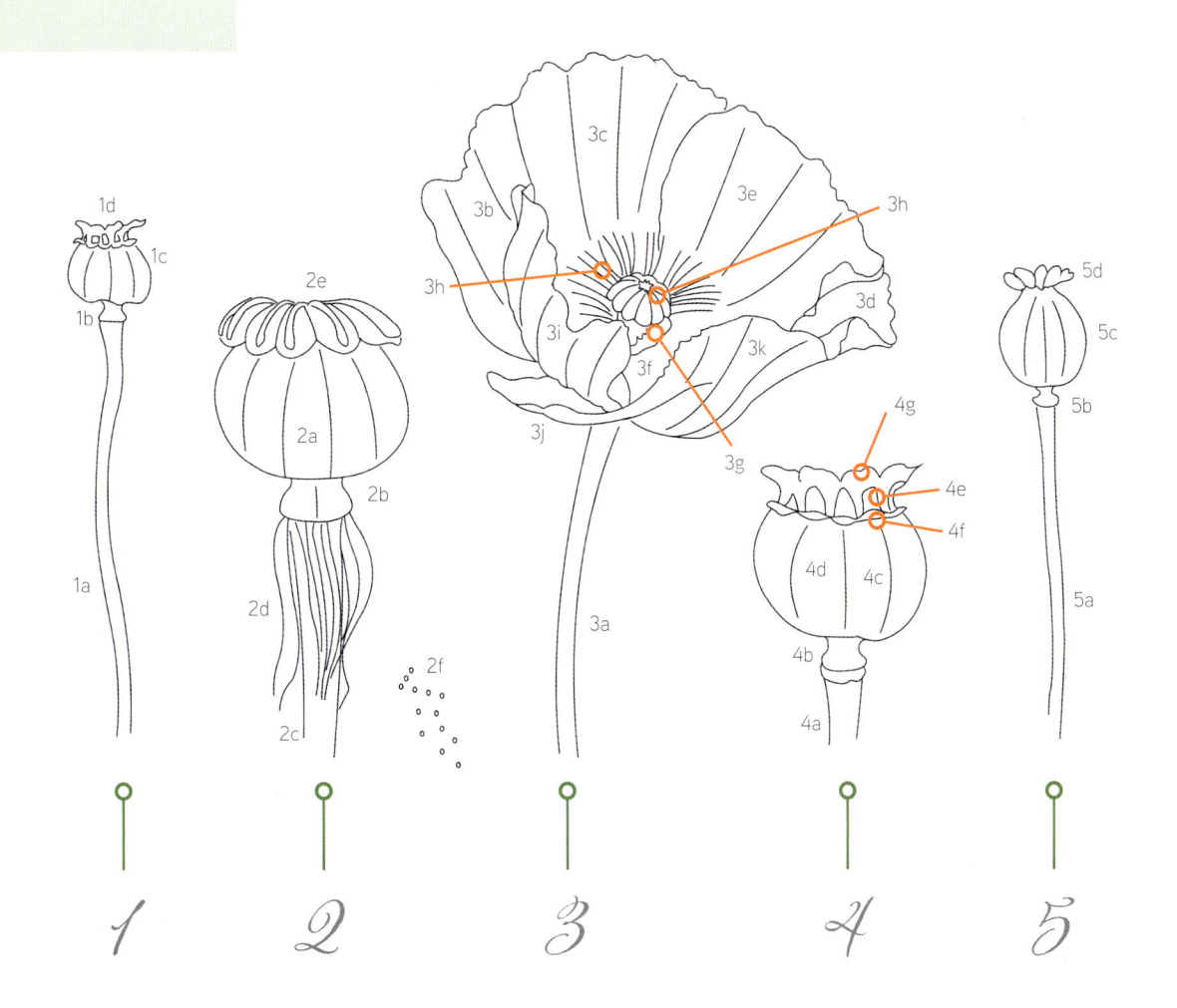

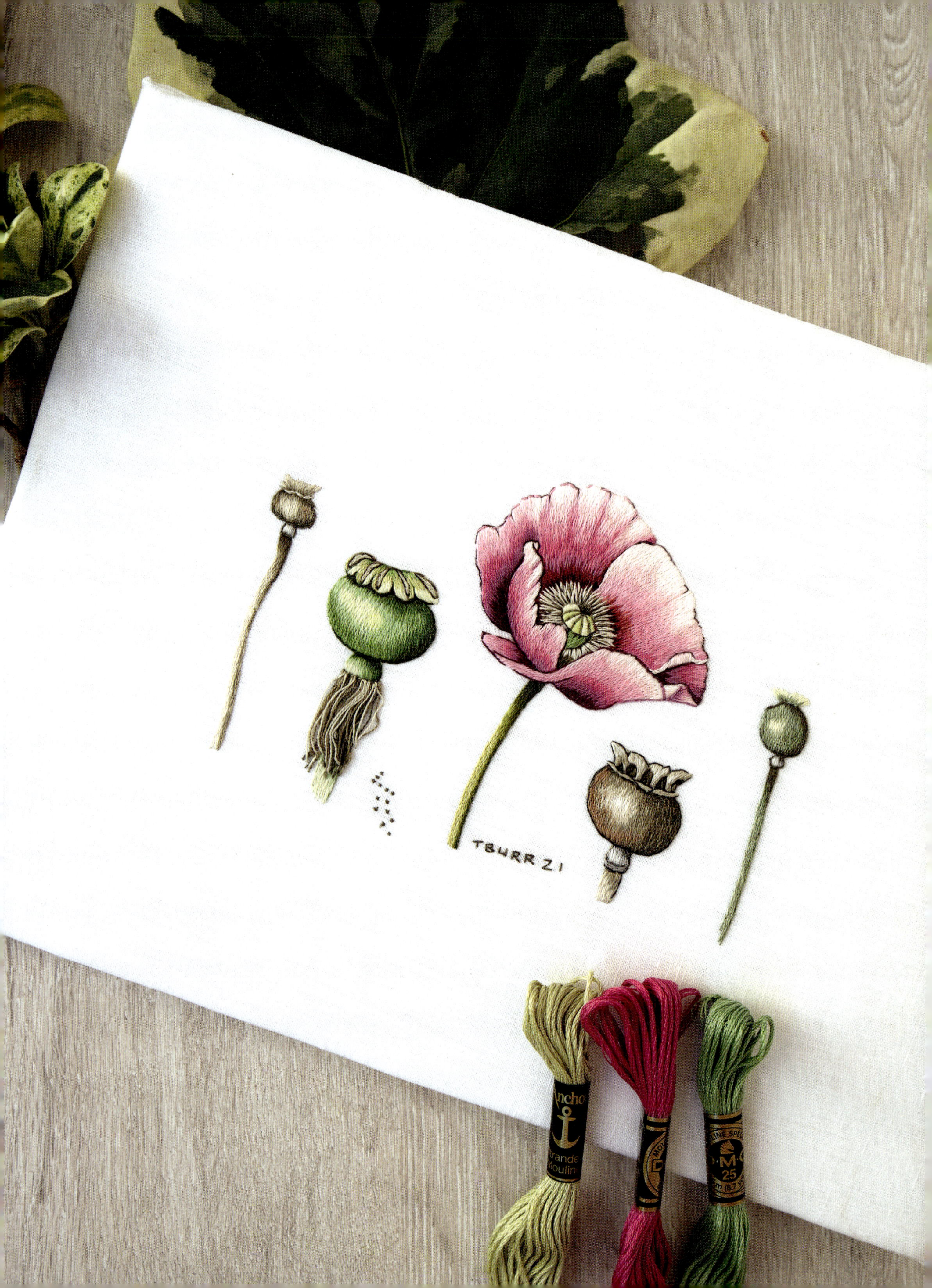
TBURR 21

1

STEP 01: SEEDHEAD 1

1a. Fill the stem with long-and-short stitch.
1b. Fill with long-and-short stitch.
1c. Fill with long-and-short stitch.
1d. Fill with irregular long-and-short stitches.

Add all outlines in split stitch using thread 3021.

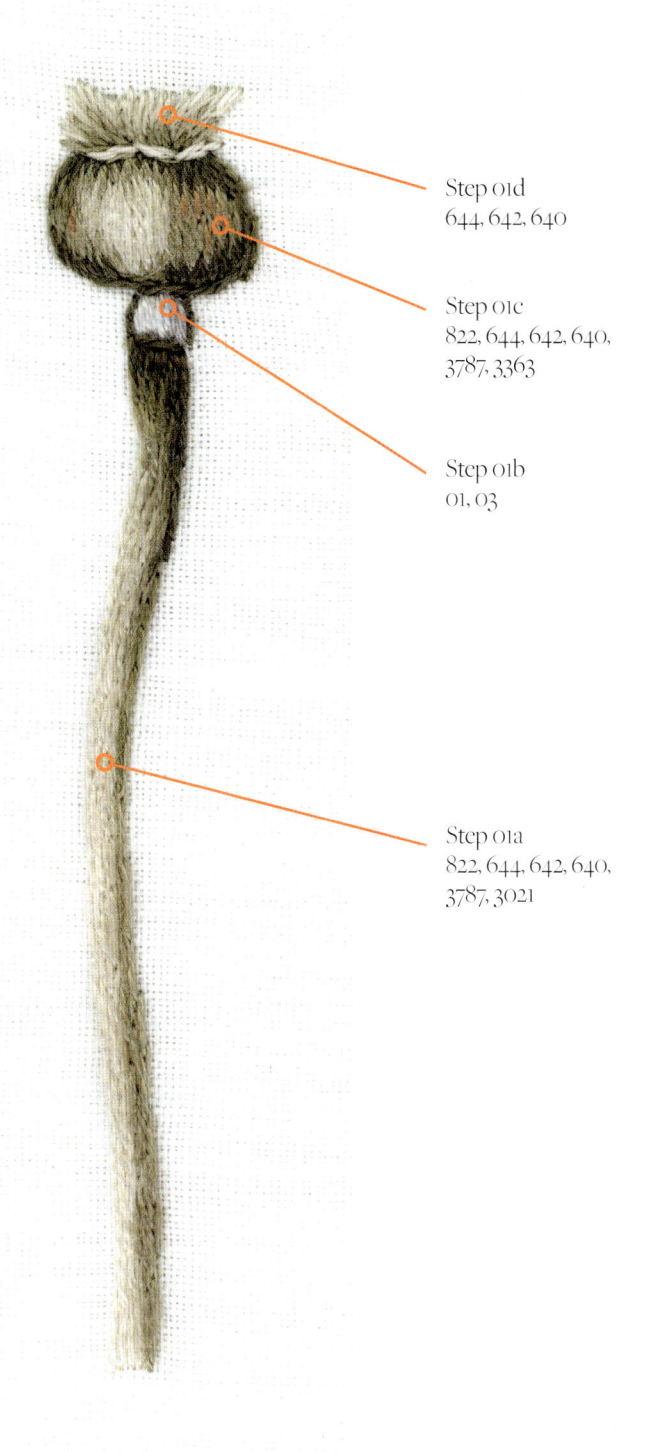

Step 01d
644, 642, 640

Step 01c
822, 644, 642, 640, 3787, 3363

Step 01b
01, 03

Step 01a
822, 644, 642, 640, 3787, 3021

2

STEP 02: SEEDHEAD 2

2a. Outline with split stitch. Fill with long-and-short stitch – this should be worked over the outline. Add outline with split stitch in 935.

2b. Outline with split stitch. Fill with long-and-short stitch – this should be worked over the outline. Add outline with split stitch in 935.

2c. Fill with long-and-short stitch.

2d. Add long, straight stitches in 3021 on top of the previous long-and-short stitch, as shown. These will create a dark background for the floating threads. Next, take a strand of 640 and create a few floating threads, as explained below. Add 642 and repeat. Add 644 and repeat.

2e. Use the photographs below as a guide to colour placement. Fill each section with long-and-short stitch, then add the lines and outlines.

2f. Add tiny stitches (dots).

Step 02e
10, 3348; lines 644, 640; outline 3021

Step 02a
10, 772, 14, 164, 989, 988, 987, 935; outline 935

Step 02b
772, 164, 989, 987, 935; outline 935

Step 02d
644, 642, 640, 3787, 3021

Step 02f
3787

Step 02c
772, 164, 989, 988, 987, 935

Floating threads:

1. Secure a piece of thread at one end.

2. Twist the thread over a crochet hook, pencil or similar.

3. Make a tiny stitch to secure at the other end.

4. Remove the hook/pencil.

80

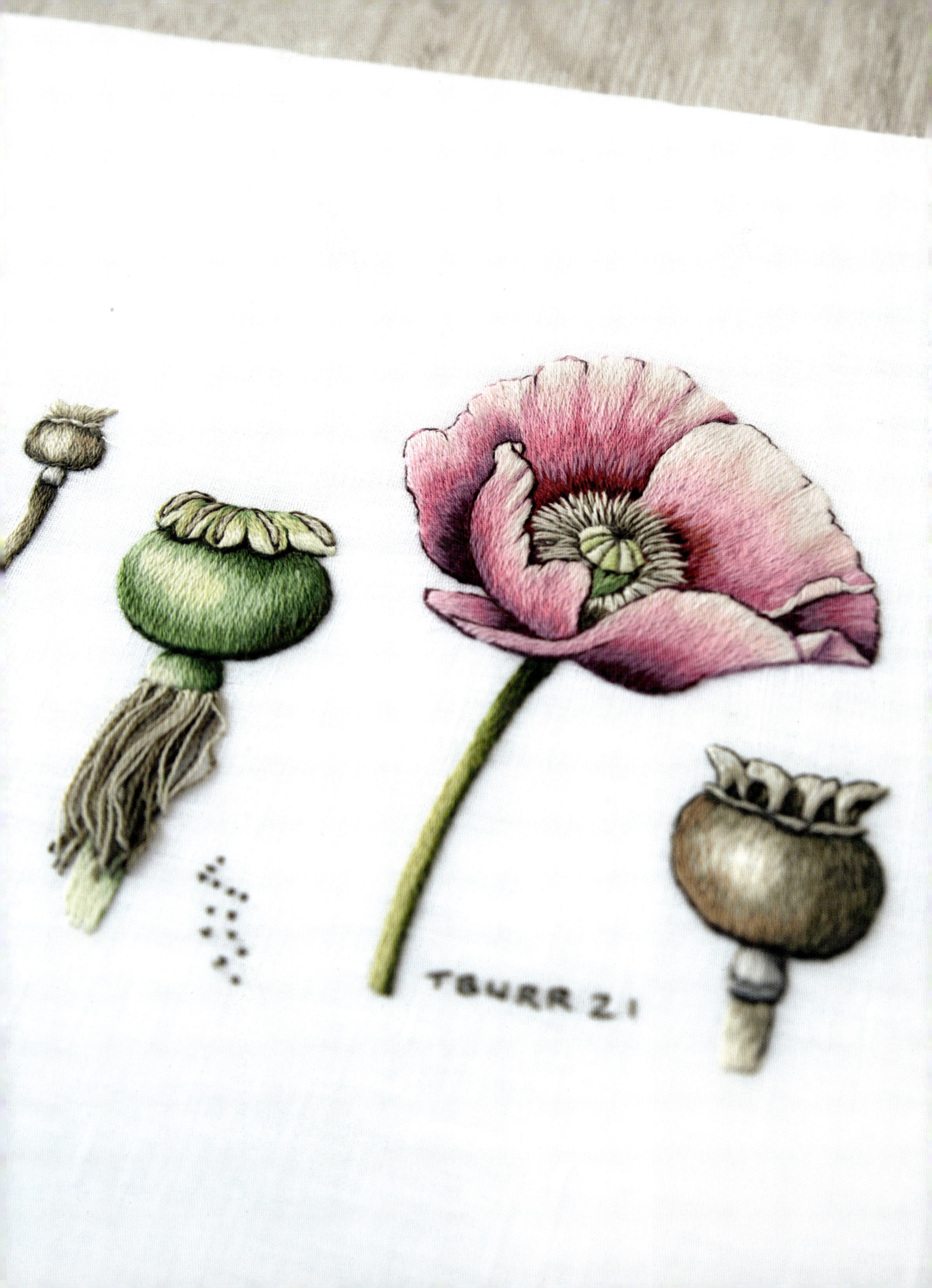
TBURR 21

STEP 03: POPPY

3a. Fill with adjacent rows of split stitch.
3b. Fill with long-and-short stitch; outline with split stitch.
3c. Fill with long-and-short stitch; outline with split stitch.
3d. Fill with long-and-short stitch; outline with split stitch.
3e. Fill with long-and-short stitch; outline with split stitch.
3f. Fill with long-and-short stitch.
3g. Fill with satin stitch.
3h. Fill each section in the centre with satin stitch; outline with split stitch in 3787. Add straight lines around the centre. Add outlines in split stitch in 3021.
3i. Fill with long-and-short stitch; outline with split stitch.
3j. Fill with long-and-short stitch; outline with split stitch.
3k. Fill with long-and-short stitch; outline with split stitch.

Step 03c
23, 3689, 3609, A86, A87, 33, 3834

Step 03b
23, 3689, 3609, A86, A87, 33, 3834

Step 03e
23, 3689, 3609, A86, A87, 3803

Step 03i
23, 3689, 3609, A86, A87, 33

Step 03e
3689

Step 03h
Centre 10, 15, 3787; lines around centre 640, 822; outlines 3021

Step 03d
A86, A87, 33, 3834

Step 03j
3609, A86, A87, 33, 3834

Step 03g
989

Step 03f
640, 3787

Step 03k
3689, 3609, A86, A87, 33, 3834

Step 03a
3348, 471, 469, 936, 935

83

STEP 04: SEEDHEAD 3

4a. Fill with long-and-short stitch; outline in split stitch.
4b. Fill with long-and-short stitch; outline in split stitch. Add band in split stitch.
4c. and **4d.** Complete on either side, but ensure that the stitches join so that one solid shape is formed. Fill with long-and-short stitch; outline in split stitch.
4e. Fill with long-and-short stitch; outline in split stitch.
4f. Fill with split stitches; outline in split stitch.
4g. Fill with straight/split stitches. Outline in split stitch.

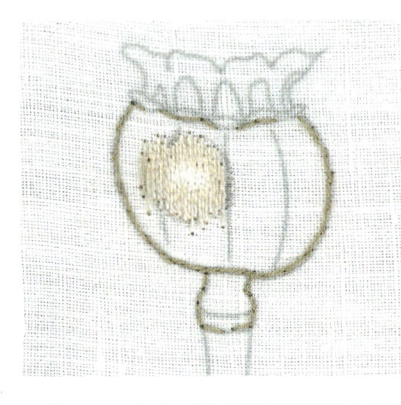

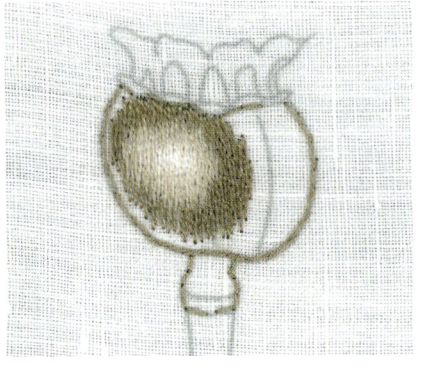

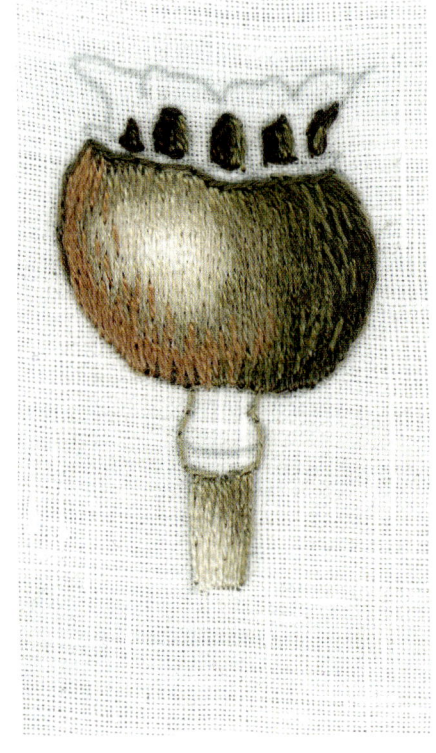

Step 04g
822, 644, 642, 640;
outline 3021

Step 04e
640, 3787, 3021

Step 04f
822, 644; outline 3021

Step 04d
3865, 644, 642, 3863;
outline 3021

Step 04c
642, 640, 3787; outline 3021

Step 04b
01, 03, 535;
outline 3021

Step 04a
822, 644, 642; outline 3021

5

STEP 05: SEEDHEAD 4

5a. Fill the stalk with adjacent rows of split stitch.
5b. Fill with satin stitch, then add a few straight stitches for shadow; outline with split stitch.
5c. Fill with long-and-short stitch; outline with split stitch.
5d. Fill with straight stitches.

Step 05d
10, 522

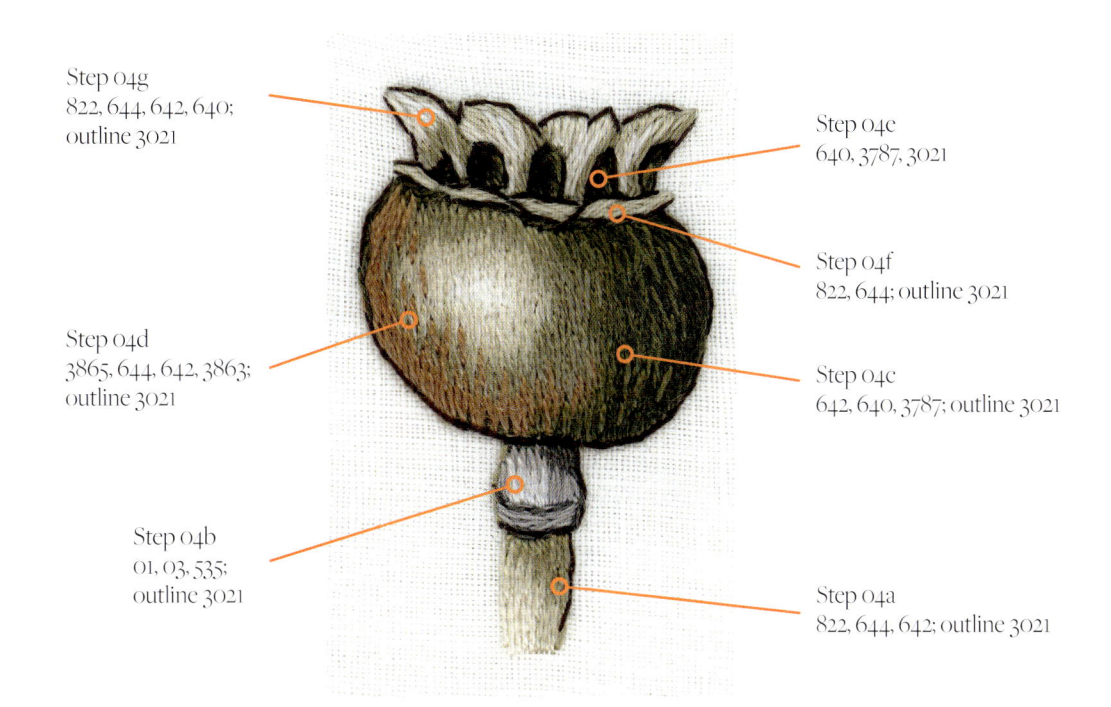

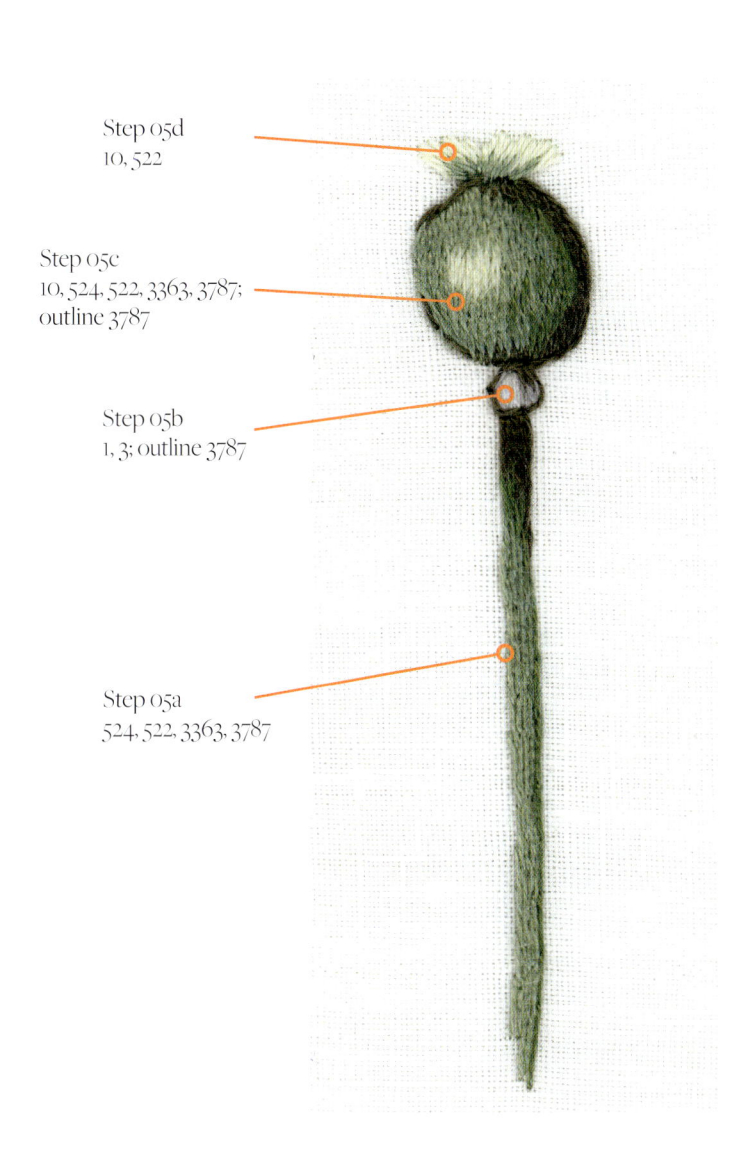

Step 05c
10, 524, 522, 3363, 3787;
outline 3787

Step 05b
1, 3; outline 3787

Step 05a
524, 522, 3363, 3787

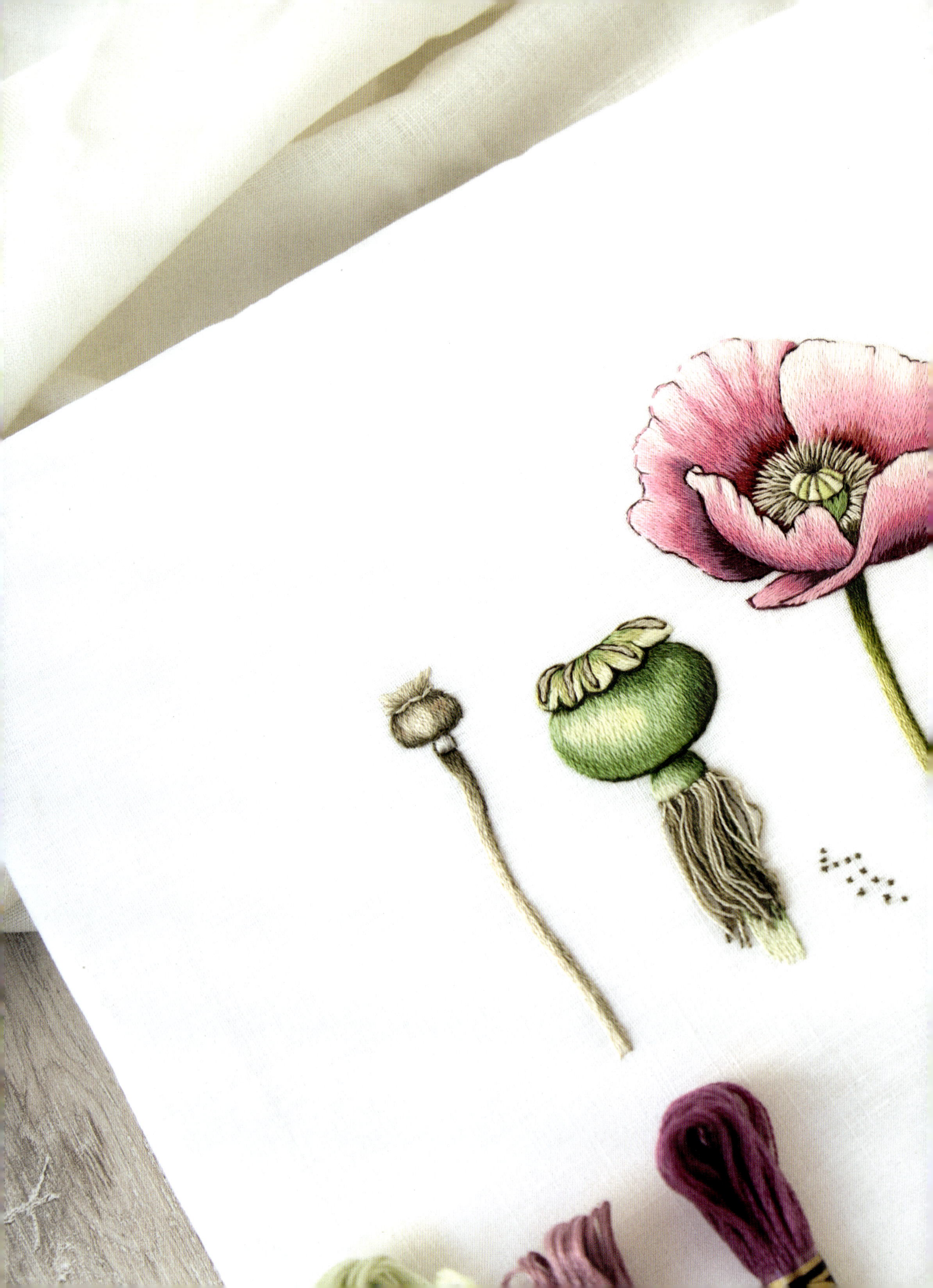

BURRZI

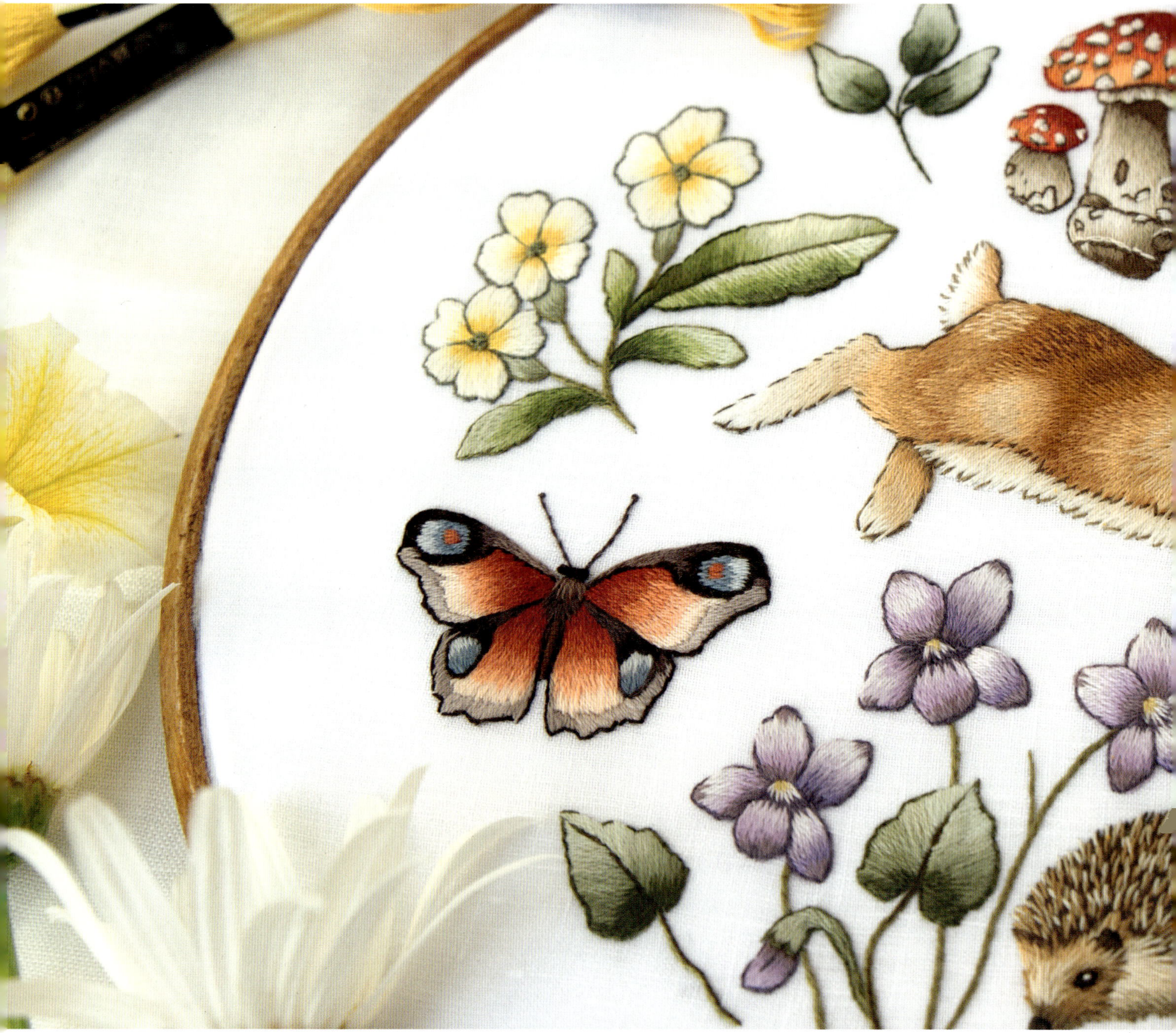

INTERMEDIATE PROJECTS

BARN OWL SAMPLER

Artwork by Amy Rose Geden.

PROJECT SIZE
21 x 11cm (8¼ x 4½in)

YOU WILL NEED
- Piece of fabric, 30 x 34cm (12 x 13½in)
- Threads as per list
- A super grip hoop, size 20cm (8in), or stretcher frame
- Template, page 171

PREPARATION

- Transfer the outline to the fabric (see pages 16 and 176).
- Add directional lines in pencil, as required (see page 23).
- Mount your fabric in the hoop or frame (see pages 16–17).
- Follow the step-by-step instructions on pages 96–103.
- Use one strand of thread throughout unless otherwise specified.
- If using a hoop, mount the first half of the design into the hoop and tack/baste up any excess fabric so it does not get in the way while stitching. When the first half is complete, take the fabric out and mount the second half of the design, tacking/basting up the excess fabric as before.

THREAD LIST

DMC
- 154
- 434
- 435
- 436
- 437
- 640
- 642
- 644
- 680
- 712
- 729
- 738
- 739
- 777
- 822
- 934
- 935
- 3011
- 3012
- 3013
- 3021
- 3326
- 3371
- 3687
- 3688
- 3689
- 3781
- 3787
- 3802
- 3803
- 3831
- 3832
- 3833
- 3862
- 3865
- 3866
- Blanc

ORDER OF WORK

The overall sampler plan is shown at a reduced size as an overview; the sampler elements are shown at an increased size for clarity when detailing the order of work. The templates at the back of the book are given at actual size (see page 171).

1   *2*   *3*   *4*   *5*   *6*

92

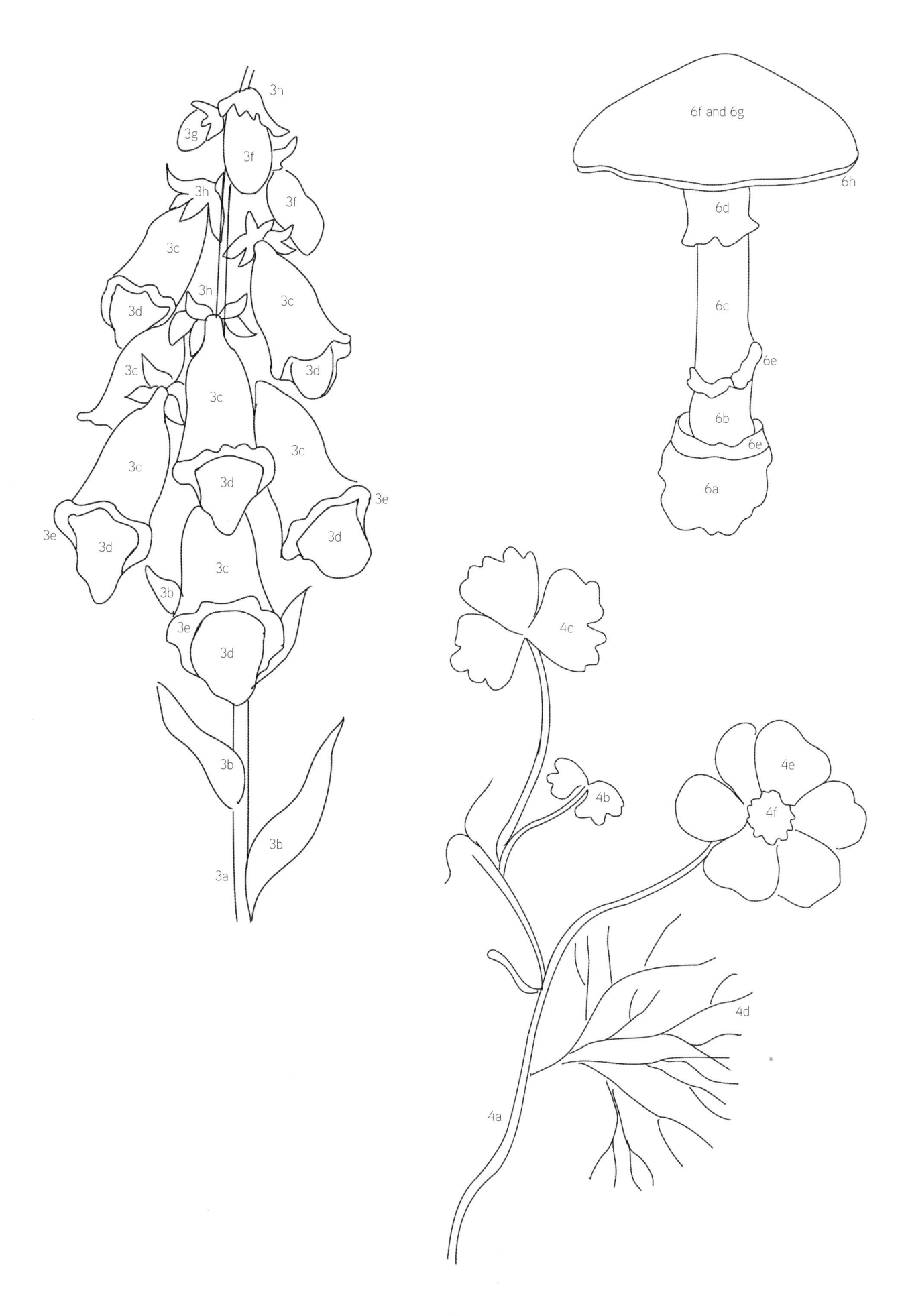

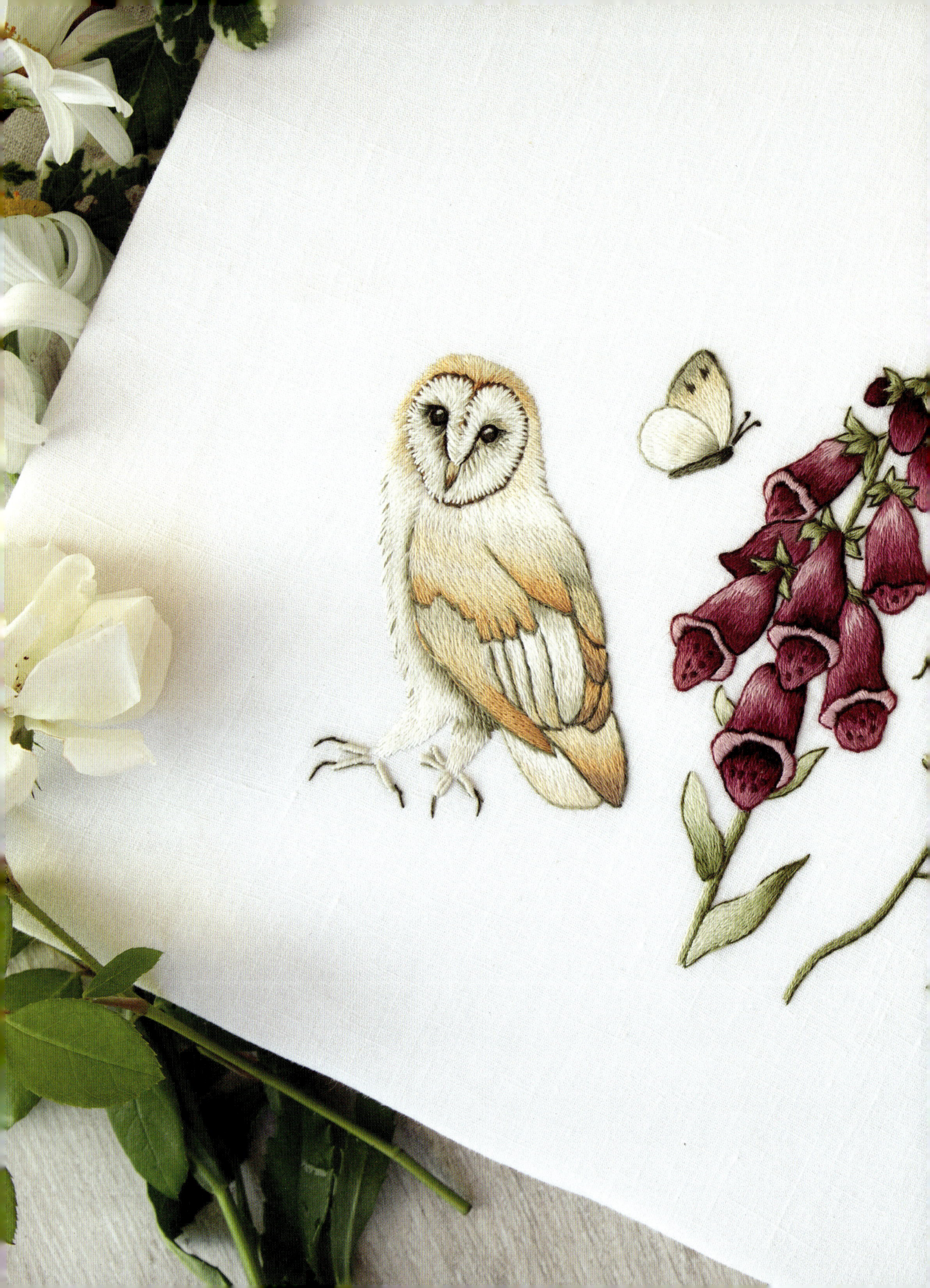

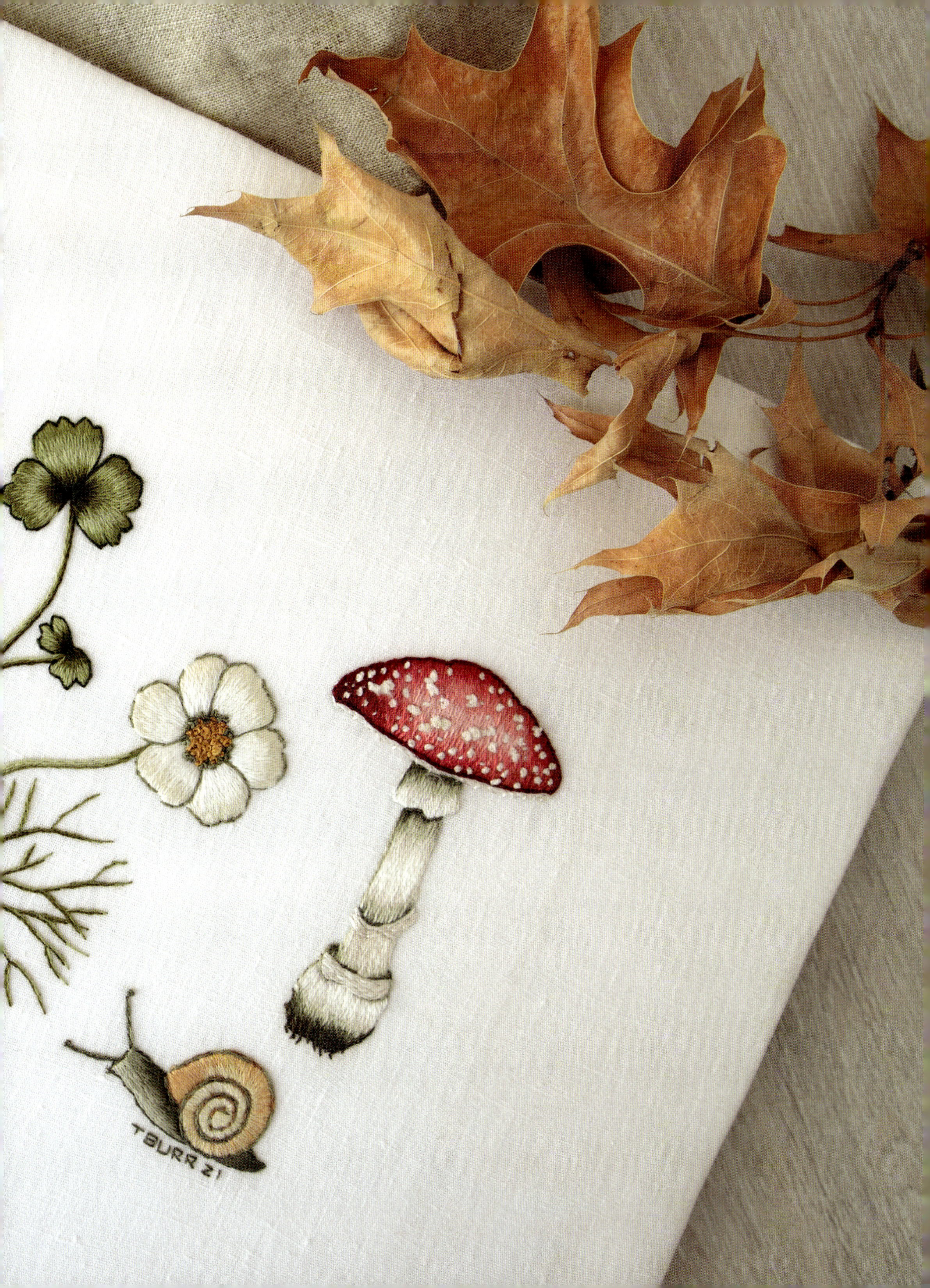
TBURR 21

1

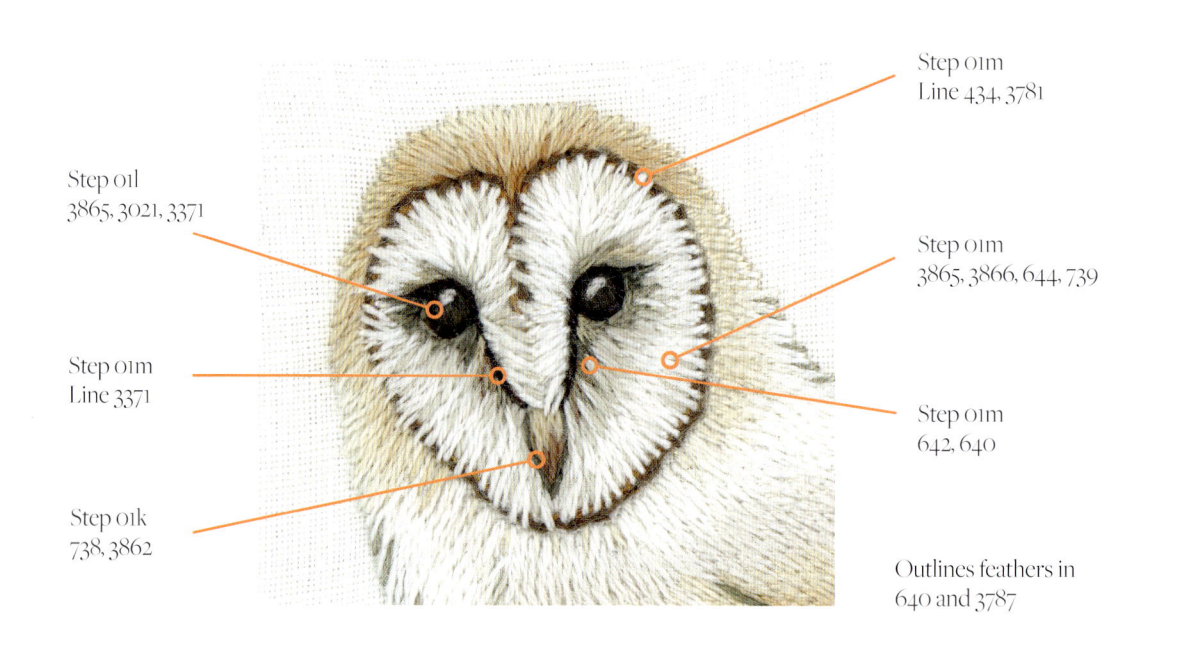

Step 01j
739, 738, 437, 435

Step 01i
739, 3866, 3865

Step 01h
3865, 3866, 644, 642, 640

Step 01f
3866, 644, 640

Step 01g
Bullions 3866; underline 640; claws 3021

Step 01e
3865, 3866, 644, 739, 738, 437, 436

Step 01d
437, 3862

Step 01c
3865, 3866, 644, 738

Step 01b
739, 738, 437, 3862

Step 01a
3865, 3866, 739

Step 01f
3866, 644, 640

Step 01m
Line 434, 3781

Step 01l
3865, 3021, 3371

Step 01m
3865, 3866, 644, 739

Step 01m
Line 3371

Step 01m
642, 640

Step 01k
738, 3862

Outlines feathers in 640 and 3787

96

STEP 01: OWL

1a. Fill with long-and-short stitch; outline in split stitch.
1b. Fill with long-and-short stitch; outline in split stitch.
1c. Fill with long-and-short stitch; outline in split stitch.
1d. Fill with long-and-short stitch; outline in split stitch.
1e. Fill with long-and-short stitch; outline in split stitch.
1f. Fill with irregular long-and-short stitch. Add outlines in straight stitches.
1g. Loosen the fabric in the hoop. Add bullion stitches using two strands of thread and about 11 twists. Add a line under each bullion. Add the claws with split stitch.
1h. Fill with irregular long-and-short stitch. Add outlines in straight stitches.
1i. Fill with irregular long-and-short stitch. Add outlines in straight stitches.
1j. Fill with irregular long-and-short stitch.
1k. Fill the beak with long-and-short stitch, outline with split stitch.
1l. For the eye, refer to the detail given below. Fill the pupil with satin stitch. Add tiny stitches in 3865 for eye glints. Add outlines in split stitch.
1m. First add a line of split stitch in 434 and 3781. Next, fill the face with irregular long-and-short stitches – these stitches need to go over the line at intervals, as shown in the photographs. Add a few shadows in 642 and 640.
Add all outlines on the wings in split stitch.

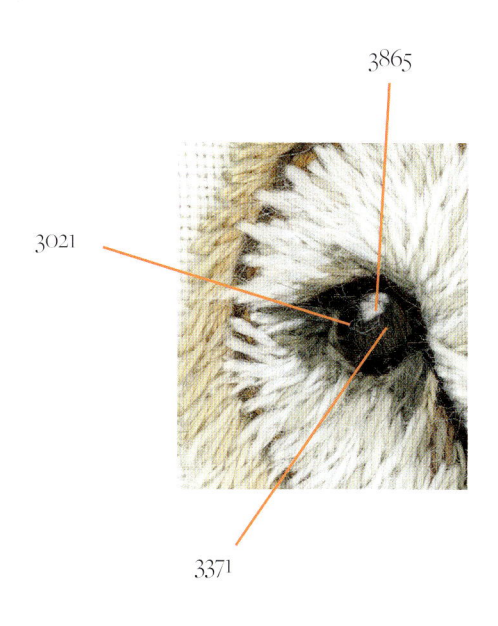

3865

3021

3371

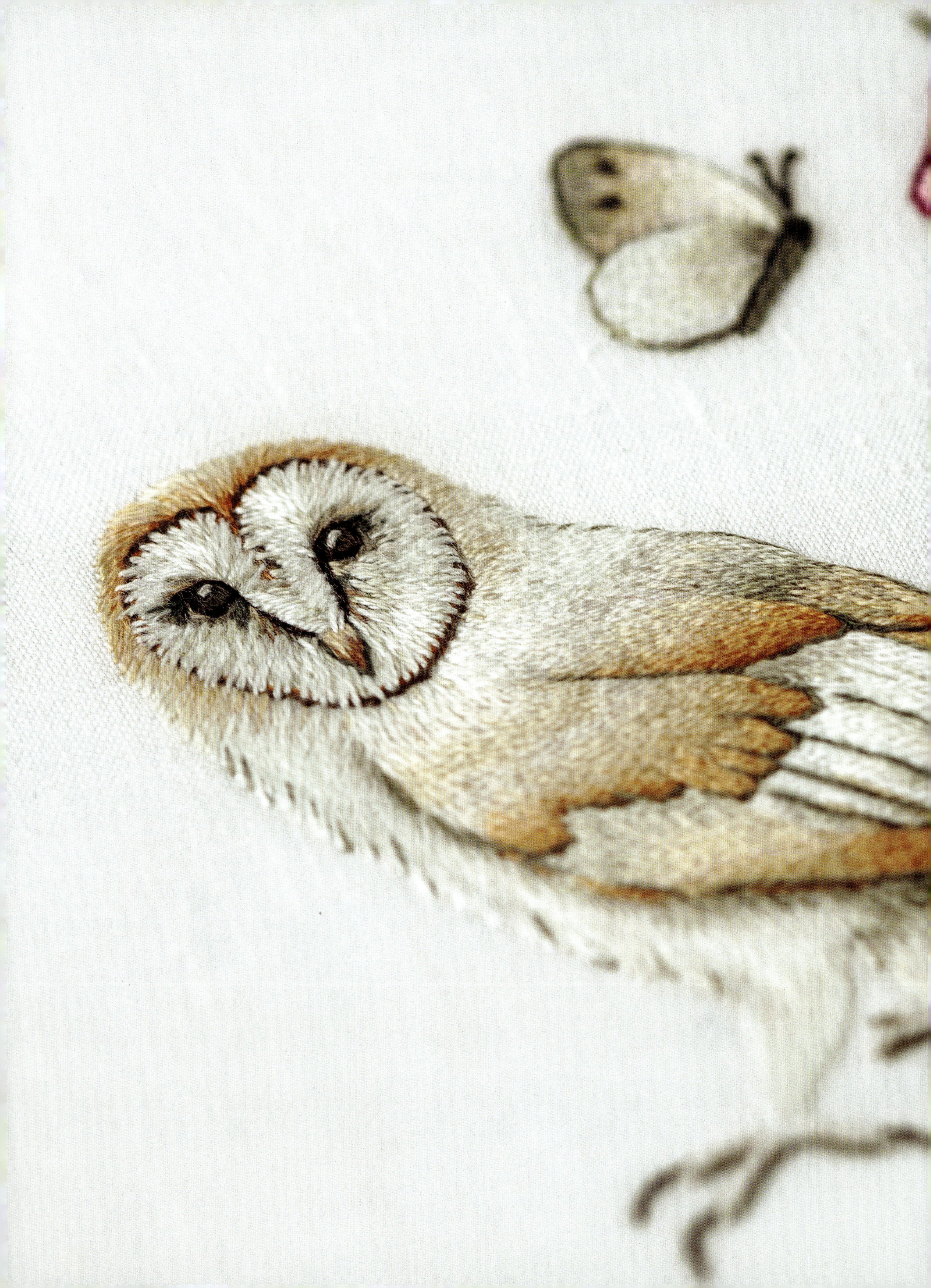

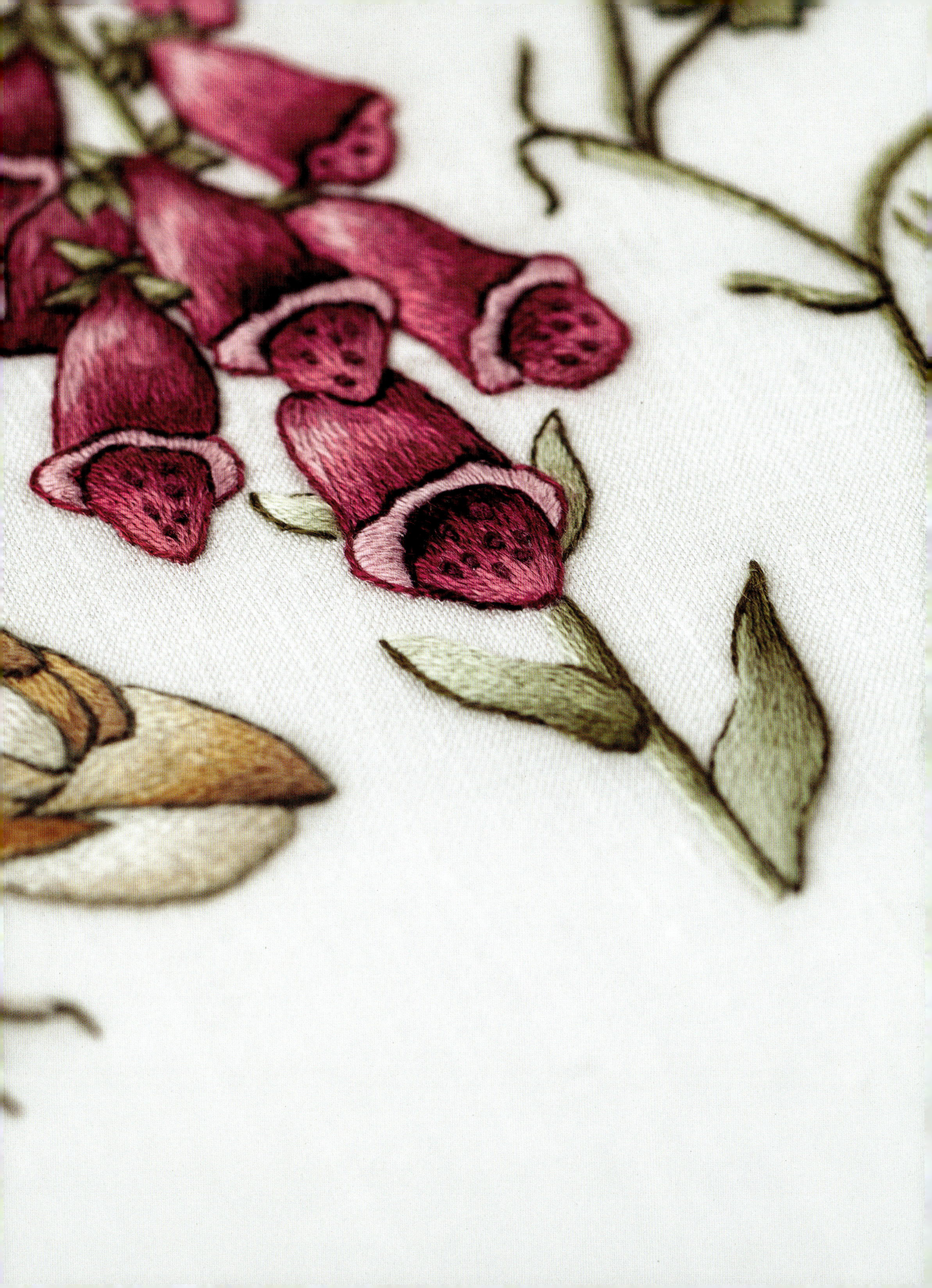

STEP 02: BUTTERFLY

2a. Fill the upper wing with long-and-short stitches. Add tiny straight stitches for the dark marks in 3021. Outline with split stitch.
2b. Fill the lower wing with long-and-short stitch; outline with split stitch.
2c. Fill with long-and-short stitch; outline in split stitch. Work the antennae in split stitch; add a French knot at the top of each.

Step 02a
712, 739, 738, 642

Step 02b
3865, 712, 644, 642;
outline 642

Step 02c
640, 3021

STEP 03: FOXGLOVE

3a. Fill the stem sections with adjacent rows of split stitch.
3b. Fill the leaves with long-and-short stitch; outline with split stitch.
3c. Fill the outside of the flowers with long-and-short stitch; outline with split stitch.
3d. Fill the inside of the flowers with long-and-short stitch; outline with split stitch. Add French knots with one strand and two twists.
3e. Fill the turnovers with satin stitch; outline with split stitch.
3f. Fill the buds with long-and-short stitch; outline with split stitch.
3g. Fill bud with long-and-short stitch; outline with split stitch.
3h. Fill sepals with long-and-short stitch; outline with split stitch.

Step 03g
3687, 3803;
outline 154

Step 03h
3013, 3012, 3011;
outline 935

Step 03c
3689, 3688, 3687, 3803;
outline 3803, 3802

Step 03f
3688, 3687, 3803;
outline 3802, 154

Step 03d
3687, 3803, 3802;
outlines 3802, 154;
knots 3802

Step 03e
3689; outlines 3802, 154

Step 03a
935, 3011, 3012, 3013

Step 03b
935, 3011, 3012, 3013;
outline 935

4

STEP 04: WATER CROWFOOT

4a. Fill the stems with adjacent rows of split stitch.
4b. Fill the leaf with long-and-short stitch; outline with split stitch.
4c. Fill the leaf with long-and-short stitch; outline with split stitch.
4d. Fill with split stitch.
4e. Pad the petals as shown right; on top of this fill the petals with long-and-short stitch. Outline with split stitch.
4f. Fill the centre with French knots. Use two strands and two twists.

Padding for flower petals.

Step 04c
3013, 3012, 3011, 935, 934;
outline 934

Step 04b
3012, 3011, 935, 934;
outline 934

Step 04a
3012, 3011, 935, 934

Step 04d
3012, 3011, 935

Step 04e
Blanc, 3865, 822;
outline 640

Step 04f
729, 680

Step 04f
3787, 640

5

STEP 05: SNAIL

5a. Fill with long-and-short stitch; outline with split stitch.
5b. Fill the shell with long-and-short stitch or satin stitch where space does not allow; outline with split stitch.
5c. Fill the eyestalks with split stitch. Add a small French knot at the top of each using one strand and one twist.

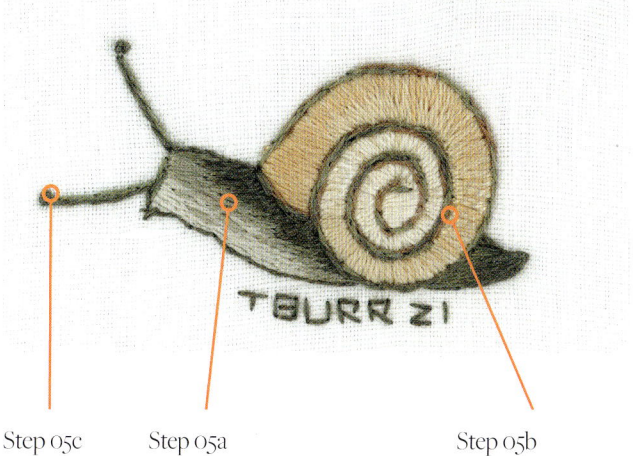

Step 05c
3787

Step 05a
644, 642, 640,
3787; outline 3787

Step 05b
739, 738, 437;
outline 3862, 640

6

STEP 06: TOADSTOOL

6a. Fill with long-and-short stitch. Add some split stitch at the base for the 'roots'; outline with split stitch.
6b. Fill with long-and-short stitch; outline with split stitch.
6c. Fill with long-and-short stitch; outline with split stitch.
6d. Fill with long-and-short stitch; outline with split stitch.
6e. Fill with split stitches.
6f. Pad the cap with felt (see below and page 35). On top of this, fill with long-and-short stitch, then outline with split stitch.
6g. Add clusters of French knots. Use two strands and two twists.
6h. Fill with split stitches.

Step 06g
French knots 3866

Step 06f
3326, 3833,
3832, 3831, 777;
outline 777

Step 06h
3865, 3866

Step 06d
3865, 3866, 644, 640,
3787; lines 3787

Step 06c
3865, 3866, 644, 640;
lines 3787

Step 06e
3865, 3866; lines 644

Step 06b
3865, 3866, 644, 640;
lines 3787

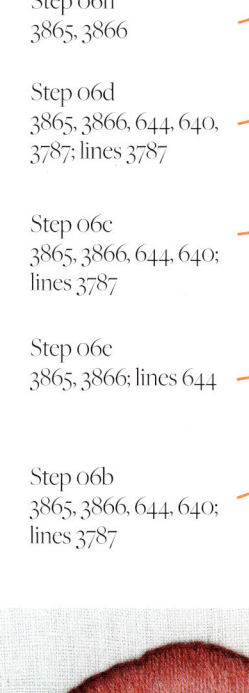

Step 06e
3865, 3866;
lines 644

Step 06a
3865, 3866, 644, 640,
3787, 3021

Padding for the toadstool cap.

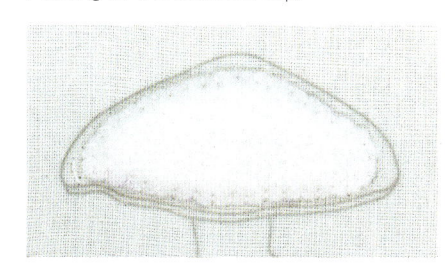

BUNNY SAMPLER

Artwork by Jane Carkill.

PROJECT SIZE
17.5 x 17.5 cm (7 x 7in)

YOU WILL NEED
- Piece of fabric, 30 x 30cm (12 x 12in)
- Threads as per list
- A super grip hoop, size 20cm (8in), or stretcher frame
- Template, page 172

PREPARATION
- Transfer the outline to the fabric (see pages 16 and 176).
- Add directional lines in pencil, as required (see page 23).
- Mount your fabric in the hoop or frame (see pages 16–17).
- Follow the step-by-step instructions on pages 109–116.
- Use one strand of thread throughout unless otherwise specified.
- Anchor threads are prefaced with an A before each number.

THREAD LIST

DMC	Anchor
- 09	- A108
- 25	- A109
- 29	- A110
- 167	- A213
- 209	- A259
- 210	- A260
- 211	- A266
- 224	- A267
- 225	- A338
- 350	- A339
- 351	- A844
- 355	- A845
- 433	- A846
- 434	- A858
- 435	- A859
- 436	- A860
- 437	- A861
- 451	- A846
- 452	- A1010
- 611	- A1014
- 612	- A1015
- 613	- A9575
- 712	
- 738	
- 739	
- 746	
- 819	
- 834	
- 922	
- 931	
- 3021	
- 3032	
- 3033	
- 3041	
- 3051	
- 3078	
- 3371	
- 3752	
- 3777	
- 3781	
- 3782	
- 3787	
- 3790	
- 3821	
- 3825	
- 3860	
- 3865	
- 3866	

105

ORDER OF WORK

The overall sampler plan is shown at a reduced size as an overview; the sampler elements are shown at an increased size for clarity when detailing the order of work. The templates at the back of the book are given at actual size (see page 172).

107

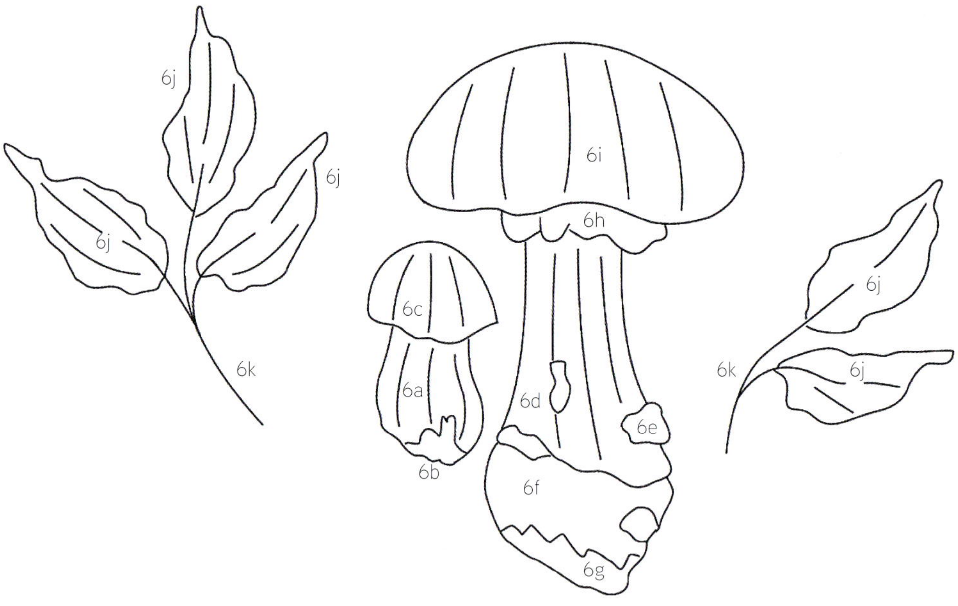
6j
6j
6i
6j
6h
6j
6c
6k
6a
6d
6k
6j
6e
6b
6f
6g

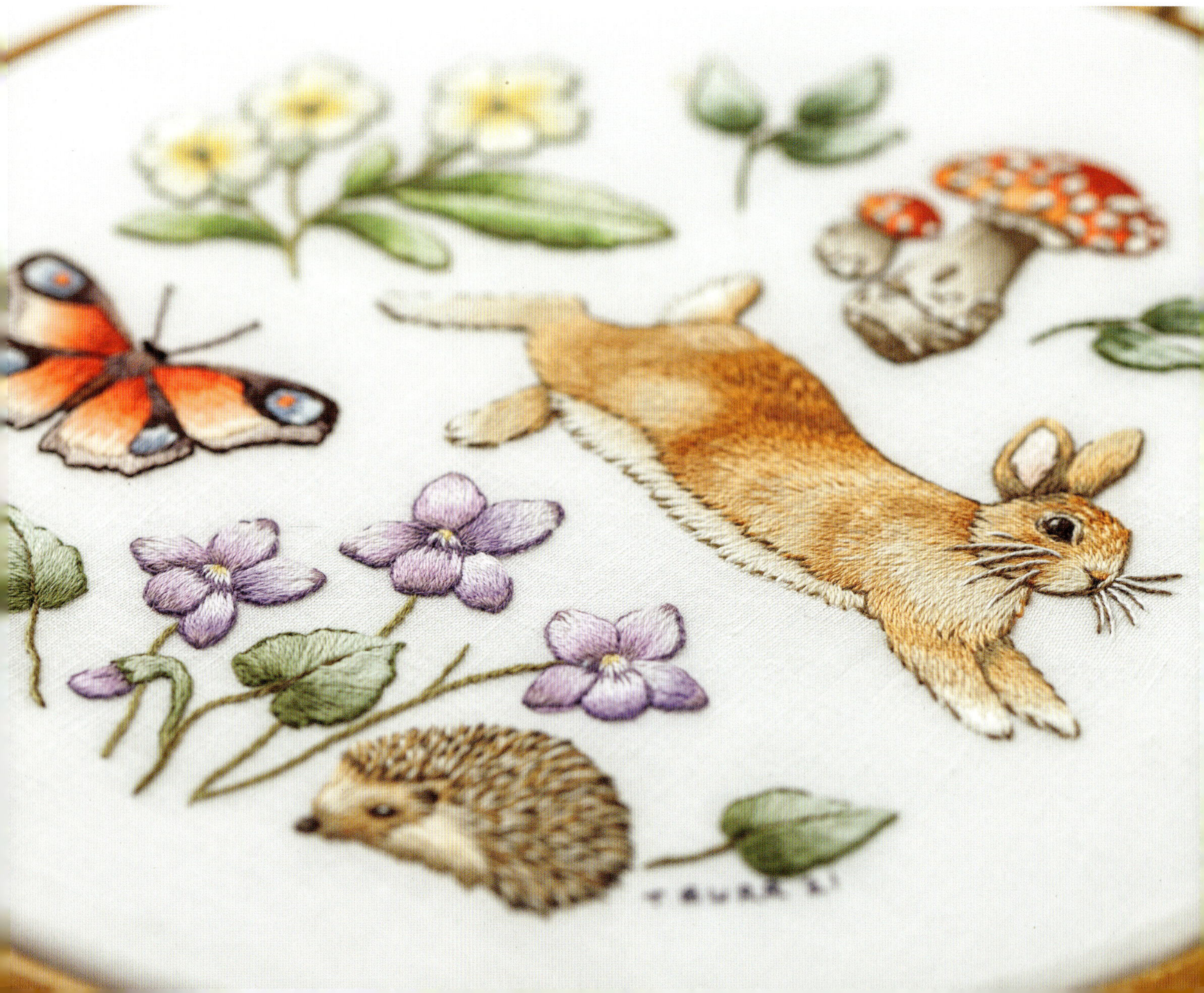

1

STEP 01: VIOLETS

1a. Fill the stems with adjacent rows of split stitch.
1b. Fill each petal with long-and-short stitch from the tip towards the centre. Outline each petal with split stitch.
1c. Fill the centre with irregular straight stitches.
1d. Fill each side of the leaf with long-and-short stitch. Add outlines and a centre line with split stitch.
1e. Fill the bud with long-and-short stitch; outline with split stitch.
1f. Fill with long-and-short stitch; outline with split stitch.

Step 01b
211, 210, 209, 3041; petal outlines 29; tips 3041

Step 01b
25, A108, A109, A110, 3041; petal outlines 29; tips 3041

Step 01b
25, 211, 210, 209, 3041; petal outlines 29; tips 3041

Step 01c
29, 25, 834

Step 01e
210, 209, 3041; outline 29

Step 01f
A858, A859, A860; outline A861

Step 01d
A213, A858, A859, A860, A861; outline A861; centre line A846

Step 01a
A844, A845, A846

109

STEP 02: HEDGEHOG

2a. Fill the nose with satin stitch; outline with split stitch.
2b. Fill the eye centre with satin stitch in 3021. Add a highlight with two tiny stitches in 3865. Outline the eye with split stitch in 3371.
2c. Fill the head with irregular long-and-short stitch from the wider part down towards the nose.
2d. Fill the ear with satin stitch, blending the stitches into the head. Outline with split stitch.
2e. Fill the chest with irregular long-and-short stitch.
2f. Fill the spiky back as follows:
Layer one = this is the background – fill with long-and-short stitch in 3021 and 3781.
Layer two = add irregular long-and-short stitches on top of layer one with 167, 612 and 613. Add the darker shades first and then the lighter shades on top.
2g. Repeat as for step 2f.

Step 02d
3781; outline 3371

Steps 02f and 02g
3781, 3021, 167, 612, 613

Step 02c
739, 738, 612, 611

Step 02a
3021; outline 3371

Step 02e
739, 738, 437, 612

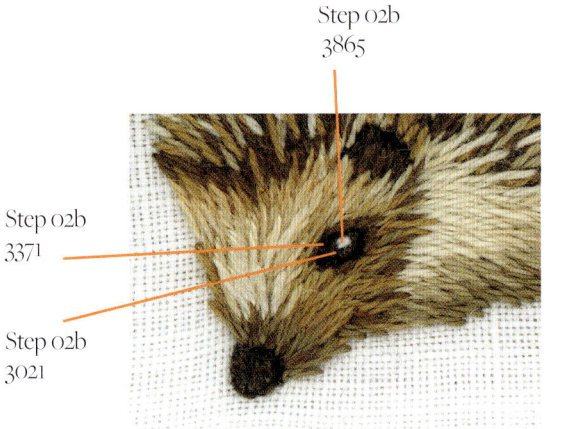

Step 02b
3865

Step 02b
3371

Step 02b
3021

110

3

STEP 03: BUTTERFLY

3a. Fill the lower wings with long-and-short stitch, from the wider edge towards the centre.
3b. Fill the spots with long-and-short stitch; outline with split stitch.
3c. Fill the area with long-and-short stitch; outline with split stitch.
3d. Fill the outer edge with long-and-short stitch. Outline lower wing with split stitch in 3371.
3e. Fill the upper wings with long-and-short stitch.
3f. Fill the spots with long-and-short stitch.
3g. Fill the area with long-and-short stitch; outline with split stitch.
3h. Fill the outer edge with long-and-short stitch. Outline upper wing with split stitch in 3371.
3i. Fill the abdomen with satin stitch; outline with split stitch.
3j. Fill the thorax with irregular long-and-short stitch.
3k. Fill the head with satin stitch. Add two French knots for eyes, using two strands and two twists. Stitch the antennae with split stitch. Add a French knot at the top of each.

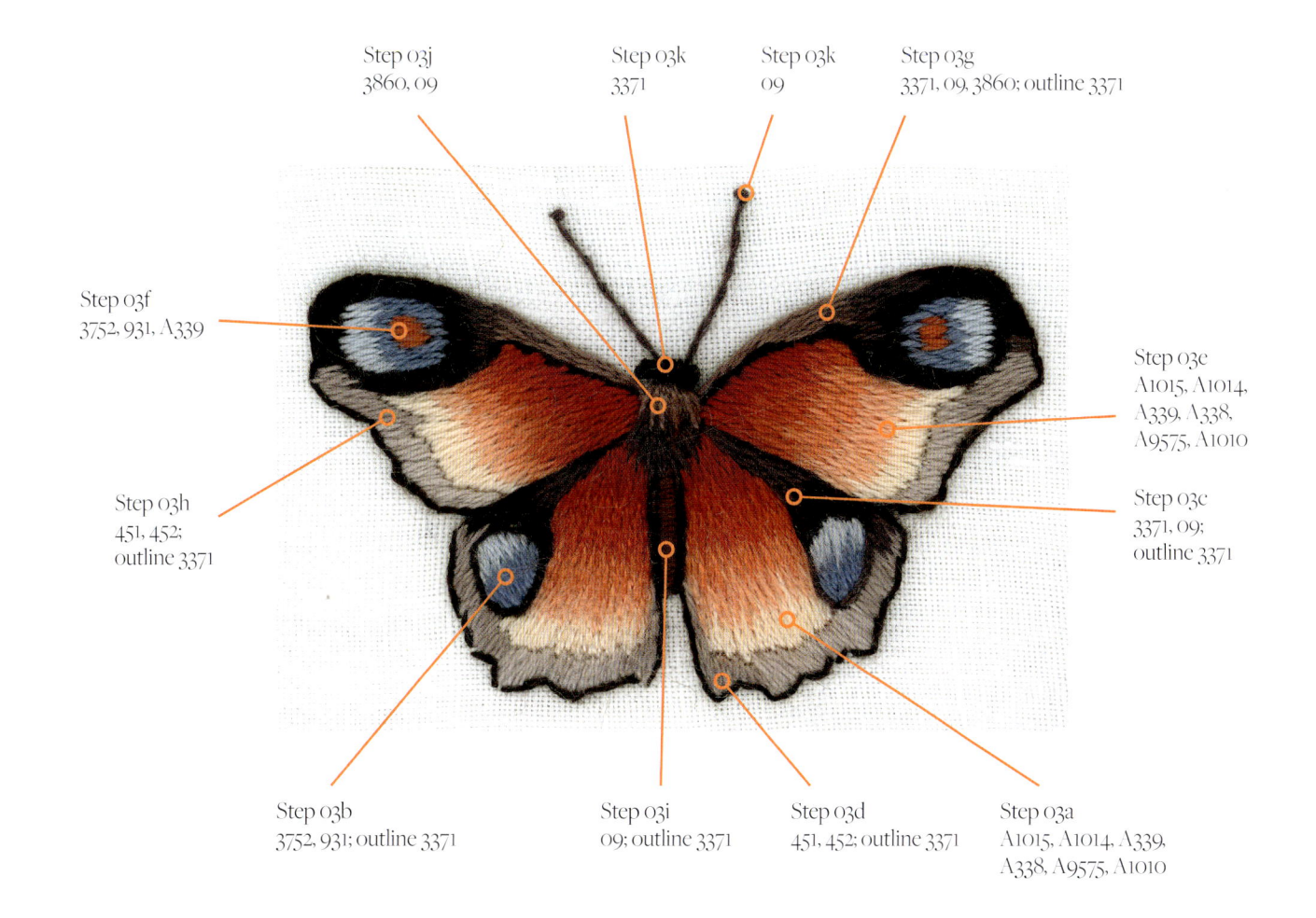

Step 03j
3860, 09

Step 03k
3371

Step 03k
09

Step 03g
3371, 09, 3860; outline 3371

Step 03f
3752, 931, A339

Step 03e
A1015, A1014, A339, A338, A9575, A1010

Step 03h
451, 452;
outline 3371

Step 03c
3371, 09;
outline 3371

Step 03b
3752, 931; outline 3371

Step 03i
09; outline 3371

Step 03d
451, 452; outline 3371

Step 03a
A1015, A1014, A339, A338, A9575, A1010

111

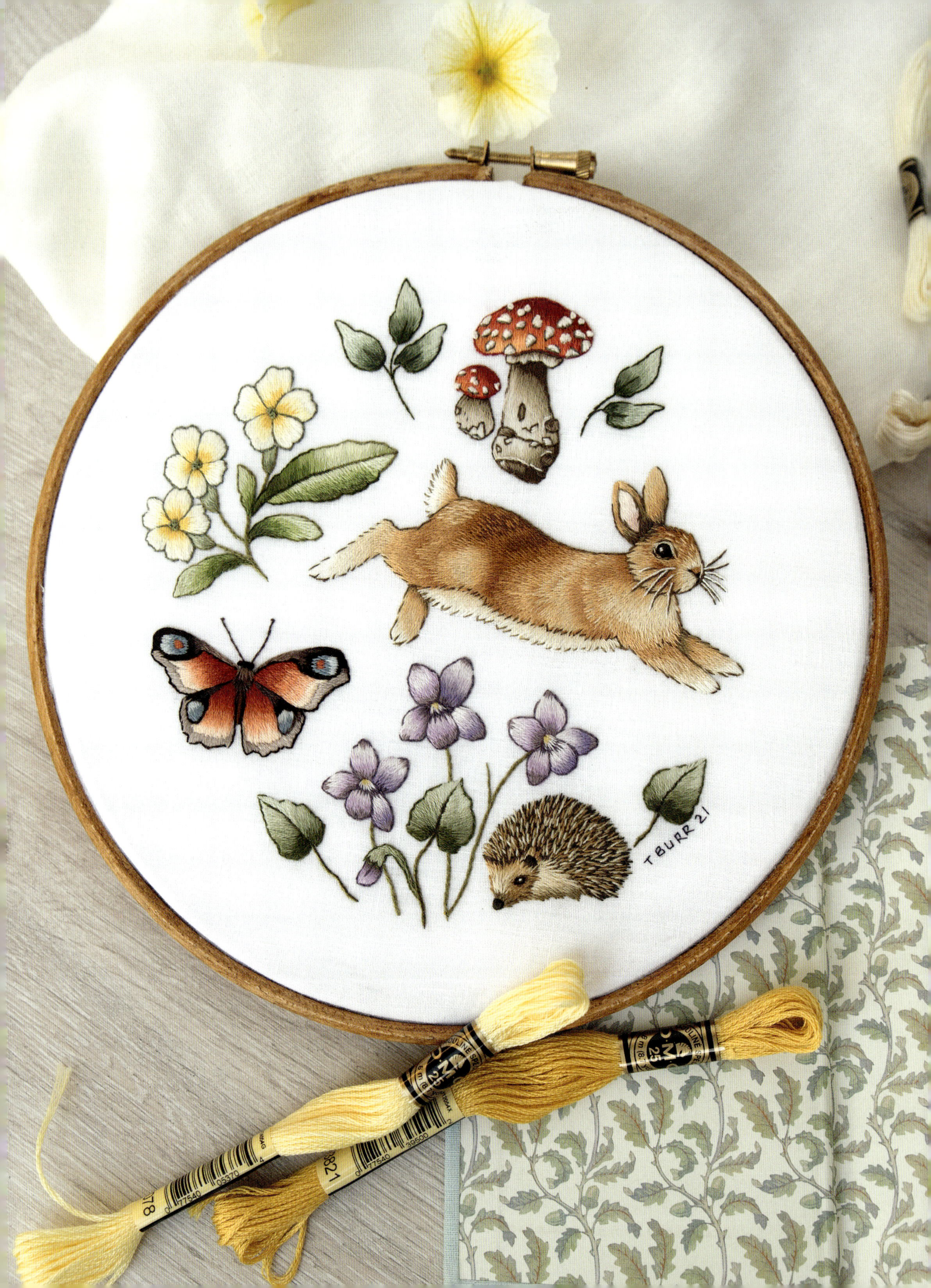
TBURR21

4

STEP 04: PRIMROSES

4a. Fill the stems with adjacent rows of split stitch.
4b. Fill with long-and-short stitch; outline with split stitch.
4c. Fill each petal with long-and-short stitch; outline with split stitch.
4d. Fill the flower centres with French knots, using two strands and one twist.
4e. Fill the small leaf with long-and-short stitch; outline with split stitch.
4f. Fill the medium-sized leaves with long-and-short stitch; outline with split stitch.
4g. and **4h.** Fill on either side of the centre vein with long-and-short stitch. Outline with split stitch and add the centre vein in split stitch.

Step 04h
A259, A260, A266, A267, 3051; outline A845, A846

Step 04g
3051, A267, A266, A260, A259; outline A845, A846

Step 04e
A260, A266, A267

Step 04c
746, 3078, 3821; outline 3787

Step 04d
A860

Step 04b
A858, A860; outline A845

Step 04a
A844, A845

Step 04f
A260, A266, A267

113

5

STEP 05: RABBIT

5a. Fill the eye with satin stitch in 3021. Add tiny stitches for the highlight in 3865. Outline the pupil in split stitch in 3371. Add lines in split stitch below the eye in 612. Add lines of split stitch above the eye in 738 and 3781.

5b. Fill the nose with satin stitch in 435. Add lines in 3371. Fill around the nose with long-and-short stitches in 739, 738 and 437.

5c. Fill the ear with long-and-short stitch; outline in split stitch.

5d. Fill the centre of the ear with long-and-short stitch; outline in split stitch. Add long-and-short stitches around the centre and outline in split stitch.

5e. Fill the paw with long-and-short stitch. Add outlines in split stitch.

5f. Fill the paw with long-and-short stitch. Add outlines in split stitch.

5g. Fill the hind paws with long-and-short stitch. Add outlines in split stitch.

5h. Fill the belly with irregular long-and-short stitch. Add lines in straight stitches.

5i. Fill the tail with irregular long-and-short stitch. Add lines in straight stitches.

5j. Fill the rump with irregular long-and-short stitch.

5k. Fill the side with irregular long-and-short stitch. Add lines in straight stitches.

5l. Fill the chest with irregular long-and-short stitch. Add lines in straight stitches.

5m. Fill the whiskers in split stitch.

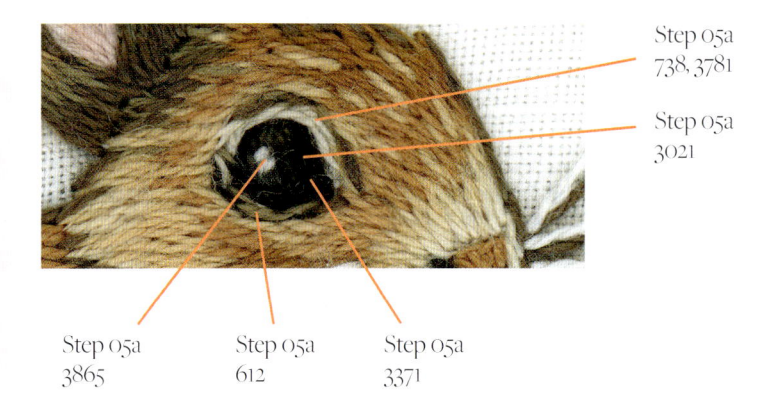

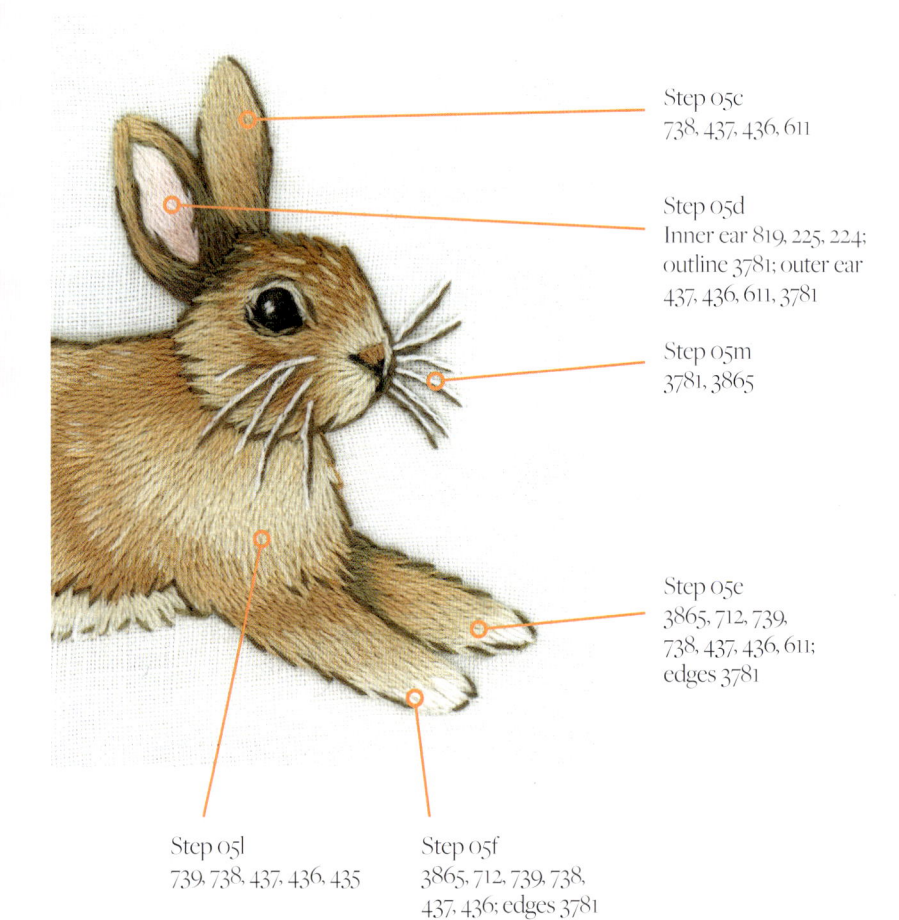

Step 05a
738, 3781

Step 05a
3021

Step 05a
3865

Step 05a
612

Step 05a
3371

Step 05b
435

Step 05b
3371

Step 05b
739, 738, 437

Step 05c
738, 437, 436, 611

Step 05d
Inner ear 819, 225, 224; outline 3781; outer ear 437, 436, 611, 3781

Step 05m
3781, 3865

Step 05e
3865, 712, 739, 738, 437, 436, 611; edges 3781

Step 05l
739, 738, 437, 436, 435

Step 05f
3865, 712, 739, 738, 437, 436; edges 3781

114

Step 05i
3865, 739, 738, 437, 436; edges 3781

Step 05k
433, 434, 435, 436, 437, 738

Step 05g
3865, 712, 739, 738, 437; edges 3781

Step 05j
436, 435, 434, 433, 435, 436, 437, 738

Step 05h
3865, 712, 739; edges 611

115

STEP 06: TOADSTOOL

6a. Fill the stalk with long-and-short stitch; outline in split stitch.
6b. Fill the notches with satin stitch; outline with split or straight stitches.
6c. Fill the cap with long-and-short stitch; outline with split stitch. Fill the spots with straight stitches and some French knots in 3866. Add lines in 3787.
6d. Fill the stalk with long-and-short stitch; outline in split stitch.
6e. Fill the notches with satin stitch; outline with split or straight stitches.
6f. Fill the bottom section with long-and-short stitch; outline in split stitch.
6g. Fill the underside with long-and-short stitch; outline with split stitch.
6h. Fill the gills with long-and-short stitch; outline with split stitch.
6i. Fill the cap with long-and-short stitch; outline with split stitch. Fill the spots with straight stitches and some French knots in 3866. Add shadow lines in 3787.
6j. Fill the leaves with long-and-short stitch; outline with split stitch.
6k. Stitch the stems with split stitch.

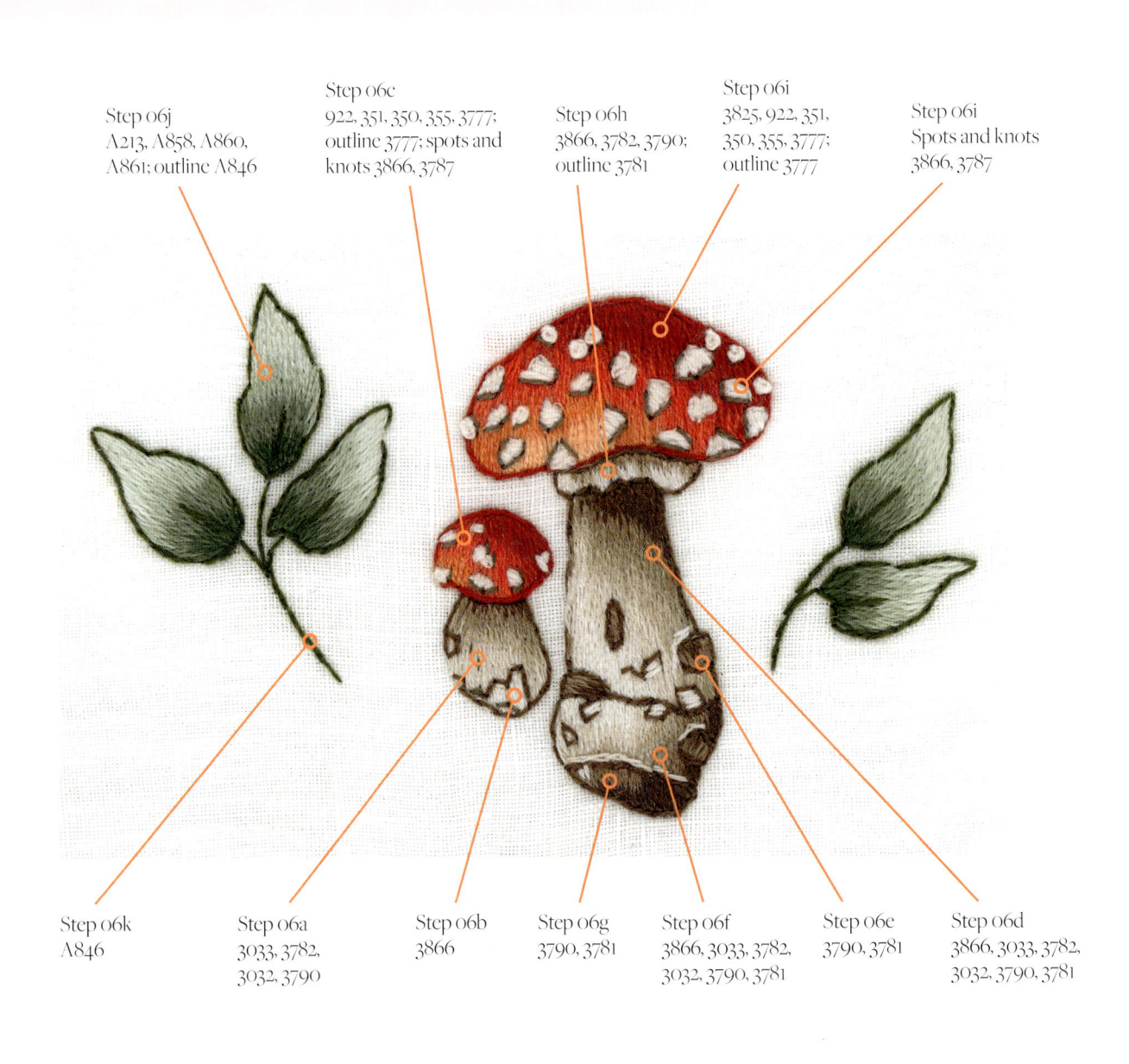

Step 06j
A213, A858, A860, A861; outline A846

Step 06c
922, 351, 350, 355, 3777; outline 3777; spots and knots 3866, 3787

Step 06h
3866, 3782, 3790; outline 3781

Step 06i
3825, 922, 351, 350, 355, 3777; outline 3777

Step 06i
Spots and knots
3866, 3787

Step 06k
A846

Step 06a
3033, 3782, 3032, 3790

Step 06b
3866

Step 06g
3790, 3781

Step 06f
3866, 3033, 3782, 3032, 3790, 3781

Step 06e
3790, 3781

Step 06d
3866, 3033, 3782, 3032, 3790, 3781

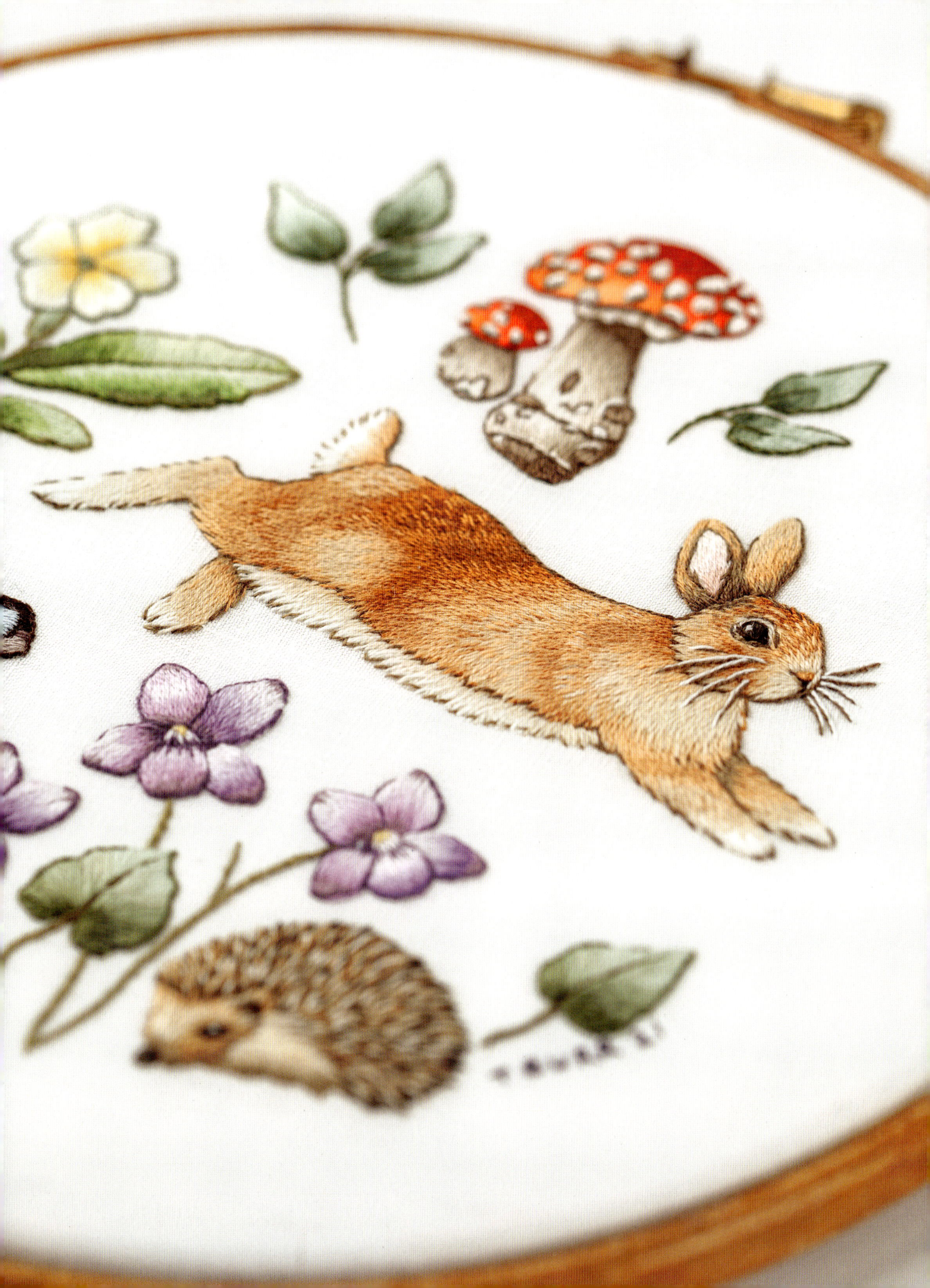

BUTTERFLY SAMPLER

Artwork by Amy Rose Geden.

PROJECT SIZE
20 x 16.5cm (8 x 6½in)

YOU WILL NEED
- Piece of fabric, 35 x 30cm (14 x 12in)
- Threads as per list
- A super grip hoop, size 20cm (8in), or stretcher frame
- Template, page 173

PREPARATION

- Transfer the outline to the fabric (see pages 16 and 176).
- Add directional lines in pencil, as required (see page 23).
- Mount your fabric in the hoop or frame (see pages 16–17).
- Follow the step-by-step instructions on pages 123–133.
- Use one strand of thread throughout unless otherwise specified.
- Anchor threads are prefaced with an A before each number.
- If using a hoop, mount the first half of the design into the hoop and tack/baste up any excess fabric so it does not get in the way while stitching. When the first half is complete, take the fabric out and mount the second half of the design, tacking/basting up the excess fabric as before.

THREAD LIST

DMC
- 27
- 28
- 31
- 152
- 223
- 433
- 434
- 435
- 436
- 437
- 543
- 611
- 612
- 613
- 640
- 642
- 644
- 676
- 677
- 738
- 760
- 761
- 780
- 782
- 801
- 819
- 838
- 839
- 840
- 841
- 869
- 935
- 936
- 948
- 977
- 3011
- 3012
- 3013
- 3021
- 3046
- 3047
- 3712
- 3713
- 3721
- 3726
- 3781
- 3787
- 3802
- 3827
- 3856
- 3857
- 3858
- 3859
- 3864
- 3865
- 3866

Anchor
- A6
- A8
- A9
- A10
- A72
- A380
- A842
- A843
- A844
- A845
- A846
- A894
- A895
- A896
- A897
- A1015
- A1022
- A1023
- A1024
- A1025
- A1027

Sewing cotton in similar shades to 3866, 3787 and 640

ORDER OF WORK

The overall sampler plan is shown at a reduced size as an overview; the sampler elements are shown at an increased size for clarity when detailing the order of work. The templates at the back of the book are given at actual size (see page 173).

120

121

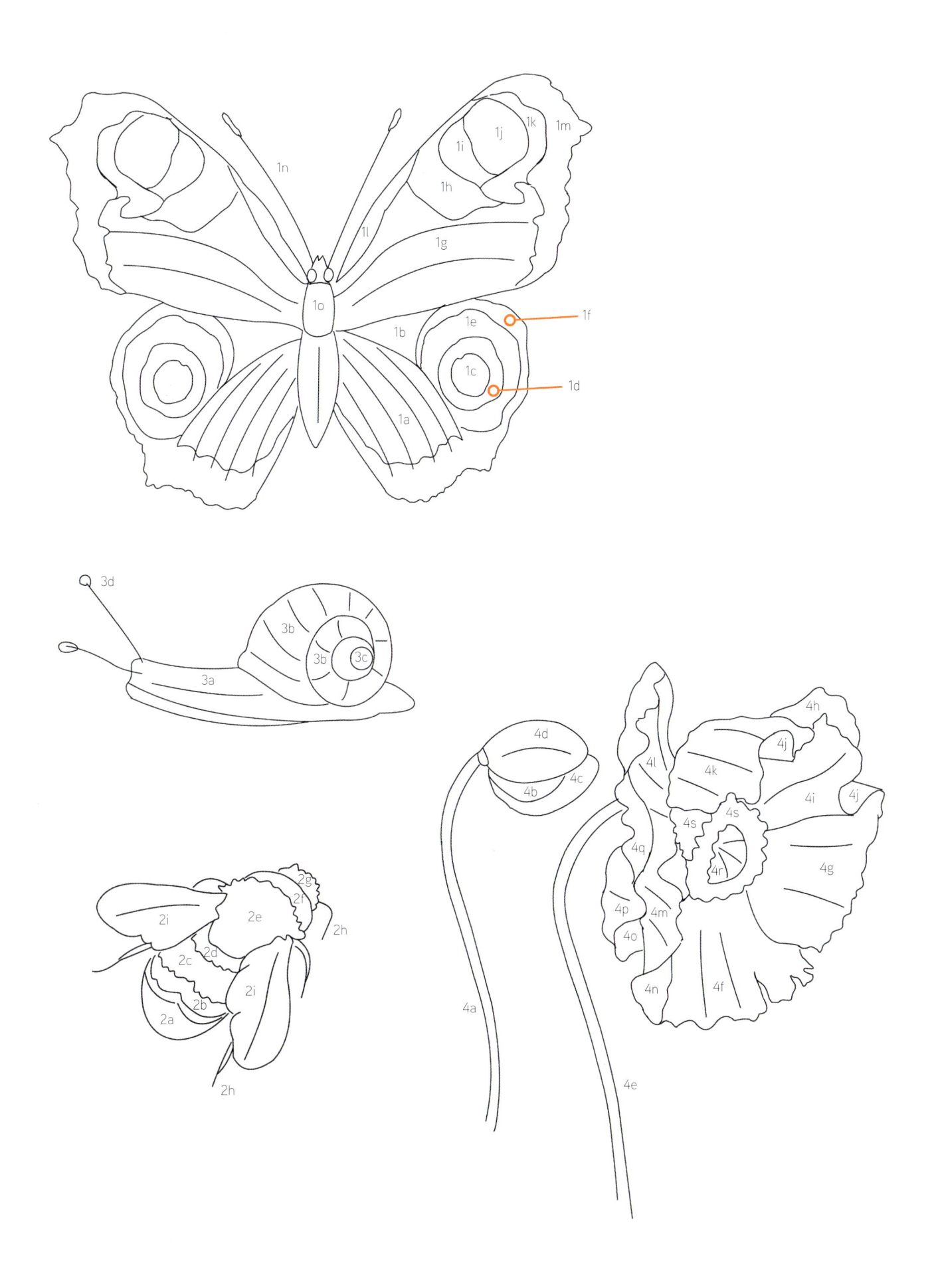

122

1

STEP 01: PEACOCK BUTTERFLY
1a. Fill with long-and-short stitch.
1b. Fill with long-and-short stitch.
1c. Fill with long-and-short stitch – you will need to encroach into the nearby shapes slightly so that the stitches overlap.
1d. Fill with satin stitch.
1e. Fill with long-and-short stitch.
1f. Fill with long-and-short stitch; add outlines in split stitch.

Continued below…

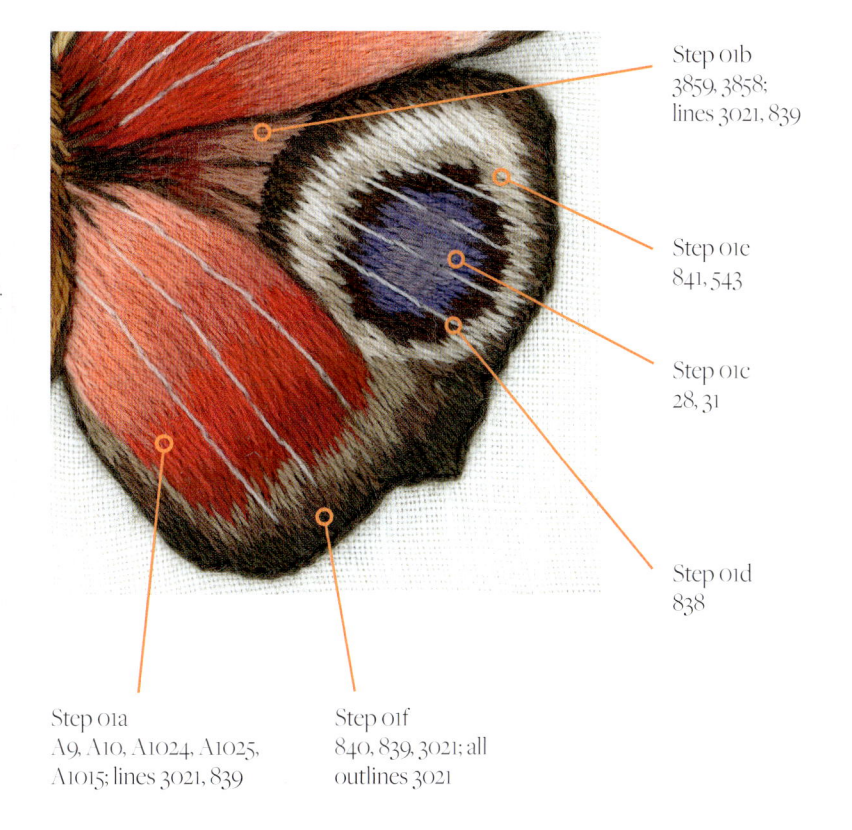

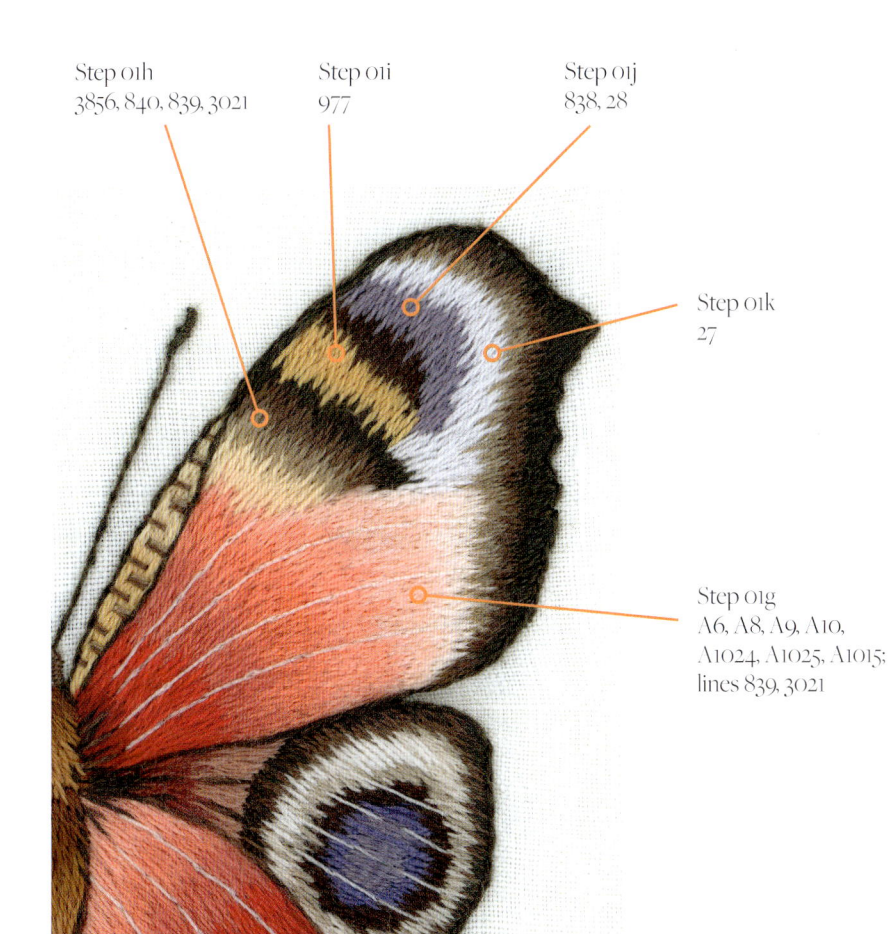

Step 01b
3859, 3858;
lines 3021, 839

Step 01c
841, 543

Step 01e
28, 31

Step 01d
838

Step 01a
A9, A10, A1024, A1025, A1015; lines 3021, 839

Step 01f
840, 839, 3021; all outlines 3021

Step 01h
3856, 840, 839, 3021

Step 01i
977

Step 01j
838, 28

Step 01k
27

Step 01g
A6, A8, A9, A10, A1024, A1025, A1015; lines 839, 3021

STEP 01: PEACOCK BUTTERFLY
CONTINUED

1g. Fill with long-and-short stitch.
1h. Fill with long-and-short stitch. Again, overlap the stitches slightly so that they encroach into each shape.
1i. Fill with long-and-short stitch.
1j. Fill with long-and-short stitch.
1k. Fill with irregular satin stitches.

Continued overleaf…

Step 01n
3021 for head and
antennae; 839 for eyes

Step 01l
3856, 3827; lines 839;
outline 3021

Step 01m
840, 839, 3021

fine lines

Step 01o
435, 434, 433;
outline 3021

STEP 01: PEACOCK BUTTERFLY *CONTINUED*
1l. Fill with long-and-short stitch; outline with split stitch. Add straight lines in a pattern as shown.
1m. Fill with long-and-short stitch; outline with split stitch.
1n. Stitch with split stitch. Add a small bullion at each tip.
1o. Fill with irregular long-and-short stitch to create a fluffy effect on the thorax; use regular long-and-short stitch on the abdomen below. Outline with split stitch. Add all outlines on edge of wings in split stitch 3021.

When all the stitching is complete. Split one strand of sewing thread in a similar shade to DMC 3866. Use this to add fine lines. Use the photograph as a guide to placement.

2

STEP 02: BEE

2a. Fill with long-and-short stitch. Add a few lines at the base in 642.
2b. Fill with long-and-short stitch. You will need to overlap the stitches slightly to encroach into each shape.
2c. Fill with long-and-short stitch as before.
2d. Fill with long-and-short stitch as before.
2e. Fill with irregular long-and-short stitch to create a fluffy effect.
2f. Fill with long-and-short stitch.
2g. Fill with irregular satin stitches.
2h. Stitch the legs and the antenna with lines of split stitch.
2i. Fill each wing with long-and-short stitch. Add outlines and veins in split stitch in sewing cotton. You will need to split the sewing cotton to get a very fine thread.

Step 02e
839, 3021

Step 02g
3021

Step 02f
782, 780

Step 02d
839

Step 02c
677, 676, 782

Step 02i
3865, 3866, 642;
lines in sewing
cotton similar
to 640

Step 02b
780, 839, 3021

Step 02a
3865, 642

Step 02h
3021

125

TSUBAZI

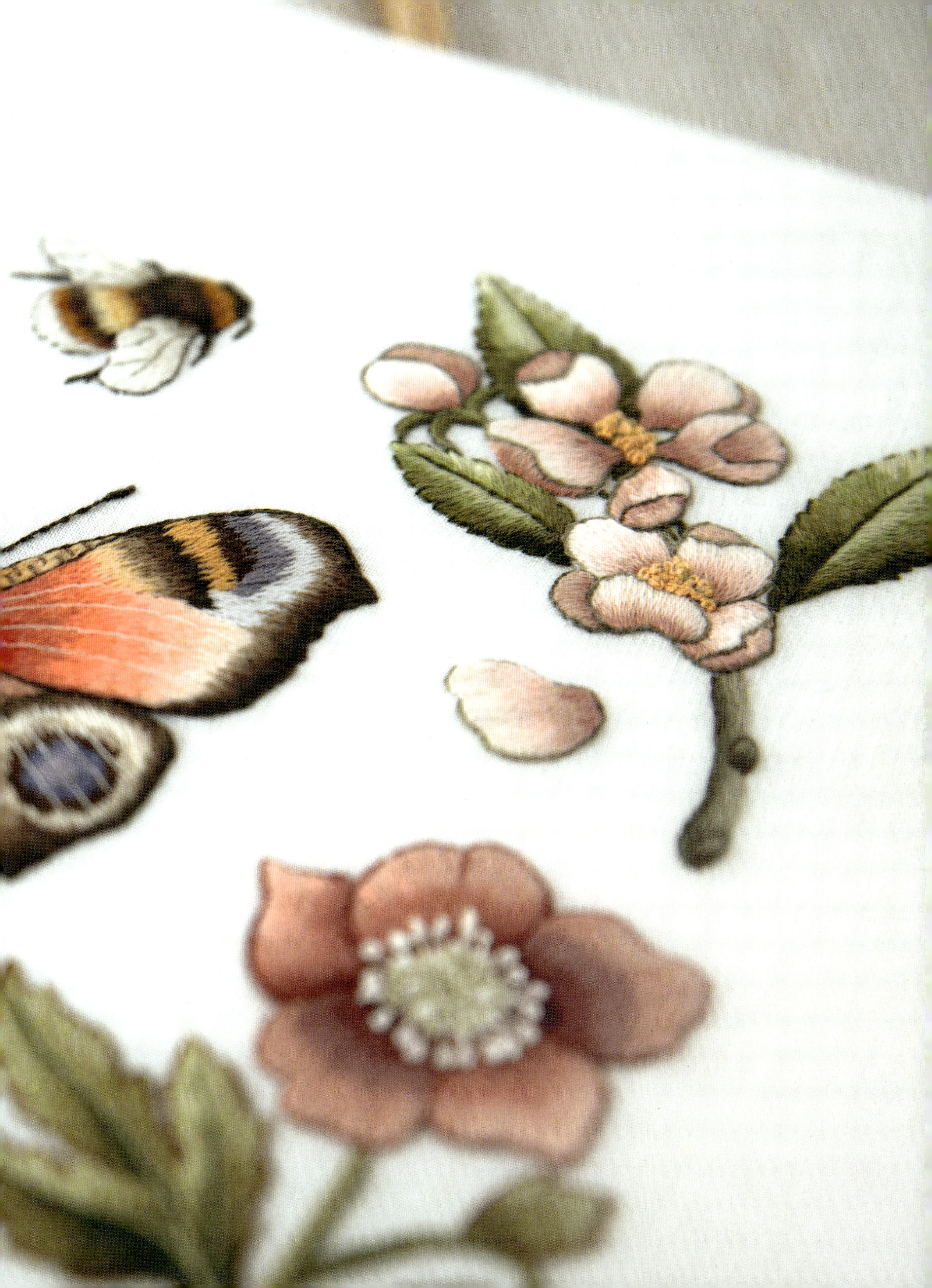

3

STEP 03: SNAIL

3a. Stitch the underside with lines of split stitch in 612. Fill the top with long-and-short stitch; outline with split stitch.

3b. Fill the shell with long-and-short stitch – adjust the shades as you work around the smaller area of the spiral. Use the photograph as a guide. Outline with split stitch.

3c. Fill with padded satin stitch. Outline with split stitch.

3d. Fill the eyestalks with lines of split stitch. Add a French knot at the top of each.

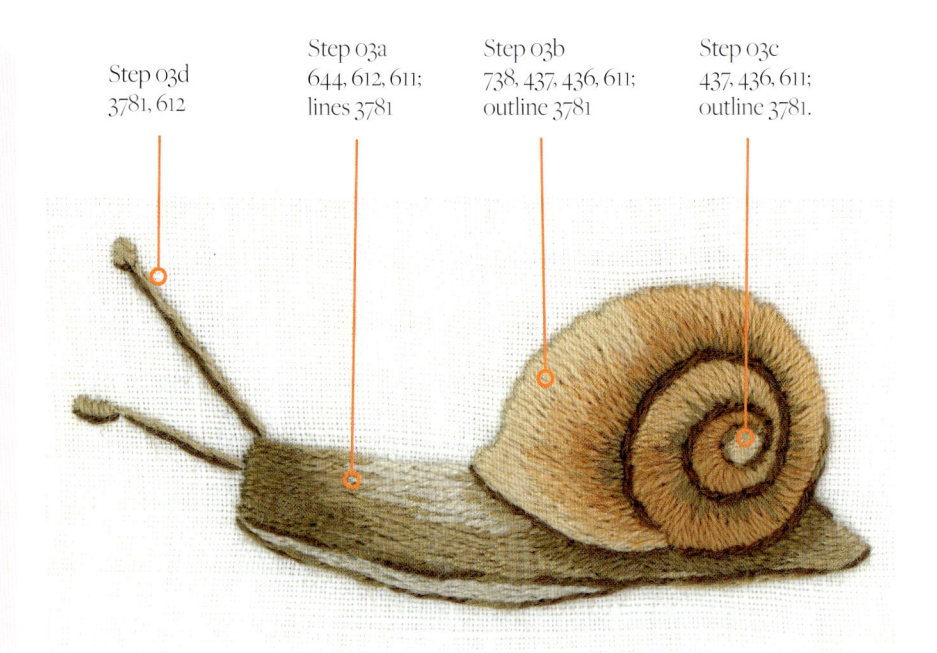

Step 03d
3781, 612

Step 03a
644, 612, 611;
lines 3781

Step 03b
738, 437, 436, 611;
outline 3781

Step 03c
437, 436, 611;
outline 3781.

4

STEP 04: POPPY AND BUD

4a. Fill with long-and-short stitch; outline with split stitch. Add fine hairs in sewing thread in a similar shade to 3787. You will need to split the sewing thread to achieve a fine thread.

4b. Fill with long-and-short stitch.

4c. Fill with long-and-short stitch; outline with split stitch.

4d. Fill with long-and-short stitch; outline with split stitch. Add hairs as for step 4a.

4e. Fill with long-and-short stitch. Add fine hairs in sewing thread.

Continued overleaf…

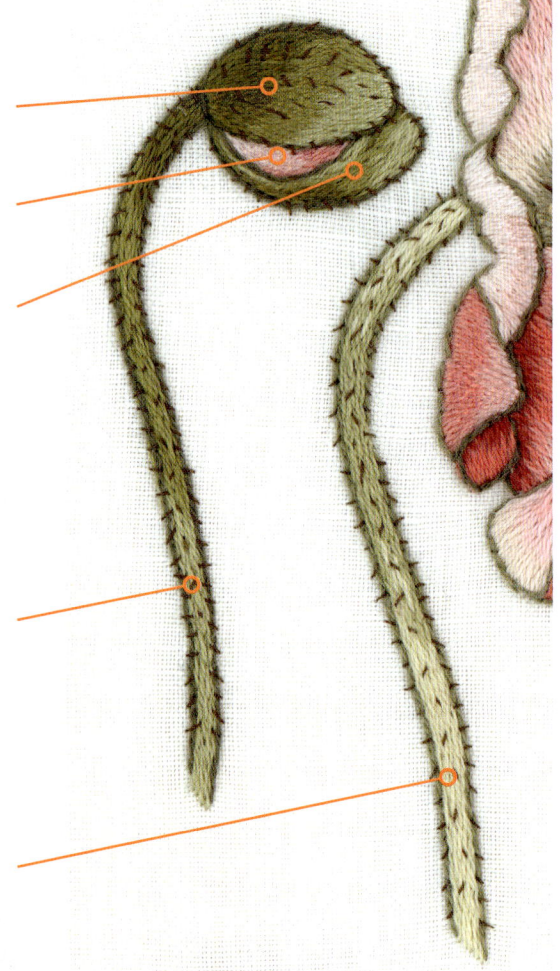

Step 04d
3013, 3012, 3011;
outlines 935

Step 04b
3713, 761, 760

Step 04c
3013, 3012, 3011

Step 04a
3013, 3012, 3011;
add fine hairs in
sewing thread
similar to 3787

Step 04e
3047, 3013; outline
640, sewing thread
similar to 3787

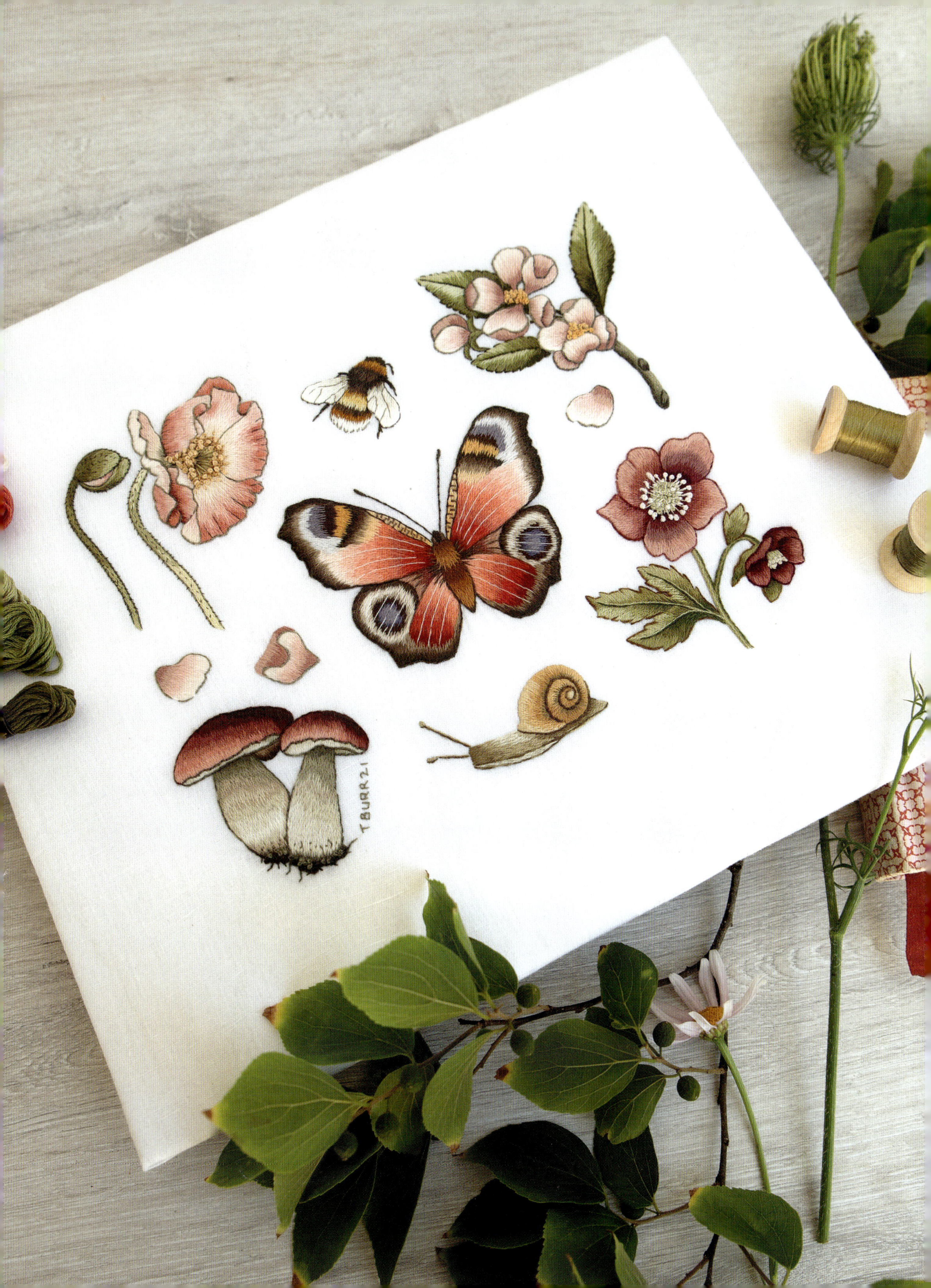
TBURR21

Step 04l
761, 3713, 948,
642; outline 640

Step 04s
436, 437, 3856

Step 04r
3046, 611;
sewing thread
similar to 3787

Step 04i
948, 819, 3713, 761,
760; outline 640

Step 04q
819, 3713;
outline 640

Step 04k
3713, 761, 760,
3712; outline 640

Step 04j
3712, 760;
outline 640

Step 04h
760, 3712;
outline 640

STEP 04: POPPY AND BUD
CONTINUED

4f. Fill with long-and-short stitch; outline with split stitch. Add fine lines on the edge of all the petals with split sewing thread.
4g. Fill with long-and-short stitch as for step 4f.
4h. Fill with long-and-short stitch; outline with split stitch.
4i. Fill with long-and-short stitch as for step 4f.
4j. Fill with long-and-short stitch; outline with split stitch.
4k. Fill with long-and-short stitch; outline with split stitch. Add fine lines in sewing thread as for step 4f.
4l. Fill with long-and-short stitch; outline with split stitch.
4m. Fill with long-and-short stitch; outline with split stitch.
4n. Fill with long-and-short stitch; outline with split stitch.
4o. Fill with long-and-short stitch; outline with split stitch.
4p. Fill with long-and-short stitch; outline with split stitch.
4q. Fill with satin stitch. Add second shade in long-and-short. Outline with split stitch.
4r. Fill with straight stitches that radiate from the centre out towards the right-hand side.
4s. Fill with French knots using two strands and two twists.

Step 04p
761, 760;
outline 640

Step 04n
948, 3713, 761;
outline 640

Step 04f
948, 819, 3713, 761,
760, 3712; outline 640,
sewing thread similar
to 3787

Step 04o
3712, 3721;
outline 640

Step 04m
761, 760, 3712,
3721; outline 640

Step 04g
948, 819, 3713, 761,
760, 3712; outline 640

130

5

STEP 05: MUSHROOM

5a. Fill with long-and-short stitch. Add lines for the 'roots' and French knots in one strand with two twists.

5b. Fill with long-and-short stitch; outline with split stitch.

5c. Fill cap with long-and-short stitch; outline with split stitch.

5d. Fill gills with satin stitches; outline with split stitch.

5e. Fill with long-and-short stitch. Add lines for the 'roots' and French knots in one strand with two twists.

5f. Fill gills with long-and-short stitch, or satin stitch where space does not allow. Outline with split stitch.

5g. Fill with satin stitch; outline with split stitch.

5h. Fill cap with long-and-short stitch; outline with split stitch.

Step 05d
3866, 644, 642;
outline 3787

Step 05c
A1022, A1023, A1027,
A896, 3857, A380;
outline A380, 3787

Step 05b
840, 839, 3021;
outline 3787

Step 05h
A1022, A1023, A1027, A896,
3857, A380; outline A380, 3787

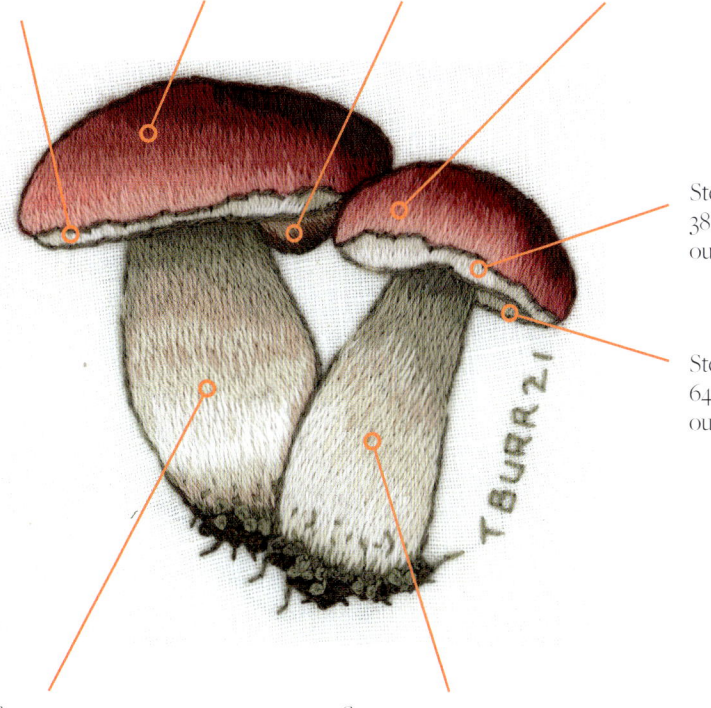

Step 05f
3866, 644, 642;
outline 3787

Step 05g
644, 642;
outline 3787

Step 05a
3866, 613, 3864, 642, 640, 3787;
outline 3787; knots 3021

Step 05e
3866, 613, 644, 3864, 642,
640; outline 3787; knots 3021

STEP 06: APPLE BLOSSOM

6a. Fill the stem with long-and-short stitch. Add outline in split stitch.
6b. Fill with satin stitches; outline with split stitch.
6c. Fill each side of each leaf with long-and-short stitch, from the outside edge in towards the centre vein. Add outlines in straight stitches. Add centre line in split stitch.
6d. Fill the sepals with lines of split stitch; outline with split stitch.
6e. Fill the petals and turnovers with long-and-short stitch; outline with split stitch.
6f. Fill with long-and-short stitch; outline with split stitch.
6g. Fill with French knots. Use two strands and two twists.

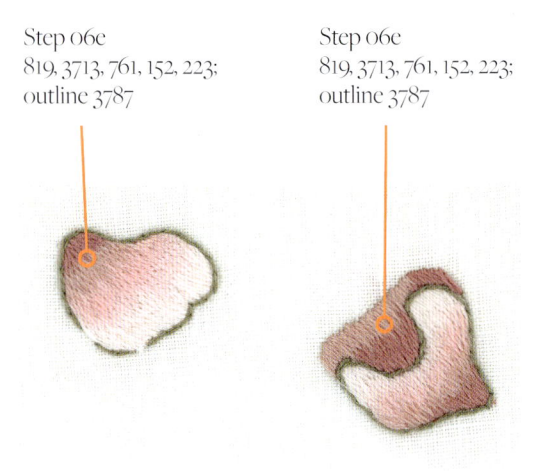

Step 06d
A843, A844, A845;
outline A846

Step 06e
819, 3713, 761, 152, 223;
outline 640, 3787

Step 06c
A842, A843, A844, A845,
A846; outline A846

Step 06f
152, 223

Step 06g
977, 3827

Step 06b
3021, 640

Step 06a
642, 640, 3787;
outline 3021

Step 06e
819, 3713, 761, 152, 223;
outline 3787

Step 06e
819, 3713, 761, 152, 223;
outline 3787

ℱ

STEP 07: HELLEBORE

7a. Fill the stem with lines of split stitch.
7b. Fill on either side of the centre veins in long-and-short stitch. Fill the centre veins in split stitch – one dark and one light on top of this. Add the outlines in split stitch.
7c. Fill with long-and-short stitch; outline in split stitch.
7d. Fill with long-and-short stitch; outline in split stitch.
7e. Fill with long-and-short stitch; outline in split stitch.
7f. Fill with long-and-short stitch; outline in split stitch.
7g. Fill the centre with French knots using two twists and two strands in 613. On top of this, add straight lines from the centre outwards in 3013. Add French knots at the end of the lines in 3865 using one strand and two twists. These should also be scattered around the centre. Use the photograph below right as a guide to placement.
7h. Fill with long-and-short stitch; outline in split stitch.
7i. Fill with long-and-short stitch; outline in split stitch.
7j. Fill with satin stitches; outline in split stitch.
7k. Add straight lines – at the ends of these, add French knots using one strand and two twists.

Step 07e
A894, A895, A1027, A896, A897; outline A897, A896

Step 07g
Knots 613, 3865; lines 3013

Step 07f
A894, A895, 3726, 3802, A72; outline A897, A896

Step 07c
3013, 3012, 3011; outline 869

Step 07b
3013, 3012, 3011, 936; lines 3013, 935; outlines 801, 869

Step 07a
3013, 3012, 3011, 936

Step 07d
3012, 3011, 936; outline 869

Step 07h
A1027, A896, A897, A72; outline A72

Step 07i
A1027, A896; outline A72

Step 07j
A1027; outline A72

Step 07k
Lines 613, 3013, 3012; knots 613

133

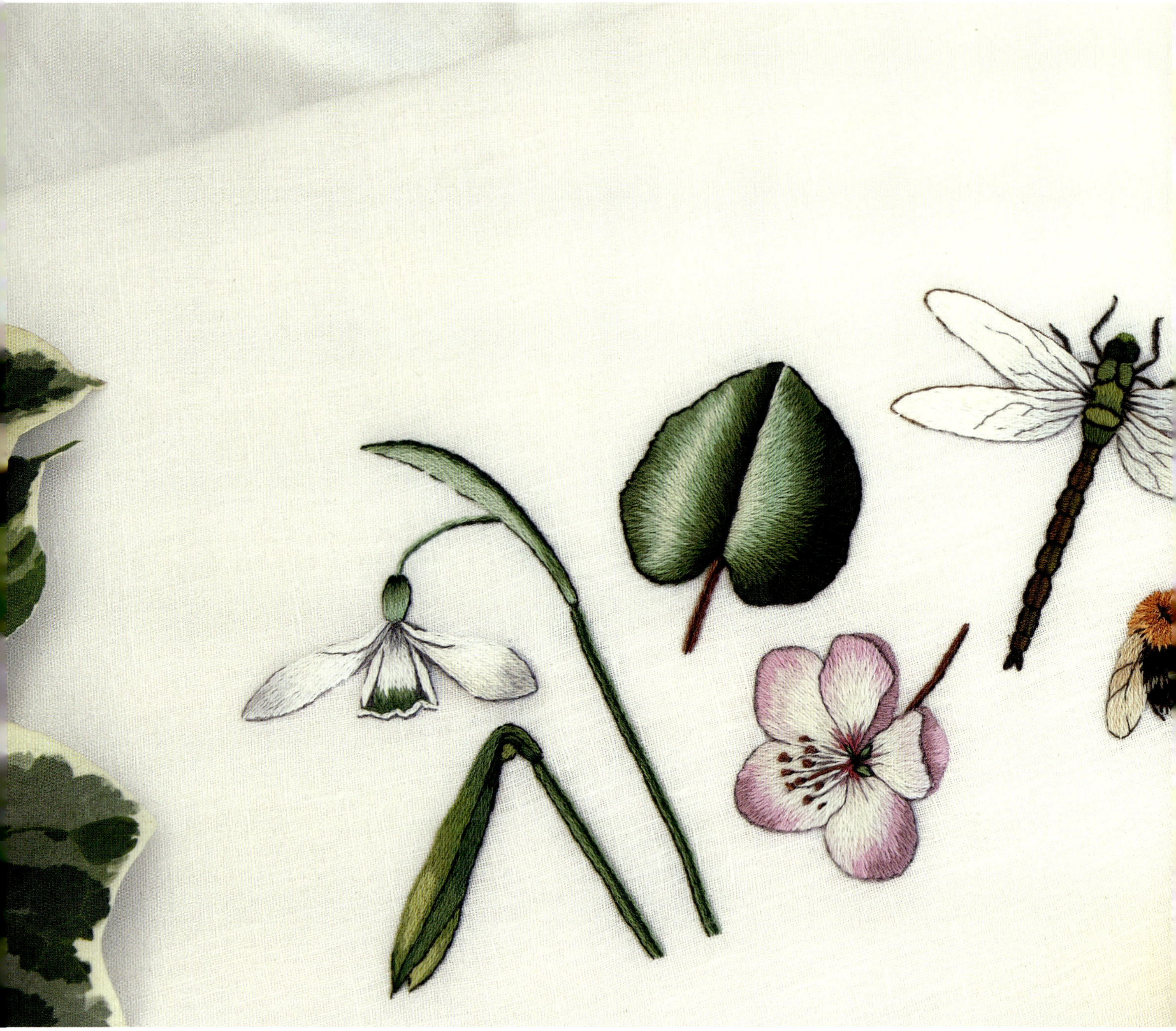

ADVANCED PROJECTS

PELARGONIUM SAMPLER

Artwork by Carolyn Jenkins.

PROJECT SIZE

25 x 12cm (10 x 4¾in)

YOU WILL NEED

- Piece of fabric, 35 x 28cm (14 x 11in)
- Threads as per list
- A super grip hoop, size 20cm (8in), or stretcher frame
- Template, page 174

PREPARATION

- Transfer the outline to the fabric (see pages 16 and 176).
- Add directional lines in pencil, as required (see page 23).
- Mount your fabric in the hoop or frame (see pages 16–17).
- Follow the step-by-step instructions on pages 141–149.
- Use one strand of thread throughout unless otherwise specified.
- Anchor threads are prefaced with an A before each number.
- If using a hoop, mount the first half of the design into the hoop and tack/baste up any excess fabric so it does not get in the way whilst stitching. When the first half is complete, take the fabric out and mount the second half of the design, tacking/basting up the excess fabric as before.

THREAD LIST

DMC
- 14
- 15
- 24
- 25
- 28
- 29
- 33
- 34
- 35
- 150
- 152
- 153
- 154
- 159
- 164
- 221
- 223
- 224
- 225
- 319
- 320
- 356
- 367
- 368
- 369
- 434
- 437
- 469
- 470
- 471
- 472
- 520
- 554
- 564
- 601
- 602
- 603
- 640
- 642
- 644
- 734
- 738
- 746
- 754
- 758
- 772
- 777
- 801
- 814
- 822
- 926
- 927
- 928
- 930
- 935
- 936
- 937
- 948
- 987
- 988
- 989
- 3021
- 3041
- 3042
- 3046
- 3047
- 3348
- 3350
- 3371
- 3607
- 3608
- 3609
- 3721
- 3722
- 3747
- 3756
- 3778
- 3787
- 3799
- 3803
- 3827
- 3831
- 3834
- 3835
- 3836
- 3862
- 3863
- 3865

Anchor
- A68

Sewing thread in a similar colour to 369

ORDER OF WORK

The overall sampler plan is shown at a reduced size as an overview; the sampler elements are shown at an increased size for clarity when detailing the order of work. The templates at the back of the book are given at actual size (see page 174).

1   2   3   4   5   6   7

1a, 1b, 1c, 1d, 1e, 1f, 1g, 1h, 1i, 1j, 1k

3a, 3b, 3c, 3d

4a, 4b, 4c, 4d, 4e

138

139

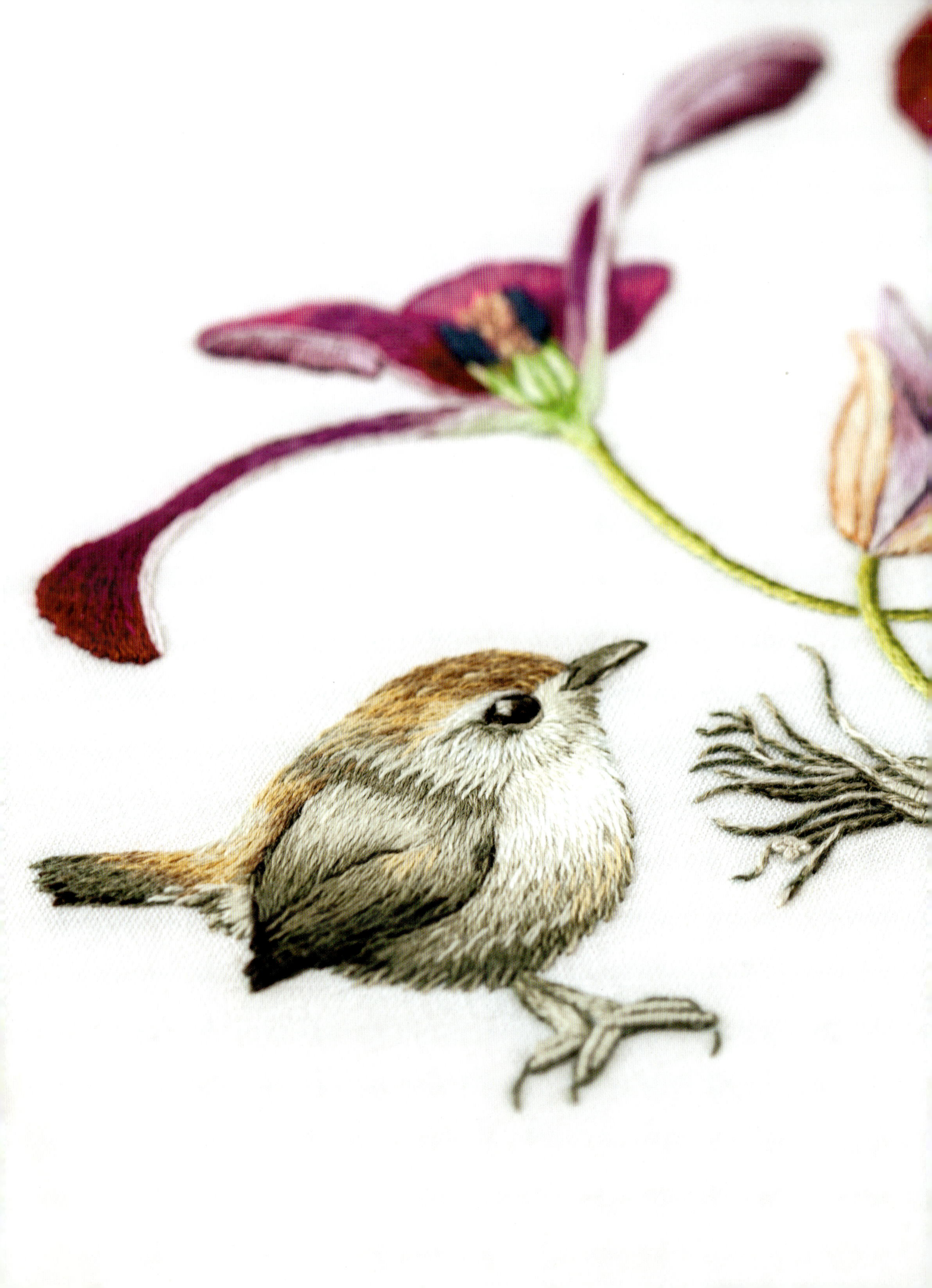

1

STEP 01: WREN

1a. Fill the body with irregular long-and-short stitches. Add tiny lines along the edge to create shadows.
1b. Fill the tail area with long-and-short stitch. Add lines in split stitch.
1c. Fill with long-and-short stitch. Add outlines in split stitch.
1d. Fill with long-and-short stitch. Add lines in split stitch.
1e. Fill with long-and-short stitch. These stitches should encroach into neighbouring areas.
1f. Fill the bottom half and the top half of the eye in satin stitch in 3021 and 3371 (see the detail photograph below). Add tiny stitches for the highlight in 3865. Outline the eye in split stitch with 3371.
1g. Fill the beak with long-and-short stitch; outline in split stitch.
1h. Fill with irregular long-and-short stitches.
1i. Fill the head with irregular long-and-short stitches.
1j. Fill the legs with adjacent lines of split stitch; outline in split stitch.
1k. Loosen the hoop. For the toes, add bullions in 644, using two strands, with two bullions side by side for each toe and approximately 10 twists. Then add claws and outlines in split stitch with 3021.

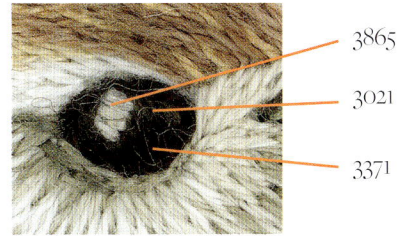

Step 01b
3787, 640, 3863, 437, 738, 822; lines 3021

Step 01e
644, 642, 640

Step 01i
738, 437, 3863, 3862

Step 01c
822, 644, 642, 640, 3787; outlines 3021

Step 01h
3865, 822, 644, 642

Step 01g
644, 640; outline 3021

3865
3021
3371

Step 01d
644, 642, 640, 3787; lines 3021, 3371

Step 01j
644, 642, 640; outline 3021

Step 01k
Bullions 644; outlines 3021

Step 01a
3865, 822, 644, 642, 640, 3787; lines 3021

141

2

STEP 02: CLEMATIS

Use the photograph as a guide for placement of the outlines – some are highlights stitched in light shades and some are outlines stitched in dark shades.

2a. Fill the stem with adjacent rows of split stitch.
2b. Fill the stem with adjacent rows of split stitch.
2c. Fill with adjacent rows of split stitch. Fill bases with satin stitch. Add French knots in 822.
2d. Fill the leaves with long-and-short stitch; outline with split stitch.
2e. Fill the petals with long-and-short stitch; outline with split stitch.
2f. Fill with long-and-short stitch. Add outlines and lines in split stitch.
2g. Fill with long-and-short stitch. Add outlines and lines in split stitch.

Continued opposite...

Step 02g
746, 948, 754, 758;
lines 356, 3778

Step 02e
25, 153, 3836, 3041;
outline 3041

Step 02f
25, 153, 3836

Step 02c
822, 642, 3787, 3021

Step 02a
472, 471, 469

Step 02b
642, 640, 3787, 3021; outline 3371, 3021

Step 02d
471, 470, 937; outline 936

STEP 02: CLEMATIS *CONTINUED*

2h. Fill with long-and-short stitch; outline in split stitch.
2i. Fill with long-and-short stitch, or satin stitch where space does not allow. Outline with split stitch.
2j. Fill with long-and-short stitch; outline with split stitch.
2k. Fill with long-and-short stitch; outline with split stitch.
2l. Fill with long-and-short stitch; outline with split stitch.
2m. Fill with long-and-short stitch; outline with split stitch.
2n. Fill and outline styles with lines of split stitch. Continue petals into stems with long-and-short stitch.
2o. Loosen the fabric in the hoop. Create bullions one on top of the other, with two strands and approximately eight twists for each. Add lines in split stitch.
2p. Add bullions next to each other as shown in the photograph; add two bullions side by side, with two strands and approximately eight twists for each.

Step 02k
153, 3836, 3835, 3834; outline 3834; line 24

Step 02l
3836, 33, 34

Step 02l
24, 153, 3836

Step 02m
33, 34, 35, 814, 3836; line 24

Step 02j
3607, 33, 34, 814; outline 34, 35

Step 02i
153, 3836, 3835; outline 3834; line 24, 3836

Step 02h
3607, 34, 35; outline 35

Step 02p
930

Step 02o
223; lines 758

Step 02n
772, 15, 470; outline 937

143

3

STEP 03: BUTTERFLY

3a. Fill the lower wings with long-and-short stitch; outline with split stitch.
3b. Fill the upper wings with long-and-short stitch. Add markings in tiny straight stitches. Outline with split stitch.
3c. Fill with satin stitch. Add French knots for the eyes.
3d. Stitch the antennae with split stitch.

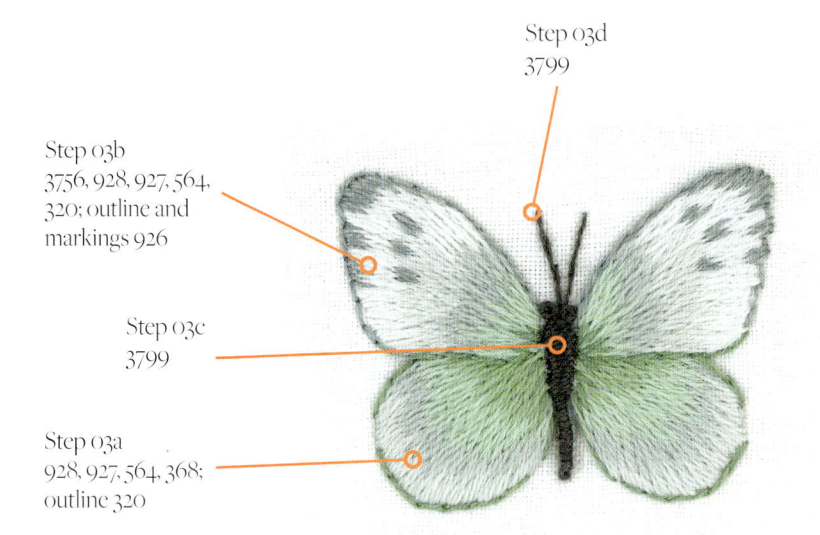

Step 03d
3799

Step 03b
3756, 928, 927, 564, 320; outline and markings 926

Step 03c
3799

Step 03a
928, 927, 564, 368; outline 320

4

STEP 04: BEETLE

4a. Fill with long-and-short stitch; outline with split stitch.
4b. Fill with satin stitch; outline with split stitch. Add French knots for eyes.
4c. Fill with satin stitch; outline with split stitch.
4d. Fill with long-and-short stitch; outline with split stitch.
4e. Fill with adjacent rows of split stitch; outline with split stitch.

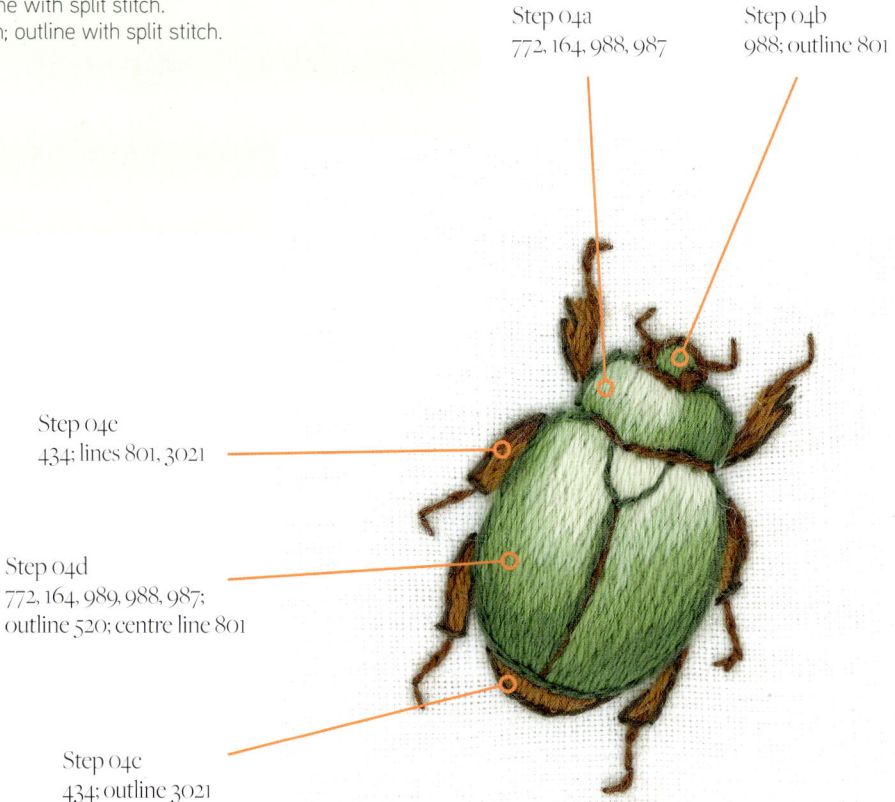

Step 04a
772, 164, 988, 987

Step 04b
988; outline 801

Step 04c
434; lines 801, 3021

Step 04d
772, 164, 989, 988, 987; outline 520; centre line 801

Step 04e
434; outline 3021

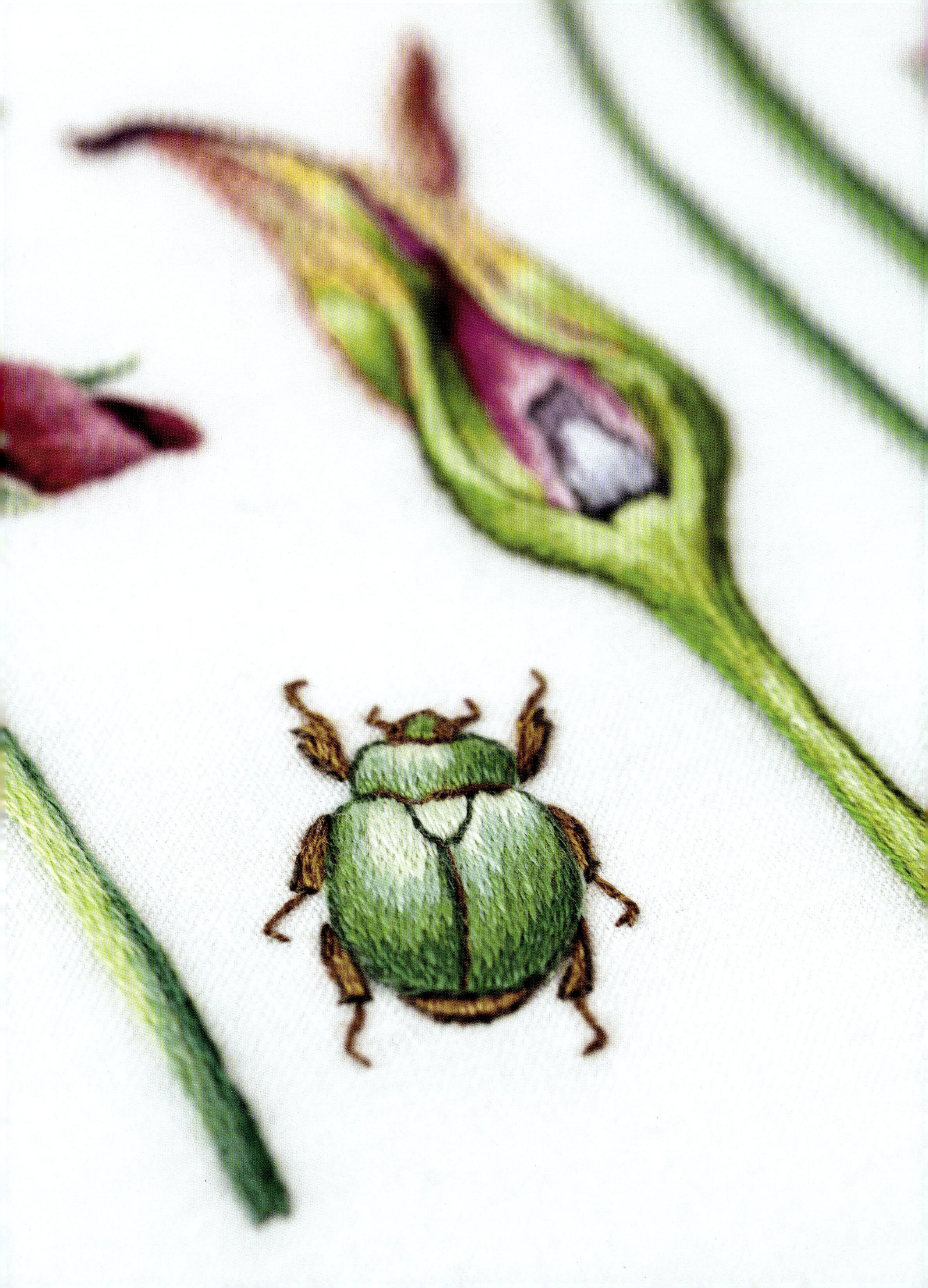

STEP 05: PELARGONIUM

5a. Fill with adjacent rows of split stitch. Take a piece of sewing cotton and split to achieve a very fine thread. Add a few hairs to the top of the stem with straight stitches.

5b. Fill with long-and-short stitch; outline in split stitch. Take a piece of sewing cotton and split to achieve a very fine thread. Add hairs in straight stitches.

5c. Fill with long-and-short stitch, or satin stitch where space does not allow. Outline with split stitch.

5d. Fill with long-and-short stitch, outline with split stitch. Add hairs in straight stitches as above.

5e. Fill with long-and-short stitch; outline with split stitch. Fill stamen with split stitch.

5f. Fill with long-and-short stitch; outline with split stitch.

5g. Fill with long-and-short stitch; outline with split stitch.

5h. Fill with long-and-short stitch; outline with split stitch.

5i. Fill with long-and-short stitch; outline with split stitch.

5j. Fill with long-and-short stitch; outline with split stitch.

5k. Fill with long-and-short stitch; outline with split stitch.

5l. Loosen your fabric in the hoop. Add bullions using between 10 and 15 twists for each.

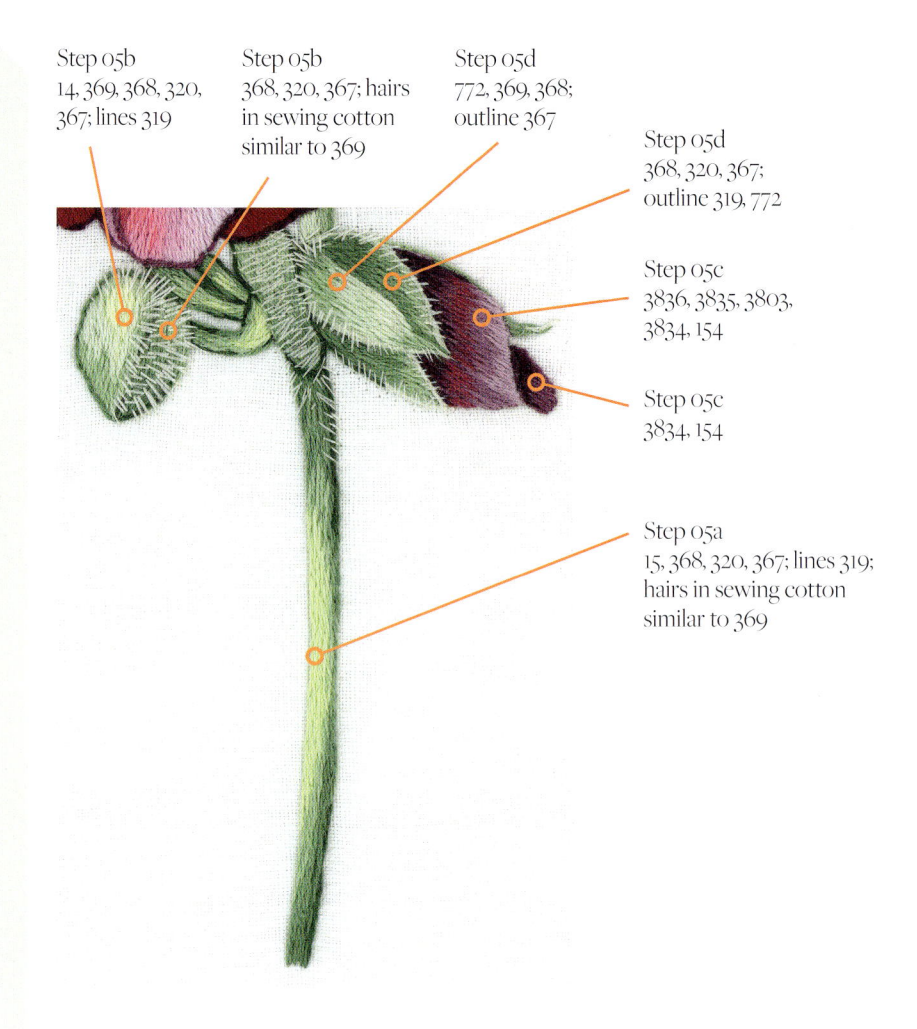

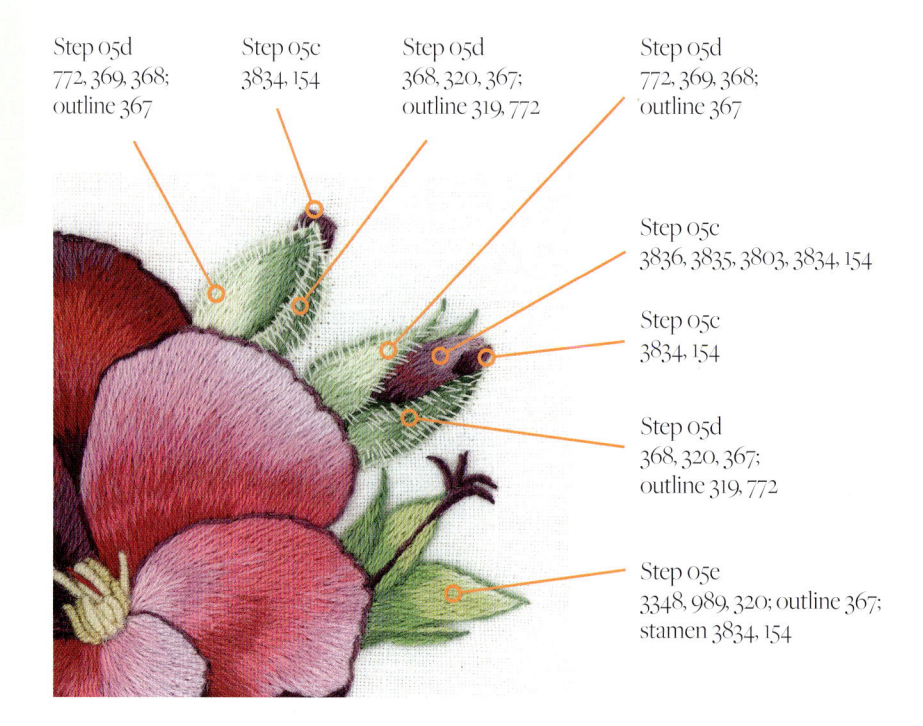

Step 05b
14, 369, 368, 320, 367; lines 319

Step 05b
368, 320, 367; hairs in sewing cotton similar to 369

Step 05d
772, 369, 368; outline 367

Step 05d
368, 320, 367; outline 319, 772

Step 05c
3836, 3835, 3803, 3834, 154

Step 05c
3834, 154

Step 05a
15, 368, 320, 367; lines 319; hairs in sewing cotton similar to 369

Step 05d
772, 369, 368; outline 367

Step 05c
3834, 154

Step 05d
368, 320, 367; outline 319, 772

Step 05d
772, 369, 368; outline 367

Step 05c
3836, 3835, 3803, 3834, 154

Step 05c
3834, 154

Step 05d
368, 320, 367; outline 319, 772

Step 05e
3348, 989, 320; outline 367; stamen 3834, 154

146

Step 05f
154, 814, 777, 3831, 3350;
highlight 3834

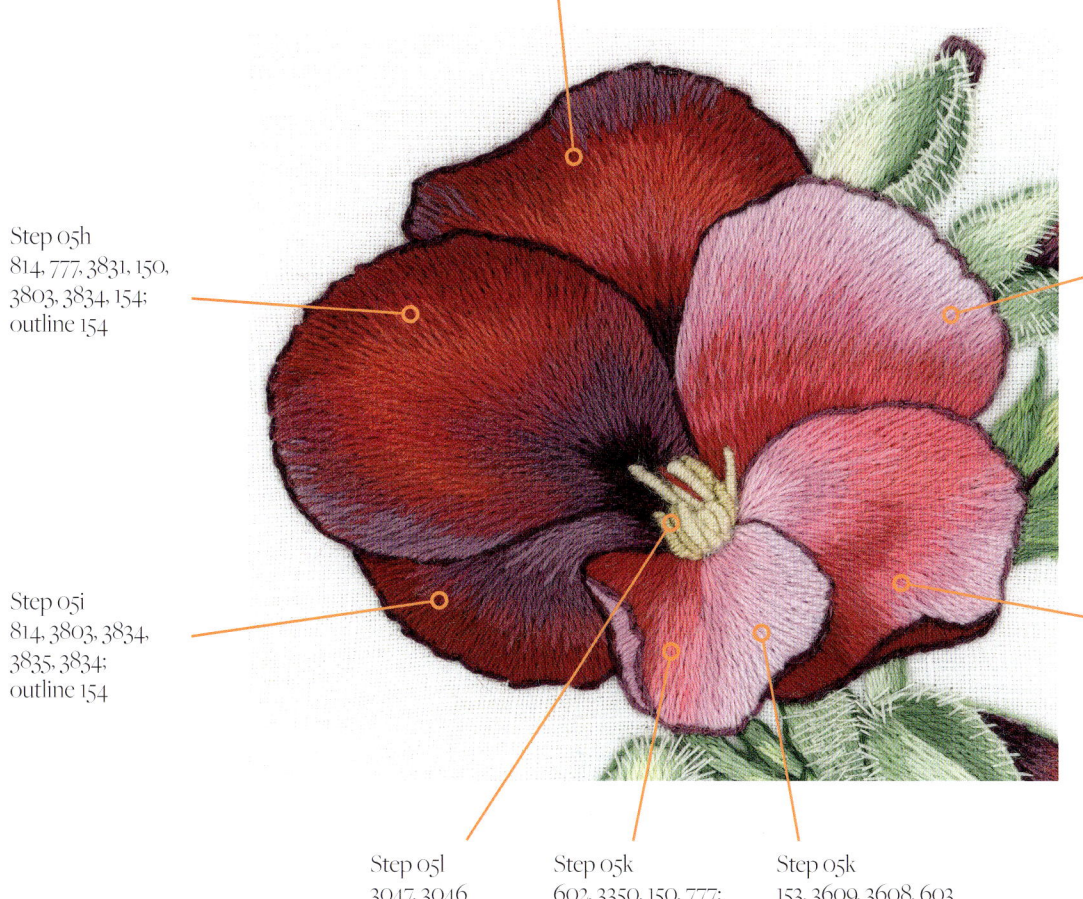

Step 05h
814, 777, 3831, 150,
3803, 3834, 154;
outline 154

Step 05g
153, 554, 3608, A68,
601, 150; outline
3835, 3834

Step 05i
814, 3803, 3834,
3835, 3834;
outline 154

Step 05j
153, 3609, 3608,
602, 3350, 150, 777,
814; outlines 154,
3834, 3835

Step 05l
3047, 3046

Step 05k
602, 3350, 150, 777;
outlines 3834, 777, 154

Step 05k
153, 3609, 3608, 603

6

STEP 06: LORDS-AND-LADIES

6a. Fill the stem with long-and-short stitch; outline in split stitch.
6b. Fill with long-and-short stitch; outline in split stitch.
6c. Fill with long-and-short stitch; outline in split stitch.
6d. Fill with long-and-short stitch; outline in split stitch.
6e. Fill with adjacent lines of split stitch; outline in split stitch.
6f. Fill with long-and-short stitch; outline in split stitch.
6g. Fill with long-and-short stitch; outline in split stitch.
6h. Fill with long-and-short stitch; outline in split stitch.
6i. Fill with long-and-short stitch; outline in split stitch.

Step 06e
35, 154, 29;
outline 154, 3721

Step 06c
15, 471, 470, 734, 3827, 3778,
3722, 3721; outlines 3721, 29

Step 06f
3722, 3721, 29;
outlines 29

Step 06d
15, 471, 470, 937, 936, 15,
734, 3827; outline 3721, 29

Step 06i
153, 554, 33, 34, 35;
outlines 35

Step 06h
28, 159; outline 3799

Step 06b
15, 471, 470, 937, 734, 3827,
3778; outline 936

Step 06g
3747, 159; outline 29

Step 06a
15, 471, 470, 937

7

STEP 07: CHIVES

7a. Fill the stems with adjacent lines of split stitch.
7b. Fill with irregular long-and-short stitch. Add lines in straight stitches.
7c. Fill with long-and-short stitch; outline in split stitch.
7d. Fill with long-and-short stitch; outline in split stitch.
7e. Fill with long-and-short stitch; outline in split stitch.
7f. Fill with long-and-short stitch; outline in split stitch.
7g. Fill with long-and-short stitch; outline in split stitch.
7h. Fill with long-and-short stitch; outline in split stitch.
7i. Fill with long-and-short stitch; outline in split stitch.
7j. Add lines of split stitch.
7k. Fill with long-and-short stitch; outline in split stitch.

Step 07g
3042, 3041, 3834; outline 29

Step 07f
24, 3836, 3041; tips 29.

Step 07j
935, 520, 320, 989

Step 07i
225, 224, 152, 28; outline 29.

Step 07h
24, 153, 3836, 28; outline 28

Step 07k
772, 164; outline 367

Step 07b
24, 153, 3836, 3835; lines 3835

Step 07c
772, 164; outline 367

Step 07e
937, 936, 221, 814; outline 154

Step 07d
221, 814; outline 154

Step 07a
989, 320, 367, 520

149

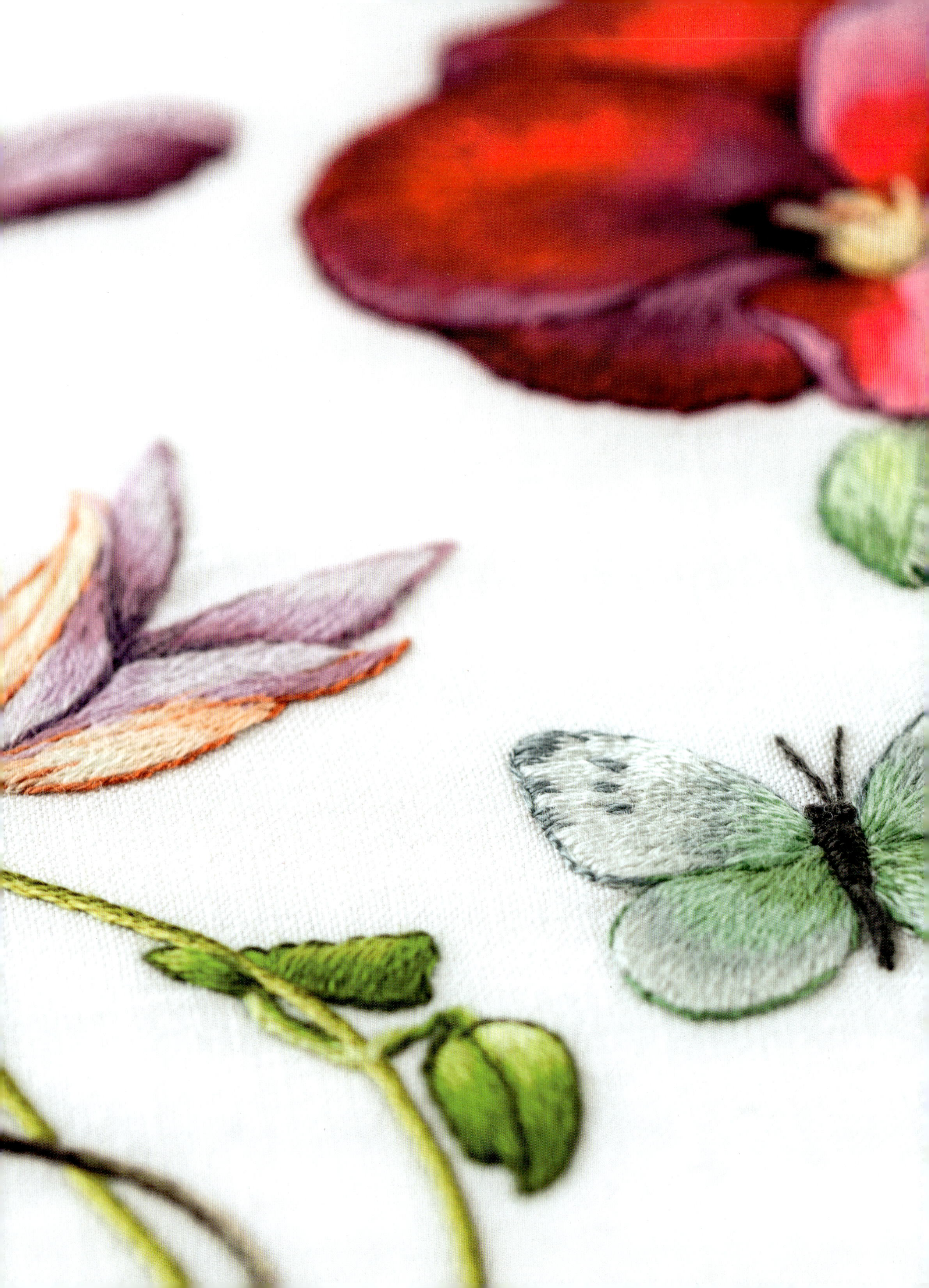

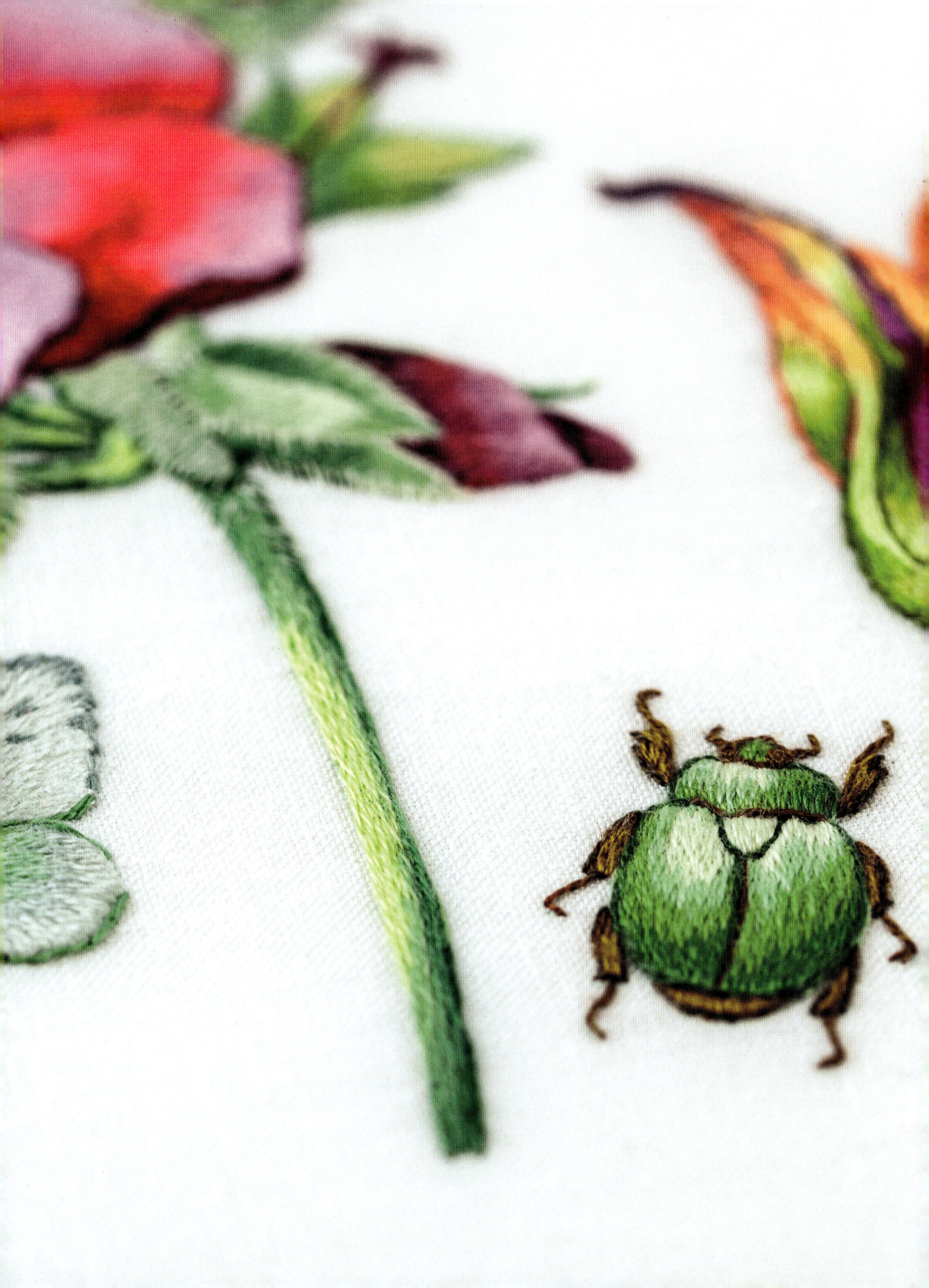

DRAGONFLY SAMPLER

Artwork by Rachel Pedder-Smith.

PROJECT SIZE

29 x 8.5cm (11½ x 3½in)

YOU WILL NEED

- Piece of fabric, 40 x 28cm (15¾ x 11in)
- Threads as per list
- A super grip hoop, size 20cm (8in), or stretcher frame
- Template, page 175

PREPARATION

- Transfer the outline to the fabric (see pages 16 and 176).
- Add directional lines in pencil, as required (see page 23).
- Mount your fabric in the hoop or frame (see pages 16–17).
- Follow the step-by-step instructions on pages 156–165.
- Use one strand of thread throughout unless otherwise specified.
- Anchor threads are prefaced with an A before each number.
- If using a hoop, you can roll up the excess fabric that is not in use and move the hoop along as you stitch.

THREAD LIST

DMC
- 1
- 2
- 3
- 10
- 23
- 24
- 164
- 316
- 369
- 470
- 471
- 472
- 524
- 580
- 632
- 642
- 730
- 738
- 739
- 762
- 772
- 818
- 822
- 829
- 830
- 831
- 832
- 834
- 898
- 934
- 935
- 936
- 937
- 975
- 976
- 977
- 986
- 987
- 988
- 989
- 3021
- 3051
- 3052
- 3345
- 3346
- 3347
- 3348
- 3371
- 3608
- 3609
- 3687
- 3689
- 3772
- 3787
- 3826
- 3827
- 3835
- 3836
- 3857
- 3858
- 3865
- Blanc

Anchor
- A85
- A87
- A259
- A260
- A263
- A265
- A845

Sewing thread in similar shades to: 645, 829, 898, 935, 936, 3021

ORDER OF WORK

The overall sampler plan is shown at a reduced size as an overview; the sampler elements are shown at an increased size for clarity when detailing the order of work. The templates at the back of the book are given at actual size (see page 175).

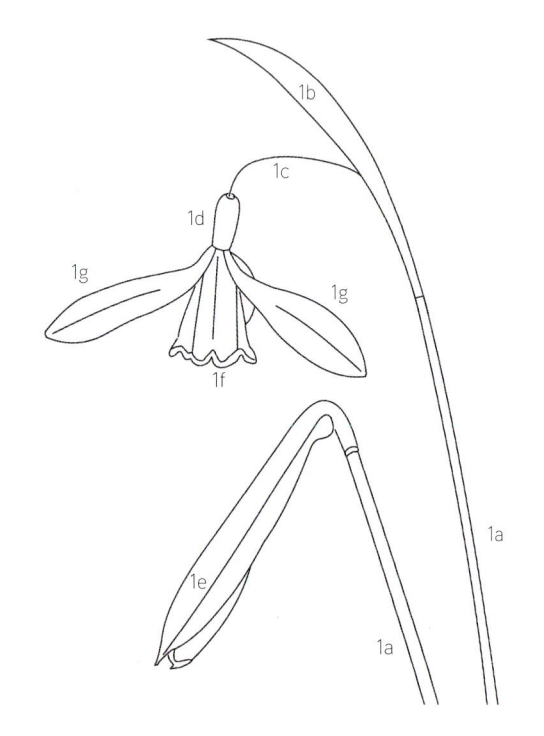

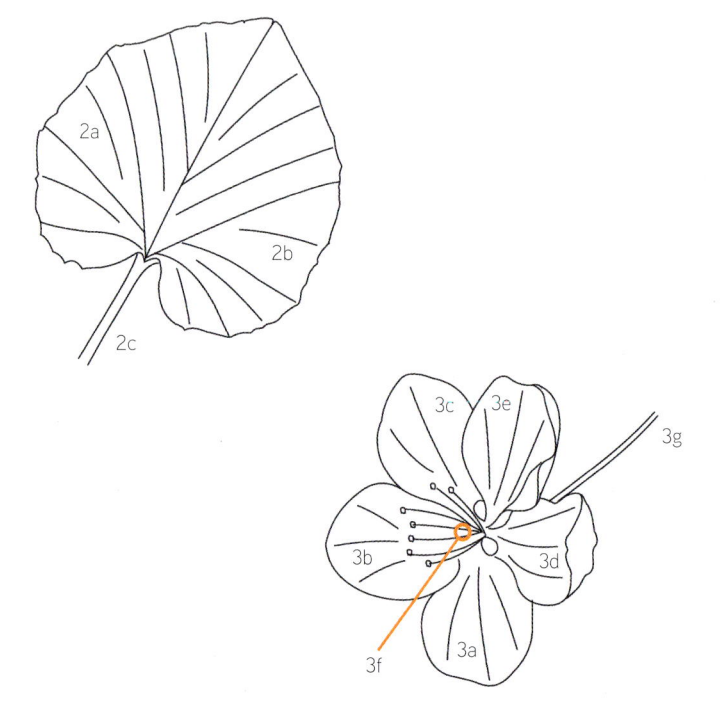

155

1

STEP 01: SNOWDROP

1a. Fill the stems with adjacent lines of split stitch.
1b. Fill the leaf with long-and-short stitch. Add lines and outlines in split stitch. Split a piece of sewing thread to achieve a fine thread.
1c. Fill with adjacent lines of split stitch.
1d. Fill with long-and-short stitch; outline with split stitch. Split a piece of sewing thread to achieve a fine thread.
1e. Fill the second leaf with long-and-short stitch. Add lines and outline with split stitch. Split a piece of sewing thread to achieve a fine thread.
1f. Fill with long-and-short stitch. Add lines and outline with split stitch. Split a piece of sewing thread to achieve a fine thread.
1g. Fill with long-and-short stitch. Add lines and outlines with split stitch. Split a piece of sewing thread to achieve a fine thread.

Step 01c
369, 164, 989, 987

Step 01b
369, 164, 989, 987; line of 986; outline in sewing thread similar to 935

Step 01d
369, 164, 989, 987

Step 01g
Blanc, 3865, 01, 02; outline in sewing thread similar to 645

Step 01f
3865, 01, 02, 03; edge 989, 987; outline in sewing thread similar to 645

Step 01e
472, 471, 470, 988, 987, 986; outline in sewing thread similar to 935

Step 01a
988, 987, 986; outline in sewing thread similar to 935

2

STEP 02: LEAF

2a. Fill the left-hand side of the leaf with long-and-short stitch; outline with split stitch.
2b. Fill the remaining side of the leaf with long-and-short stitch; outline with split stitch.
2c. Fill the stalk with adjacent lines of split stitch.

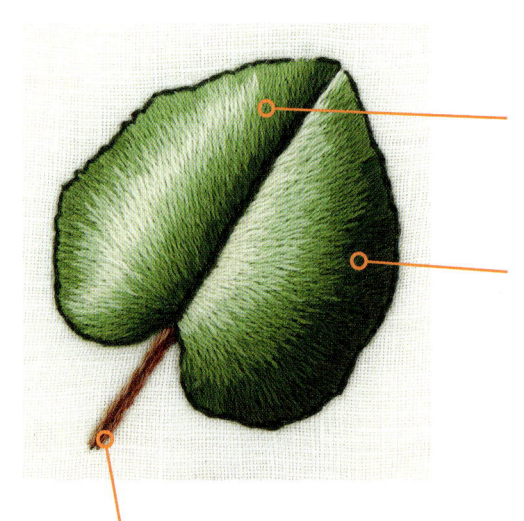

Step 02a
772, 164, 989, 3347, 3346, A263; outline 934

Step 02b
772, 164, 989, 3347, 3346, A263, 935; outline 934

Step 02c
3772, 632, 898

156

3

STEP 03: APPLE BLOSSOM

3a. Fill with long-and-short stitch. Split a piece of sewing thread to achieve a fine thread and outline with split stitch.

3b. Fill with long-and-short stitch. Split a piece of sewing thread to achieve a fine thread and outline with split stitch.

3c. Fill with long-and-short stitch. Split a piece of sewing thread to achieve a fine thread and outline with split stitch.

3d. Fill the petal and turnover with long-and-short stitch. Split a piece of sewing thread to achieve a fine thread and outline with split stitch.

3e. Fill the petal with long-and-short stitch and fill the turnover with satin stitch. Split a piece of sewing thread to achieve a fine thread and outline with split stitch.

3f. Add lines in straight stitches. Add French knots, using one strand and two twists. Add green sepals in satin stitch; outline in split stitch.

3g. Fill with adjacent rows of split stitch.

Step 03c
A85, 24, 23, 3865; outline in sewing thread similar to 645

Step 03e
A85, 24, 23, 3865; turnover 3836; outline in sewing thread similar to 645

Step 03g
632, 3021

Step 03f
316, 3687; lines 3865, sewing thread similar to 645; knots 632; sepals 935, 989

Step 03b
3836, A85, 24, 23, 3865; outline in sewing thread similar to 645

Step 03a
3836, A85, 24, 23, 3865; outline in sewing thread similar to 645

Step 03d
24, 23, 3865; turnover 3836, A85; outline in sewing thread similar to 645

STEP 04: DRAGONFLY

4a. Fill the forewings with long-and-short stitch. Split a piece of sewing thread to achieve a very fine thread and use this for outlines and veins in split stitch.
4b. Fill the hindwings with long-and-short stitch. Split a piece of sewing thread to achieve a very fine thread and use this for outlines and veins in split stitch.
4c. Stitch the legs with lines of split stitch.
4d. Fill with long-and-short stitch; outline with split stitch.
4e. Fill with satin stitch; outline with split stitch.
4f. Fill with satin stitch; outline with split stitch.
4g. Fill with satin stitch; outline with split stitch.
4h. Fill with satin stitch; outline with split stitch.
4i. Fill with satin stitch; add markings and outline with split stitch.
4j. Fill with satin stitch; outline with split stitch.

Step 04f
A263; eyes 470

Step 04d
470, 3347

Step 04e
3787, 3021

Step 04c
3347

Step 04g
471

Step 04a
Blanc, 3865, 762;
outlines in sewing
thread similar to
829, 645

Step 04h
3346

Step 04b
Blanc, 3865, 762;
outlines in sewing
thread similar to
829, 645

Step 04j
3021

Step 04i
830 and 730; lines and
outline 3021

5

STEP 05: BEE

5a. Fill the wings with long-and-short stitch. Take a piece of sewing cotton and split it to achieve a very fine thread, then add veins in split stitch.
5b. Fill with irregular long-and-short stitch.
5c. Fill with irregular long-and-short stitch.
5d. Fill with irregular long-and-short stitch.
5e. Fill with irregular long-and-short stitch.
5f. Fill with irregular long-and-short stitch.
5g. Stitch the legs with split stitch.

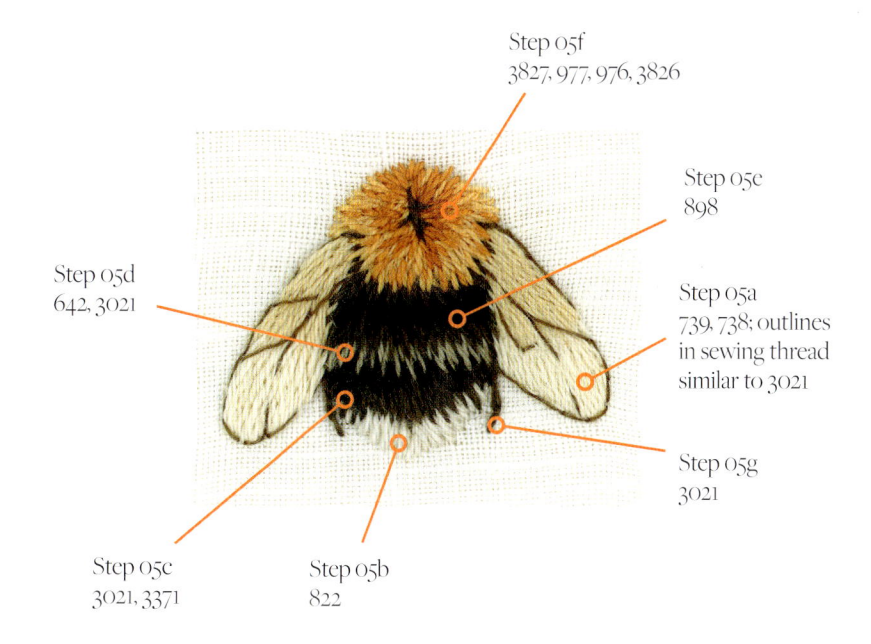

Step 05f
3827, 977, 976, 3826

Step 05e
898

Step 05d
642, 3021

Step 05a
739, 738; outlines in sewing thread similar to 3021

Step 05g
3021

Step 05c
3021, 3371

Step 05b
822

6

STEP 06: ACORN

6a. Fill the nut with long-and-short stitch; outline in split stitch.
6b. Fill the cup with French knots, using two strands and two twists.
6c. Fill with adjacent lines of split stitch; outline with split stitch.
6d. Fill with adjacent lines of split stitch; outline with split stitch.
6e. Add a few straight stitches.

Step 06a
772, 3348, 471, 470, 937, 936; outlines 470, 936

Step 06c
470, 937, 936; outline 934

Step 06e
632, 3021

Step 06b
Knots 524, 3052, 3051; outlines 934

Step 06d
471, 470, 937, 936; outlines 934

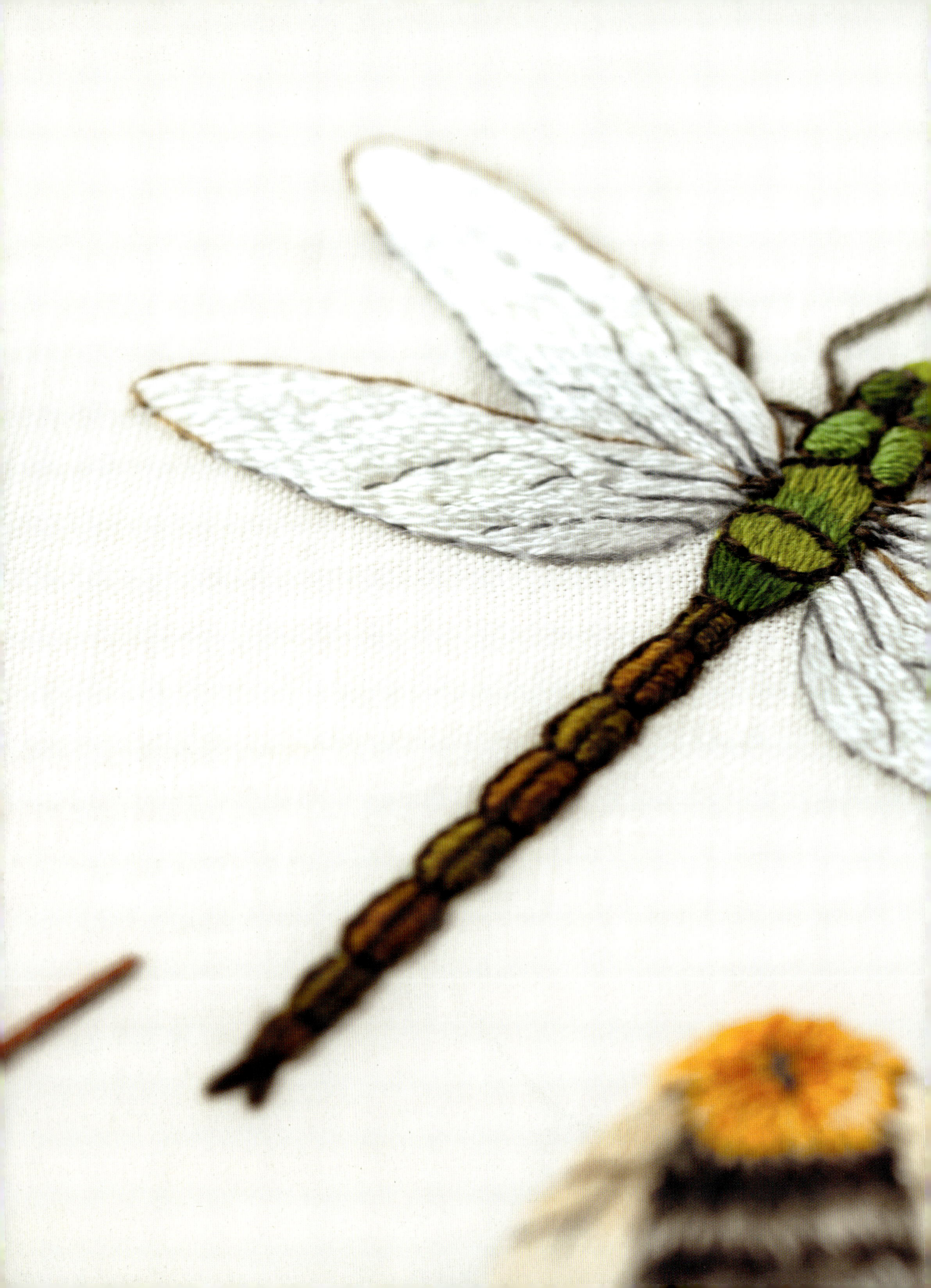

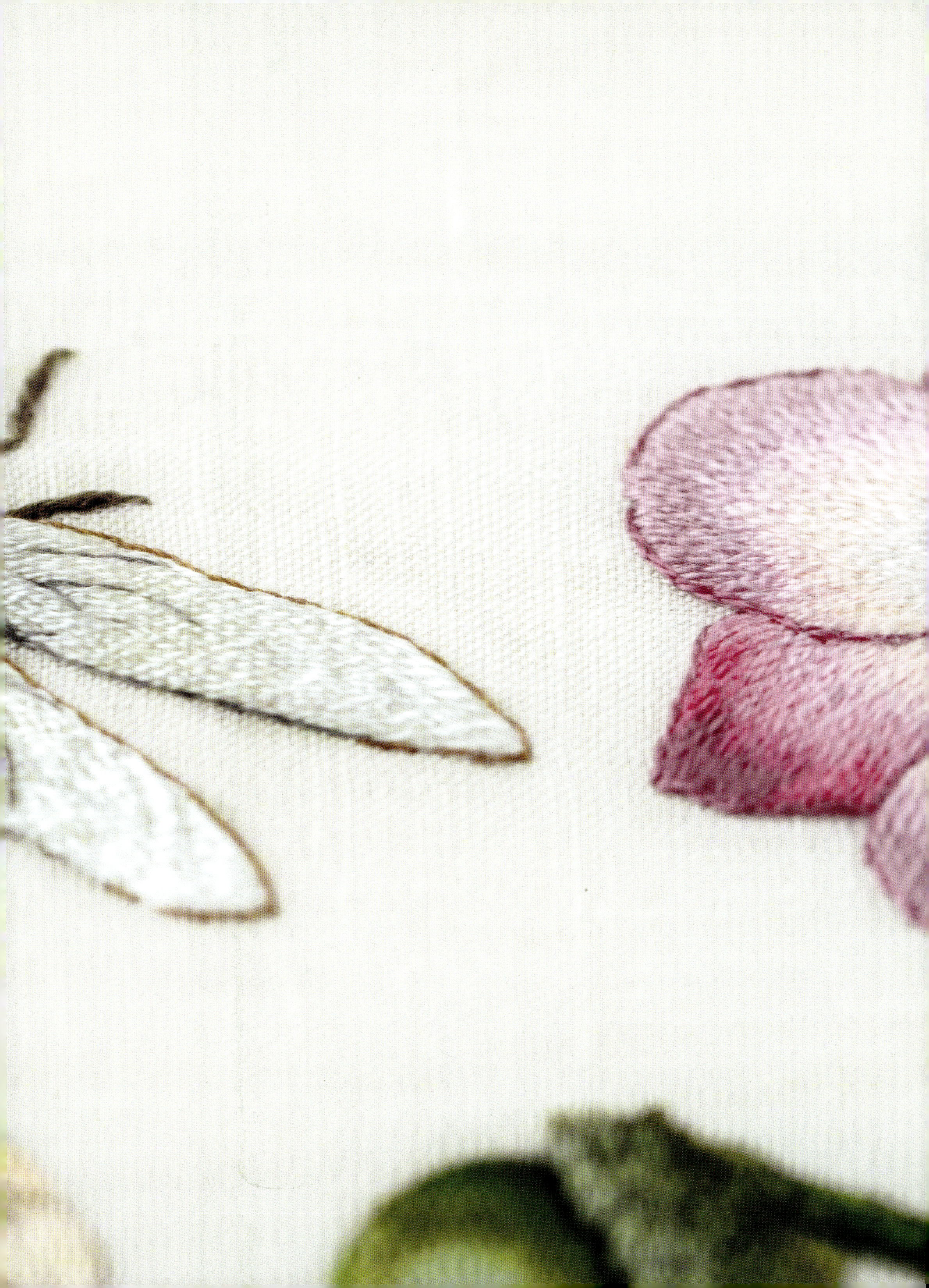

7

STEP 07: CLEMATIS

7a. Fill the stalk with adjacent lines of split stitch.
7b. Fill with long-and-short stitch; outline with split stitch.
7c. Fill with long-and-short stitch; outline with split stitch.
7d. Fill with long-and-short stitch; outline with split stitch.
7e. Fill with long-and-short stitch; outline with split stitch.
7f. Fill with long-and-short stitch; outline with split stitch.
7g. Fill with long-and-short stitch; outline with split stitch.
7h. Fill with long-and-short stitch; outline with split stitch.
7i. Fill with long-and-short stitch; outline with split stitch.
7j. Fill with long-and-short stitch; outline with split stitch.
7k. Fill with straight lines around the centre. Add French knots using one strand and one twist.
7l. Fill the centre with French knots, using one strand and two twists.

Step 07d
3608, A87, 3835

Step 07h
23, 818, 3689, 3609, 3836

Step 07k
10, 834, 831; knots 832, 829, 975

Step 07c
818, 3689, 3609, 3608, A87, 3835

Step 07i
23, 818, 3689, 3609, 3836

Step 07f
23, 818, 3689, 3609, 3836

Step 07l
Knots 472, 471, 470, 3347

Step 07j
23, 818, 3689, 3609, 3836

Step 07g
23, 818, 3689, 3609, 3836

Step 07a
471, 3347

Step 07e
818, 3689, 3609, 3608, 3836

Step 07b
3689, 3609, 3608, A87, 3835

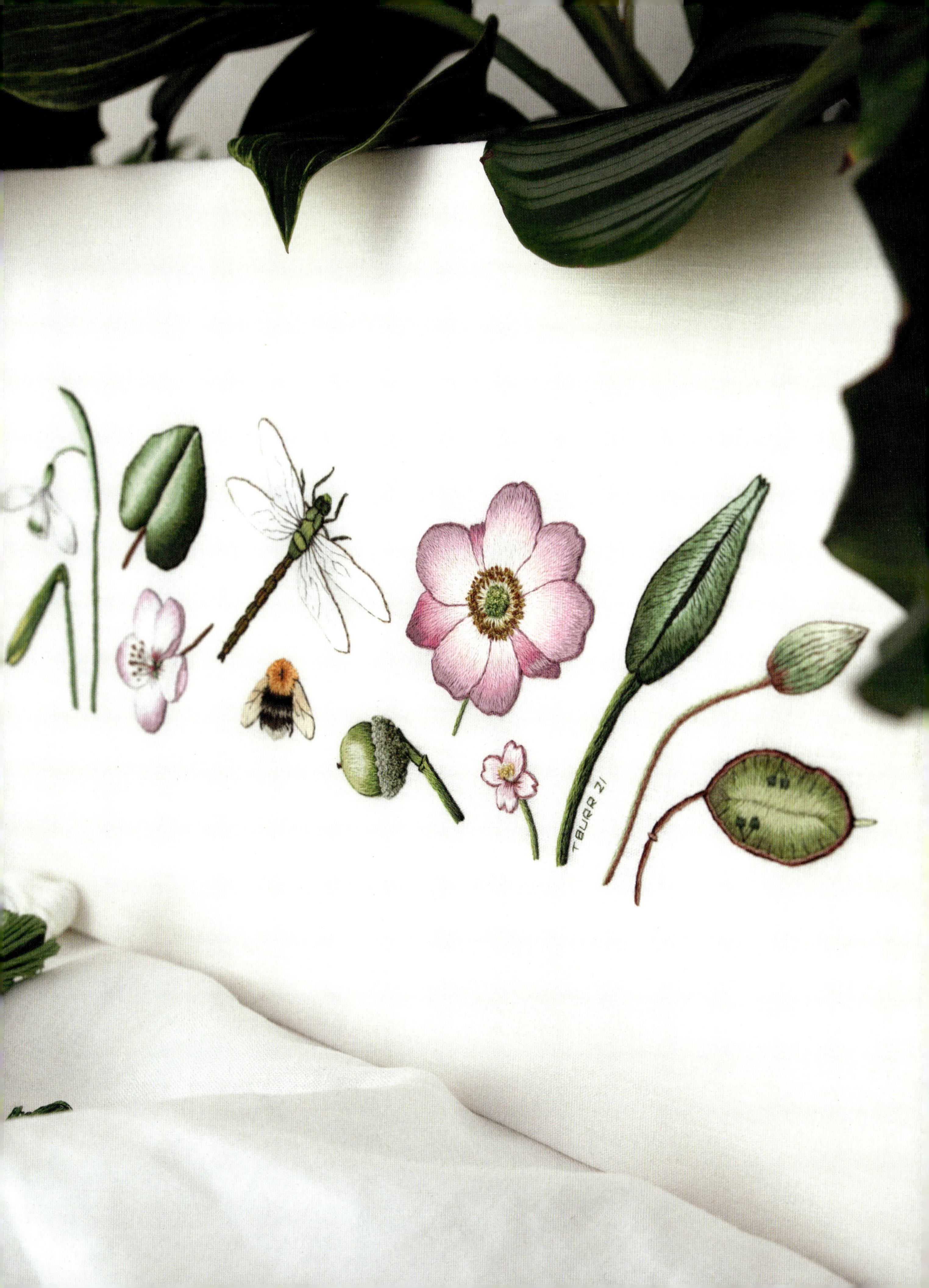
T BURR 21

8

STEP 08: SMALL FLOWER

8a. Fill the stem with adjacent lines of split stitch.
8b. Fill the petals with long-and-short stitch; outline with split stitch.
8c. Add straight lines at the base. At the top of these add French knots, using one strand and two twists.

Step 08c
10, 834

Step 08b
23, 3689; outline 3835

Step 08a
471, 3347, 936

9

STEP 09: LEAF

9a. Fill the stalk with adjacent rows of split stitch. Add lines in split stitch.
9b. Fill the centre vein with split stitch.
9c. Fill both sides of the leaf with long-and-short stitch. Outline in split stitch. Take one strand of sewing thread and split it to achieve a very fine thread – use this to add lines in split stitch.

Step 09b
935

Step 09c
164, 989, 988, 3346, A263, 935, outline 934; add lines in sewing thread similar to 935

Step 09c
164, 989, 988, 3346, A263, 935, outline 934; add lines in sewing thread similar to 935

Step 09a
471, 470, 3346, 3345, A263

164

10

STEP 10: BUD
10a. Fill the stalk with lines of split stitch.
10b. Fill the bud with long-and-short stitch. Add fine lines with sewing cotton in 898 and 936. You need to split one strand of sewing cotton to achieve a very fine strand.

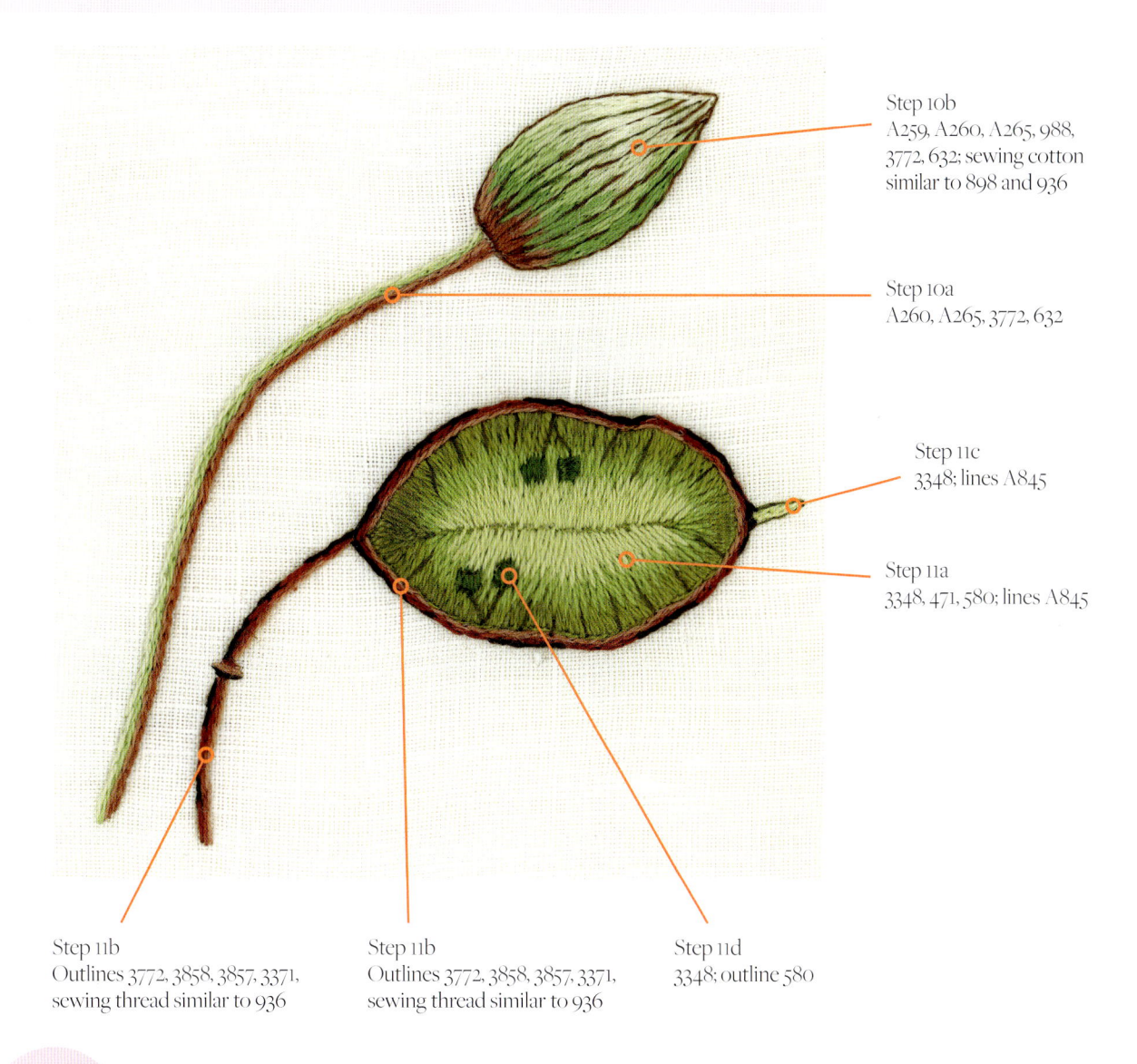

Step 10b
A259, A260, A265, 988, 3772, 632; sewing cotton similar to 898 and 936

Step 10a
A260, A265, 3772, 632

Step 11c
3348; lines A845

Step 11a
3348, 471, 580; lines A845

Step 11b
Outlines 3772, 3858, 3857, 3371, sewing thread similar to 936

Step 11b
Outlines 3772, 3858, 3857, 3371, sewing thread similar to 936

Step 11d
3348; outline 580

11

STEP 11: SEED HEAD
11a. Fill with long-and-short stitch. Add lines in straight stitch.
11b. Fill with adjacent lines of split stitch.
11c. Fill with split stitch; outline with split stitch.
11d. Fill the seeds with satin stitch.

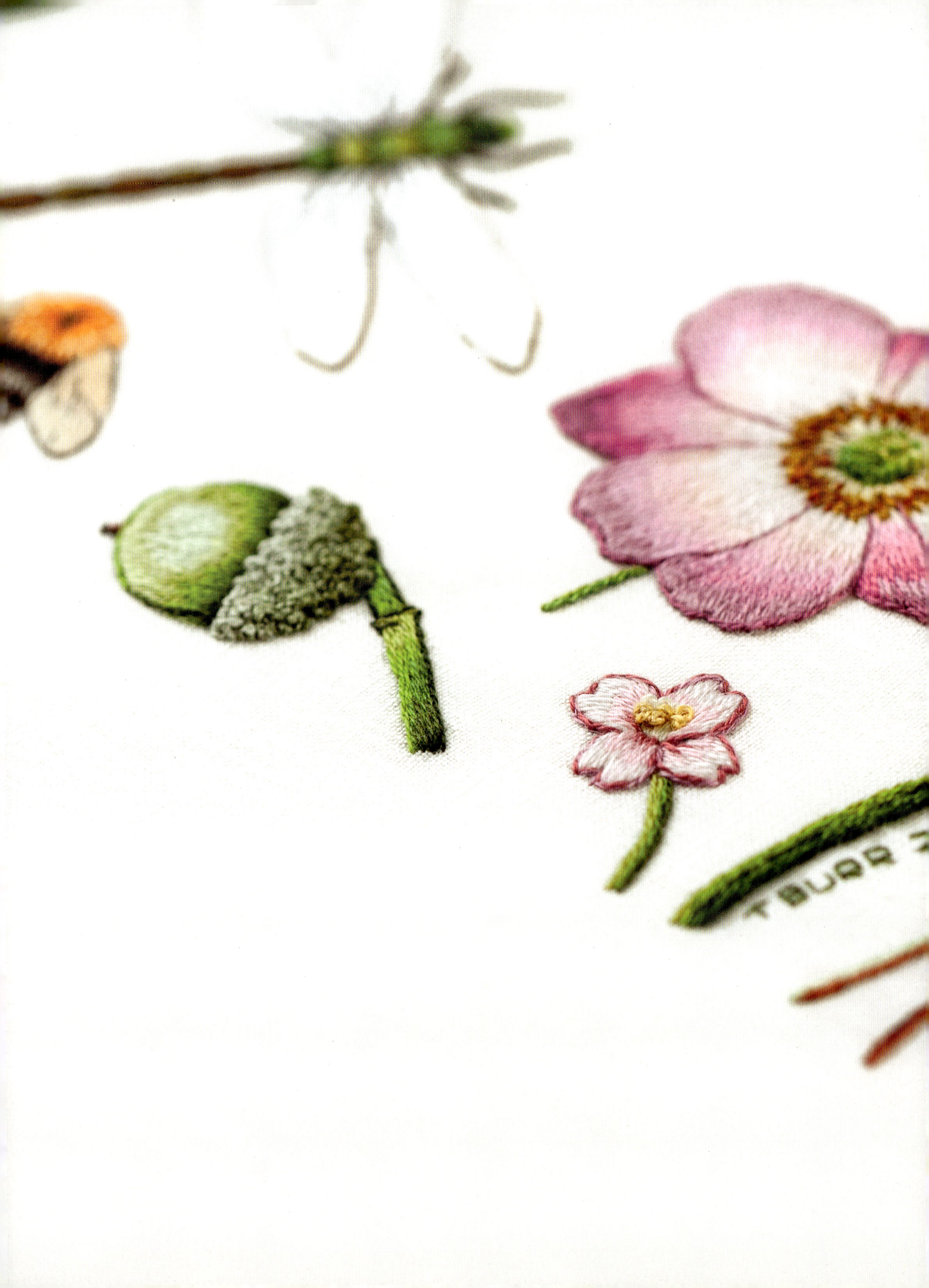
T BURR

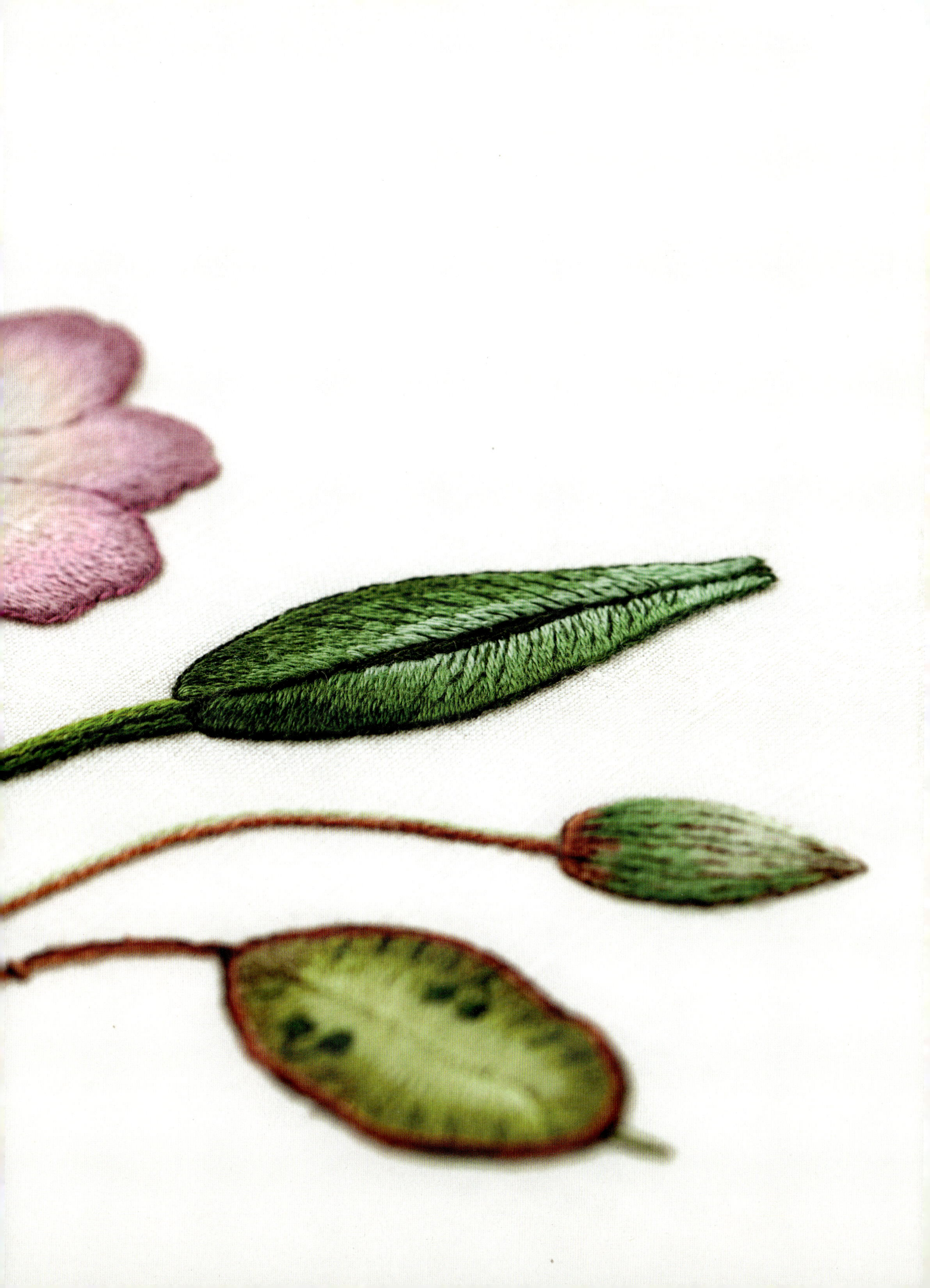

THE TEMPLATES

The templates are given here at full size – simply trace them off and transfer them to your fabric using your chosen method (see page 16). Extra copies of the templates are available to download free from the Bookmarked Hub. Search for this book by title or ISBN: the files can be found under 'Book Extras'. Membership of the Bookmarked online community is free: www.bookmarkedhub.com

STARTER STITCH SAMPLER

see pages 44–53

POPPY SAMPLER

see pages 54–59

WILDFLOWER SAMPLER

see pages 60–67

SACRED LOTUS FLOWER SAMPLER

see pages 68–75

BREADSEED POPPY SAMPLER

see pages 76–87

BARN OWL SAMPLER

see pages 90–103

BUNNY SAMPLER

see pages 104–117

BUTTERFLY SAMPLER

see pages 118–133

PELARGONIUM SAMPLER

see pages 136–151

DRAGONFLY SAMPLER

see pages 152–167.
Please note that this design has been split into two to fit on the page here at full size. Use the image on pages 152–153 as a reference to align the two sections when you transfer them onto your fabric.

USING IRON-ON TRANSFERS

Follow the method shown below to transfer the outlines to your fabric. The transfers will work the other way around (i.e. if you place the fabric on top of the transfer and then iron – this has the advantage of reducing the chance of the transfer slipping) but this can be less successful if you are using a thicker fabric, as the increased thickness makes it harder for the heat of the iron to reach the ink. Please note that iron-on transfers work best with pure linen or cotton fabric – they will not work on silk fabric. For further advice, please visit Trish's website: www.trishbembroidery.com, then go to 'Discover & Learn' and then 'Iron on transfers'.

Please note
The iron-on transfers are only available with the folder edition of this title.

STEP 1
Set the iron to the hottest dry setting and press the cotton or linen fabric to remove creases and pre-heat it.

STEP 2
Cut out the transfer.

STEP 3
Place the transfer face-down on top of the fabric. Ensure it is centred on the fabric. Insert some flat pins on either side, to hold the transfer in place, then cover the fabric and transfer with a piece of scrap cotton fabric to avoid scorching.

STEP 4
Place the hot iron on top of the transfer and hold in place for about a minute (or less depending on the heat of your iron – you want to avoid scorching your fabric). Do not move the iron around, just hold in place to prevent the lines from bleeding.

STEP 5
Lift and remove the transfer and the outline will be printed onto your fabric.

STEP 6
Iron the print one last time to set it.

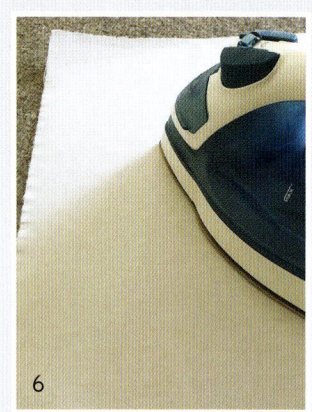

Please note
The success of the iron-on transfer process is dependent on a number of factors, including the fabric you use, the temperature of individual irons, the use of a hot, dry setting without any steam and the amount of pressure on the iron.

Although the instructions aim to minimize the scope for error, they cannot eliminate it completely, and it is suggested that you try a small test sample before use, to ensure you achieve the required results.

The transfer ink is indelible but may fade over time depending on storage conditions, so it is always advisable to iron on the transfer just prior to use.

Hint
When transferring a complete (long) sampler outline onto fabric, use flat pins to keep it in place so that it does not move around, as shown in this diagram (pins in red).

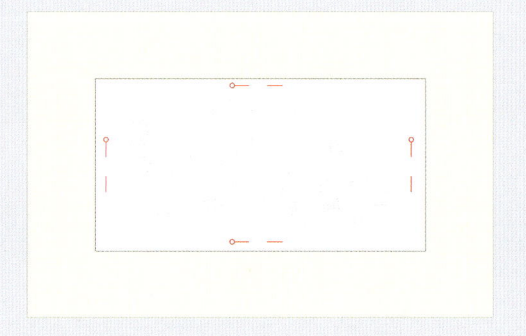

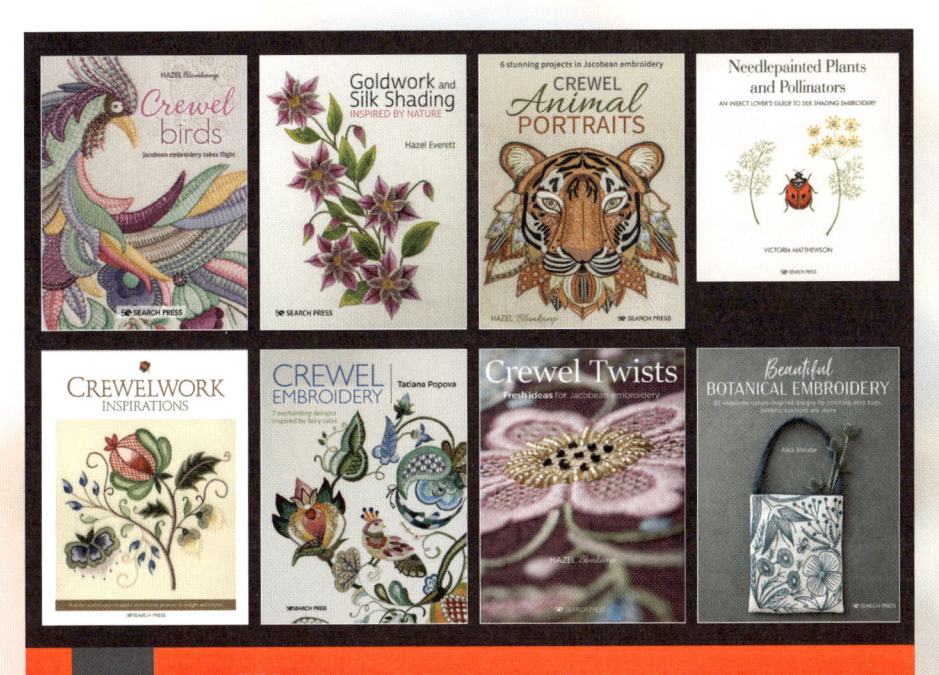

SEARCH PRESS LIMITED
The world's finest art and craft books

BOOKMARKED
The Creative Books Hub

from Search Press and David & Charles

WHY JOIN BOOKMARKED?

- Free membership of the world's leading art and craft book community
- Exclusive offers, giveaways and competitions
- Share your makes with the crafting world
- Free projects, videos and downloads
- Meet our amazing authors!

www.bookmarkedhub.com

For all our books and catalogues go to **www.searchpress.com**

www.searchpressusa.com   www.searchpress.com.au

Please note that not all of our books are available in all markets

Follow us @searchpress on:

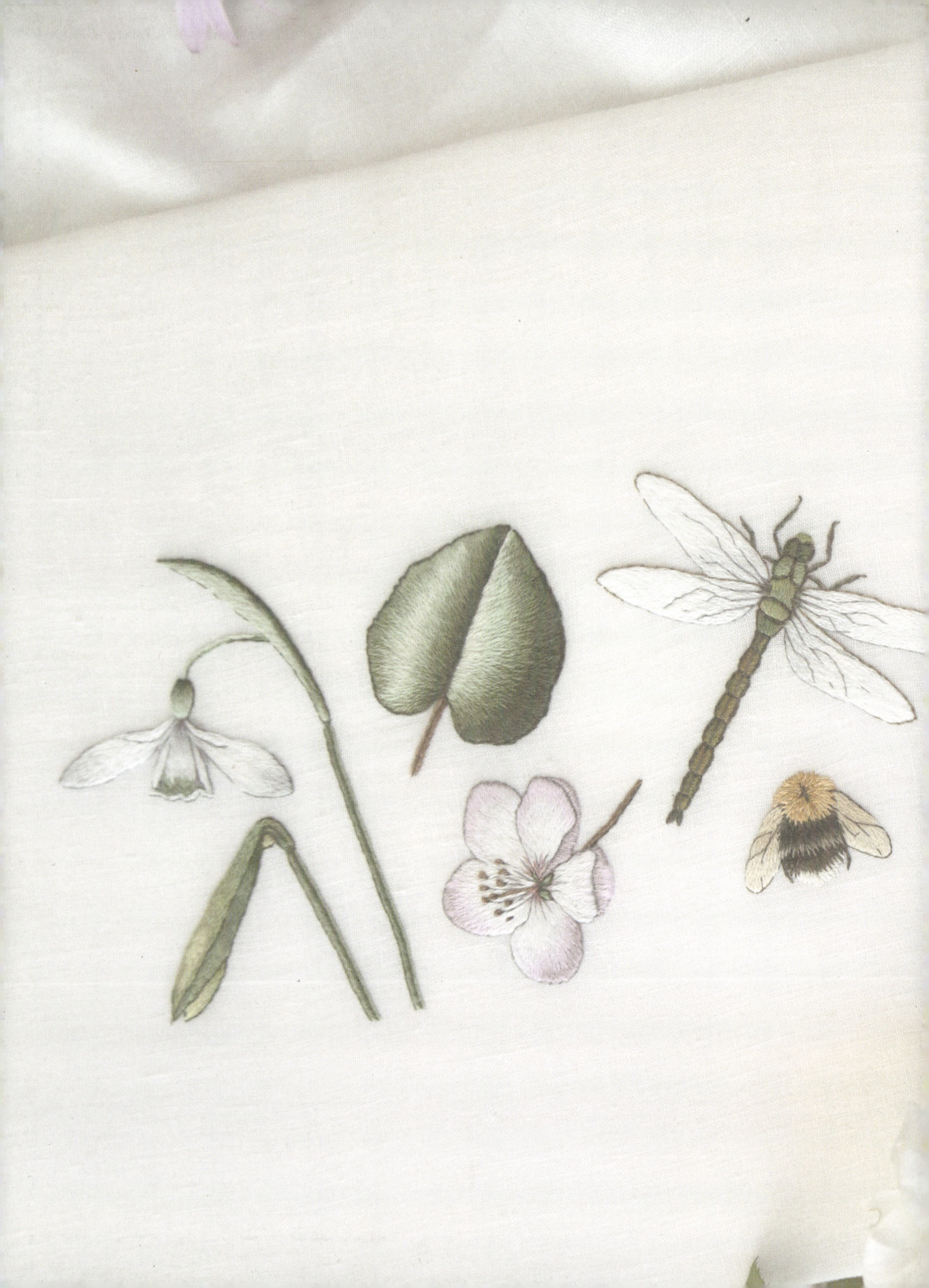